P9-DCM-238

SUBMARINES UNDER ICE

SUBMARINES UNDER ICE

The U.S. Navy's Polar Operations

Marion D. Williams

Naval Institute Press
Annapolis, Maryland

Library of Congress Cataloging-in-Publication Data
Williams, Marion D., 1909–
Submarines under ice : the U.S. Navy's Polar Operations /
Marion D. Williams.
p.   cm.
Includes bibliographical references (p.) and index.
ISBN 1-55750-943-3 (alk. paper)
1. Submarines (Ships)—United States. 2. United States. Navy—
Submarine forces. 3. Arctic Ocean. I. Title.
V858.W55 1998
359.9'3'0973—DC21   97-42584

Printed in the United States of America on acid-free paper ∞
98 99 00 01 02 03 04 05   9 8 7 6 5 4 3 2
First printing

To Dr. Waldo K. Lyon, who has generously shared his knowledge and records not only with this author, but also with everyone who has requested his assistance. To quote James Calvert (currently Vice Admiral Calvert): "Without Waldo Lyon, nothing would have happened [in the Arctic research program]."

CONTENTS

FOREWORD

The U.S. Navy has a long distinguished history of exploration and adventure. *Submarines under Ice* describes another exciting adventure by exciting men who conceived and carried out one of our nation's greatest peacetime operations. Since that day in April 1900 when the USS *Holland* became the first submarine in America's undersea fleet—the Silent Service—men have learned how to operate safely beneath the sea—but there is always much more to learn.

The skillful sailors who commanded the early sailing ships were confronted with gigantic problems in their attempts to penetrate the frozen Arctic. Pack ice was the most obvious obstacle and that was bad enough, but the problems of high-latitude navigation and sailing were nearly unsolvable. Of course, as soon as submarines became generally operational it was clear that submarines would be useful in exploration under the ice pack. Doughty Sir Hubert Wilkins made the first attempt in 1931. But the waters under the ice were uncharted. There were no instruments in those days sufficiently accurate or sensitive to inform the captain where the deep water was or where the submerged mountain peaks existed, let alone to determine how much clear water there was between the ice above and the ocean floor below.

Although in 1958 the Navy's primary goal in charting the waters above the Arctic Circle was to provide knowledge to be used in defense of the North American continent, we can also be justly proud of these modern explorers' accomplishments and contribution to the field of ocean science and technology. Developing completely new equipment and techniques required for under-ice navigation challenged the ingenuity of both the scientist and our most experienced submarine officers.

After years of struggle with the ice pack by diesel-electric boats in both the Arctic and Antarctic, it was a real personal pleasure that my responsibilities as Chief of Naval Operations enabled me to play a small role during the final years of breakthrough of the last unexplored frontier. For decades man dreamed of reaching the North Pole by ship. With the personal support of Pres. Dwight D. Eisenhower, the great *Nautilus,* our nation's first nuclear-powered submarine, gave our country one of its greatest achievements.

Since that day in 1958 when Comdr. William R. Anderson's historic message "*Nautilus*-90-North" was delivered to me at the Pentagon, the *Skate, Sargo,* and *Seadragon* went on to finish the job of charting the last corner of the world ocean. Where sailing and steam ships, and, more recently modern icebreakers, were brought to a halt by the churning, crushing pack ice, the farsighted vision of the scientist, engineer, and submarine commander, working as a close-knit team, brought final success.

It does not seem unreasonable for us now to envision even more modern submersibles which may some day carry scientists and adventurers in search of riches of the north, and perhaps even tourists on voyages to satisfy their curiosity to view the beauties above and below the ice of the North Polar Sea.

Adm. Arleigh Burke, USN (Ret.)

ACKNOWLEDGMENTS

In preparation of this arctic submarine documentary, the author acknowledges the invaluable assistance of the U.S. Navy in permitting access to unclassified and declassified documents and supplying rare photographs of submarines operating in the polar seas.

The officers and men involved in these operations gave generously of their knowledge. Special recognition is due to the following individuals for reviewing specific chapters, granting interviews, and providing papers and facts known to them alone:

Adm. Arleigh Burke, Congressman William R. Anderson (formerly Commander Anderson), Ambassador John Hay Whitney, Vice Adm. Allan McCann, Vice Adm. James Calvert, Vice Adm. John Nicholson, Vice Adm. George Steele, Rear Adm. John Maurer, Rear Adm. E. P. Aurand, Rear Adm. Joseph Icenhower, Capt. John Palmer, Capt. John H. Turner, Capt. Joseph Skoog Jr., Capt. C. Daniel Summit, Capt. Robert McWethy, Capt. James Strong, Comdr. John Bienia, and Comdr. Allen Catlin. Also Col. Joseph O. Fletcher, U.S. Air Force, Dr. Nordert Untersteiner, Elton Kelley, Dr. Eugene LaFond, Arthur Roshon, and Arthur Molloy.

Mere words cannot describe the valuable assistance of Dr. Waldo K. Lyon, physicist and arctic scientist, and Richard Boyle, research engineer, for reviewing the manuscript during its preparation and contributing extensive suggestions.

Acknowledgments

Lt. Comdr. Raymond E. Meyers, aide to Sir Hubert Wilkins, and a personal friend, supplied photographs and his journal. He also added his interesting recollections from the first *Nautilus* expedition.

Special recognition is due to Mrs. Sarah Hopkins, administrative assistant to Dr. Lyon, and Mrs. Theda Basset, librarian at the Submarine Base Library in New London, Connecticut, for many personal favors.

Finally, grateful appreciation is owed for the loyalty and support of my wife, Nell; my editor, Marjorie Moss; and typists Heather Martinez and Barbara Gillespie.

SUBMARINES UNDER ICE

1

A MAN AND HIS SUBMARINE

"You guys are nuts! What are you going to do when you get under the ice? How are you going to get up?"

In the spring of 1930, Ray Meyers had just read an article in a Sunday edition of the *Philadelphia Inquirer* describing an expedition Sir Hubert Wilkins was planning to the North Pole by submarine. The article also stated that an old friend, Master Diver Frank Crilley, was going along as diving officer. Now Meyers was writing to Crilley what he thought of the idea.

Meyers remembered Crilley as a daredevil who didn't know the meaning of fear. He and Crilley had been members of the Navy's first deep-sea diving squad.

Instead of replying by letter, Crilley sent Meyers a telegram:

MEET ME IN THE BELLEVUE STRATFORD HOTEL, IN
PHILADELPHIA, NEXT WEDNESDAY AT 1030.

Meyers walked into the hotel lobby to be greeted by a group of men whose records were deeply impressive: Sir Hubert Wilkins, veteran polar airman, who had recently been knighted by King George V of England; Simon Lake, a submarine inventor, whom Meyers had met before; and Lt. Comdr. Sloan Danenhower, U.S. Naval Reserve, a graduate of the Naval Academy. Danenhower was the son of famous polar explorer John W. Danenhower, Master of Lieutenant

De Long's *Jeannette,* which was crushed in the arctic ice pack in 1879. Sloan Danenhower and Meyers had been shipmates on the submarine *C-5.*

The fourth man of the group was Chester W. Nimitz. As a young lieutenant (jg), Nimitz had taken command of the 105-foot, 275-ton *C-5,* his first submarine, on 2 January 1909. Three years later he was commanding officer of the larger *E-1,* a 135-foot, 342-ton boat that was the first submarine to cross the Atlantic Ocean under its own power.

Meyers sat down with the four men to hear their story. They talked convincingly enough for an hour and a half that Meyers signed up to go on the expedition as the electrical officer.

Wilkins first needed a submarine. Because Meyers had a friend in the Navy Department, he was selected to go to Washington to see the secretary of the Navy. They hoped Sir Hubert could get one of the submarines scheduled for decommissioning in accordance with the Limitations of Arms Conference. Meyers hand-carried a letter to the Navy Department, in which Sloan Danenhower requested a submarine be transferred for charter in connection with an "International Geophysical Expedition" within the arctic regions. Since in 1930 Wilkins was not a U.S. citizen and the Transarctic Submarine Expedition was not yet incorporated, the service of an intermediary was required to procure the vessel. Lake and Danenhower, Inc., at that time a corporation existing under the laws of the state of New York, became the intermediate agent.

The letter also stated that no great unbroken ice floes had been observed in the Arctic Ocean, and that there were no icebergs there of great size. It was believed that more than 25 percent of the distance from Spitzbergen, Norway (a group of islands in the Arctic Ocean belonging to Norway), to the Bering Sea would be sailed in open water. On much of the remainder of the planned route, estimates placed the depth of the ice at 10 feet.

The secretary of the Navy approved the request and invited Wilkins's group to "take any one you want. There's a whole bunch of them tied up in the back channel of the Philadelphia Navy Yard. You either bring the boat back to the United States to be scrapped, or you sink it in 200 fathoms of water where it cannot be used by another government."

Wilkins and Danenhower together selected the *O-12*. The old boat had been in the back channel a long time. After years of service in the fleet, all of the bearings were so badly worn that some were now egg-shaped. The old submarine was mechanically quite decrepit. The *O-13* was a better boat, but its number was considered unlucky.

O-12 was originally built for the Navy by the Lake Torpedo Boat Company, Simon Lake's firm, at a cost believed to be more than $1,000,000. She was commissioned 19 October 1918 and was due to be scrapped in accordance with the London Naval Treaty. A charter party was concluded on 15 July 1930 between the U.S. Shipping Board and Lake and Danenhower, Inc. *O-12* was to be delivered "as is" at the Navy Yard at the port of Philadelphia and would be reconditioned for special arctic service. In turn, the submarine was chartered to the Transarctic Submarine Expedition, Inc., headed by Wilkins for a trip across the top of the world from Spitzbergen to the Bering Strait, via the North Pole. Throughout the charter the submarine remained a public vessel of the United States, to be used only to conduct an expedition for the purpose of scientific research.

The *O-12* was 175 feet long, 640 tons displacement, total range 7,000 miles, 125 miles submerged at three knots with one battery charge. Its surface speed was 14.7 knots. It had two 500-horsepower diesel engines and a new 15-kilowatt Winton hand-starting diesel generator set. A new 120-cell Exide battery had been installed. Air capacity would sustain 20 men for five days. The hull was designed to stand pressure at 200 feet below sea level.

Sir Hubert named his polar submarine *Nautilus,* the name of Captain Nemo's fictional submarine in Jules Verne's *Twenty Thousand Leagues under the Sea.* That story had inspired Wilkins to make the trip.

Lake and Danenhower contracted to have the submarine modified and ready for trials in January 1931. It left Camden in a partly finished condition under its own power on 22 March, but the engines broke down and it was towed to the New York Engineering Company's dock at Yonkers, New York, where it was repaired.

With little to do except get the batteries and motors in operating condition, Meyers was given the role of personnel officer. The submarine's crew required all kinds of people and many were eager to go on this expedition.

Danenhower and Meyers made a firm rule. Every man who wanted to go along had to be experienced in his own particular trade and also had to be an ex-Navy-qualified submariner. Most applicants wanted to go along as the cook, but they knew nothing about submarines.

Meyers signed up a quartermaster, Willard I. Grimmer, who was also a radioman. He had been married only three days when he signed up.

Ray Meyers kept a personal journal:

> *28 October 1930: Went to work this date after conference with Captain Danenhower at the Sylvania Hotel last night. Boat at Philadelphia Navy Yard undergoing fitting out. Crew consists of Captain Danenhower; Ralph Shaw, chief engineer; William Danenhower [brother of the captain], assistant engineer; Frank Crilley, master diver, and myself as chief electrician of the boat. Inspected all electrical equipment and made report to the Captain.*

Meyers later recalled,

> The *O-12* was in pretty sad shape, but we went to work on her. After we had been working in the Navy Yard for a couple of weeks I was given the job as treasurer of the expedition. William Randolph Hearst gave us $25,000 for exclusive news rights. Pathe News gave us $25,000. William D. Leeds, a millionaire sportsman and son of a Greek princess, gave us another $25,000. Donations came from many sources but the money started to go fast. In government, it is expensive to get things done.
>
> "If you fellows want to exist," I told Wilkins, "we'd better get out of here and go to a private shipyard." Wilkins agreed and we prepared to move the *O-12* across the river to the Mathis Shipyard. It was a small boat yard at Camden, New Jersey, capable of finishing our work.

His journal continued:

> *7 January 1931: Took up every floor plate and gave the boat a darn good cleaning. Inspection at 1130. Captain remarked how nice she looked. Sir Hubert inspected and seemed pleased. Captain talked like*

I will go as radioman. Oh, boy! What a great and glorious feeling, for that is where I shine—and how!

8 January 1931: Put all material aboard. Filled my car with small stuff and shoved off for Camden. Beat the ship over and had power lines on the dock. Using two-phase 220 here . . . ran three-wire system to the board . . . hope no one tried to hook up anything on board because 220 AC is not so good for 110V DC motors.

Meyers later related,

During the following weeks, we finally finished up our work in the private shipyard, as far as we could, and had to go back to Philadelphia to get our batteries charged. Our plotted charge rate began at 3,000 amperes, tapering off to 2,100. This little shipyard, which had 48-volt batteries for direct current power to do its work, couldn't handle the job. We also needed some navigation equipment: running lights, fog horns, sirens, and compasses.

Just as we were about to leave Camden, it started to snow. The reporters were down there asking, "How about a story, Ray?" "I can't talk," I told them, and suggested they see Sir Hubert.

"I'm sorry," Wilkins told them, "I can't talk, I have exclusive news feature arrangements with Mr. Hearst."

"You will be sorry."

It was snowing. And there was no way to alert ships on the river that *Nautilus* was coming. There were no foghorns or sirens. But there was a schedule to meet.

His journal continued:

16 March: Left Camden 1530 for Marcus Hook, but stopped at Philadelphia due to heavy snow, poor observation. No running lights.

It took 2 hours and 15 minutes to make the short distance to Philadelphia from Camden. The ferry boat normally made the trip in 12 minutes.

The reporters had kept their word. The *Philadelphia Call-Bulletin* already had an extra edition on the street with its headline reading:

THE ARCTIC SUBMARINE NAUTILUS LOST IN SNOWSTORM IN THE DELAWARE RIVER!

Meyers' journal read:

18 March: Left Philadelphia for Marcus Hook.

19 March: Marcus Hook—oiling.

21 March: 0730—Underway, towed by tug Caspian *bound for New York Navy Yard.*

We started down the Delaware River under tow by a large tug. The *O-12* was going to the New York Navy Yard to be christened. En route, we ran into another very bad storm off Asbury Park. Willard Grimmer was crawling around the narrow deck cleaning the sides of the submarine while the boat was being tossed about by choppy seas. Suddenly a huge wave rolled against the rounded hull and crashed over the low deck. Grimmer was picked up, thrown against the lifeline, then lifted bodily thrashing into the river.

22 March: (time) 1453—rough seas. Grimmer, W.I., quartermaster, fell overboard when lifeline carried away. I had just given him a match. Ship stopped and attempted to get him, but due to tow line it was impossible to break away from tug. Plane circling overhead. Shame he don't see him.

Meyers recalled,

Grimmer didn't have a chance. We were on the end of a tow line and couldn't do anything about it. The Ward Line steamer *Morro Castle* was about a half mile away. I immediately dropped into the radio room and broadcast a message, asking if they would send a lifeboat to pick him up. They didn't get my message. The radioman was out on deck watching this strange-looking submarine cruising up New York harbor instead of on his watch.

A Coast Guard amphibious plane flew over about this time. The *Nautilus* crew waved wildly while pointing to Grimmer struggling in the cold water. The pilot merely waved back without changing course.

22 March: 1630—Gave up the search. Captain Danenhower said a prayer, which was very impressive, and asked us to carry on. Coast Guard patrol boat crew mans the rail.

New York City radio stations broadcast the sad news and a newspaper article described the accident:

The first voyage of the *Nautilus*—the submarine Sir Hubert Wilkins hopes to journey to the North Pole—was touched by tragedy this afternoon. Willard I. Grimmer, quartermaster, fell from the narrow deck of the sub sea boat and was lost as the submarine was off West Bank Light, below quarantine.

Lt. Comdr. Sloan Danenhower, commanding the *Nautilus,* told in a radio report to Sir Hubert of the dramatic efforts to rescue Grimmer whose home town is Philadelphia. The radio said, "Regret that Willard Grimmer was lost overboard while *Nautilus* was proceeding in tow of a tug and was unable to maneuver. The *Nautilus* dropped life buoy and went full speed astern. Gave signal to tug, and with full power of *Nautilus* motors, dragged tug back to spot where Grimmer sank. Searched vicinity assisted by airplane, Coast Guard, and police boats without sighting man. After police and Coast Guard agreed it was no further use to continue search, a memorial service was held at the spot where Grimmer sank." It was a downhearted gang that pulled into Stapleton to make a formal report to the Coast Guard.

Reaching Staten Island, the crew rushed for the nearest telephones. Some radio stations had broadcast the news that one of the *Nautilus* crew had been washed overboard without giving his name. Everyone wanted to report home.

Meyers had started down the gangway when Sir Hubert stopped him.

"You better stick around, Ray," he said, "until somebody else comes back because it will be bad for us. The souvenir hunters will steal the wallpaper."

Nautilus had inch and a half thick cork insulation covering the inside of the boat. People would actually come on board, pull off a piece and ask, "Will you please autograph this?"

23 March: 0630—Underway for New York Navy Yard under motors. Have the wheel watch. Our after mast carried away by tug. Navy Yard tugs meet us off Battery and take us to yard. Arrive 1220.

Nautilus went into the Navy Yard to await the christening ceremony. Jean Jules Verne, grandson of the famous author, had arrived from Paris to help christen the old submarine named after the vessel that the elder Verne had guided through two novels.

"What man can imagine, man can do! My grandfather told me that," Verne told Sir Hubert, "and I transmit it to you. I was a boy of 12 when he died, but I have never forgotten it. I wish to express my admiration for you in attempting this feat. It almost surpasses anything that my grandfather dreamed of. I am sure you will succeed. The *Nautilus* is not as luxurious, but more practical than my grandfather's storybook boat. I am confident the voyage to the North Pole will be successful."

Wilkins asked if he would like to join his polar party. Verne, a small thoughtful man, brightened, and then explained, "But I am the district attorney of Rouen and my duty is there. Besides," he added, "is not the full crew enlisted?"

Wilkins smilingly assured him that there was no room for another man.

24 March: Christened "Nautilus" by Lady Wilkins, assisted by Jean Jules Verne.

The crew had an novel way of christening the boat. A bucket of ice cubes was rigged over the bow. At the proper time Lady Wilkins pulled a blue and gold lanyard attached to the bucket, dropping the ice cubes on the bow of the submarine, and said, "I christen thee *Nautilus!*"

Nautilus sailed for Yonkers, New York, and tied up at Mahlsted's Lumberyard docks to have the ice drills put on board. The submarine was rebuilt. Its deck now gave the appearance of a razorback hog. Sled runners ran across the deck from bow to stern. The submarine was designed to slide along underneath the ice.

The depth gauge would help them determine the thickness of the ice. A radio antenna was attached to a trolley pole above the narrow deck. Two 10-inch ice drills in 10-foot sections could be extended up to 100 feet. The ice drills also were intended to serve as snorkel tubes. One was to bring in fresh air and the other to expel carbon dioxide and other gases.

A third ice drill was 34 inches in diameter, rising to $15\frac{1}{2}$ feet above the deck and topped by a circular cathead cutter. The theory was if the ice layer was less than 15 feet thick the crew could drill through the ice, crawl out through the center of the drill, and reach the surface.

Danenhower decided to go up the Hudson River off Poughkeepsie for a test dive to learn how the submarine would act in fresh water. It was possible that they would run into pockets of fresh water in the polar region where huge quantities are produced by melting ice in summer. Fresh water has a different buoyancy than salt water.

On 2 May *Nautilus* was ready to sail. Herman Gieski, a cub reporter, was anxiously hanging around the dock looking for a story. He asked to go along.

"I would like to go aboard and write my experiences," he told Sir Hubert. "And how it feels to be in a submarine when it dives."

"You'd be in the way, Herman!" replied Wilkins.

"Oh, let him come along," said Meyers. "He can sit in the radio room. He won't be any trouble."

2 May: 1030—Underway for Poughkeepsie. Arrived off Groton Point 2300.

Herman made himself comfortable. Seated at the typewriter in the boat's small radio room he prepared to write his story while the crew checked out the boat. *Nautilus* was old and badly rusted. The crew especially was interested in any small leaks that might be found.

On the first dive following a submarine overhaul, each crewman was routinely given a piece of blue chalk. Everyone was on the look-out for a "teardrop" that might appear on each rivet in the bulkhead. If a drop of water was found, they circled the rivet with blue chalk. Back in the yard caulkers plugged each hole.

Nautilus had two periscopes; one was designed to work like a jack-knife. If the deck struck ice while submerged, the periscope would be forced backwards and lie down. After passing clear of the protruding ice ridge, the periscope would spring back to its upright position.

An engineer from the New York Engineering Company was not quite pleased with the operation of this periscope. It had not been working well and before departing for the test dive he had removed it and filled the open hole with a huge wooden plug sealed with a bit of canvas and red lead.

Nautilus had been submerged about two hours when too much pressure built up inside the boat. The wooden plug popped out and a torrent of water poured into the control room like a stream from a four-inch hose. Danenhower immediately ordered the submarine to the surface. The boat was returned to the dock and the periscope reinstalled.

Herman Gieski spotted Crilley emptying water from his pockets.

"My God! What happened?"

"We submerged and left the conning tower hatch open," Crilley replied jokingly.

The cub reporter wrote his story. When *Nautilus* returned to the dock, Gieski quickly disappeared.

"Where's Herman?" asked Sir Hubert.

"I don't know," Meyers replied.

Gieski had left by way of the forward hatch and immediately telephoned his story to the Hearst newspaper. The article was in the morning edition.

Nautilus was ready to go to New London, Connecticut, for her deep test dive.

"We still don't have a cook," Meyers told Sir Hubert.

"I know a fellow down in Asbury Park," said Crilley. "He's a survivor of the *S-5*. [The *S-5* had foundered off Delaware Cape 1 September 1920. The stern was raised and the crew had escaped through a hole cut in the hull.] I'm sure he'll go along with us."

"Give Frank a couple hundred dollars, Ray," said Wilkins. "Let him go down and see the man."

The next morning Crilley called. "We got the guy . . . if!"

"If what?"

"If we permit his pantry boy to go along."

"Well, who is the pantry boy?"

"He's a little Swiss boy named Jacob Fleutch."

"What does he know about submarines?"

"Nothing!"

"What does he know about the sea?"

"Nothing!"

"Well, we can't take him!" concluded Wilkins.

"Well," said Crilley, "you can't have the cook. He refuses to go unless you take the pantry boy."

Wilkins and Meyers discussed the situation.

"All right," Meyers told Crilley, "bring him along."

The two men joined the crew and *Nautilus* headed for New London to prepare for a deep dive. The new cook was seen making hamburgers. This fellow was a production cook. Stripped down to the waist, the 240-pound ex-submariner dipped both hands into a big tureen filled with chopped meat, rolled the meat neatly into hamburger patties, slapped them on his bare stomach, and flipped them into the frying pan. The cook was fired and the crew kept the pantry boy.

"Jake, you're going to be a submarine man."

"What do I do?"

"When you hear the claxton, close the hatch over the galley. Don't open it until you get orders!"

"We held a rehearsal," related Meyers. "We sounded the diving alarm. Jake closed the hatch with a big smile on his face."

"'Did I do all right?'

"'You do fine, Jake. Now you can open it.'"

Nautilus headed for the sea for the deep dive and the crew made ready. The submarine rescue ship *Falcon* was standing by with her skipper, Bill Laughlin. Laughlin had been a member of the *F-4* salvage team off Pearl Harbor and was still crippled from the effects of a broken hip. Frank Crilley had saved his life when Laughlin became entangled in his diving lines.

"I hope I can return the favor you fellows did me in Pearl Harbor," he told Crilley.

"We hope you don't have to. Just stand clear."

"Flood everything!" ordered Captain Danenhower.

The O-type submarines were designed to stand sea pressure up to a depth of 210 feet, a little more than 92 pounds per square inch. The 566-ton ex-*O-12* plunged to the bottom out of control in about 240 feet of water, pushing her keel deep into the muddy bottom. Danenhower immediately ordered all tanks blown to get maximum positive buoyancy. Nothing happened. *Nautilus* lay stuck firmly on the bottom.

The crew did everything they knew to get the keel loose from the suction hold of the mud. They ran forward, then aft, and tried running back and forth athwartship, hoping their combined weight would rock the submarine sideways. All efforts failed. *Nautilus* remained firmly on the bottom.

Over the submarine oscillator Meyers tapped out a message, informing the *Falcon* of the situation and instructing Laughlin to remain clear. With positive buoyancy Danenhower did not want the rescue vessel directly overhead if *Nautilus* suddenly broke loose.

Jake Fleutch approached Ray with a worried expression. "Hey, Mr. Meyers! When we come up?"

"I don't know, Jake."

"You know, we better come up soon. I forgot to bring bread today."

He knew nothing about submarines and wasn't worried.

The crew assembled in the control room for a conference. Sitting around, everyone was quiet, wondering what to do next. Should they ask *Falcon* to send a diver down and try to blow the mud away?

"My God!" someone yelled. "Look at the depth gauge!"

Nautilus had broken loose by herself and was rising to the surface. Without stopping to learn what had caused her to go down so fast, Danenhower and Wilkens decided the submarine was ready for the Arctic.

Once the boat was returned to the New London dock, the tanks were filled with fuel oil in preparation for the Atlantic crossing. The Thames River soon became covered with leaking oil, quickly spreading far downstream.

At first Texaco was accused of being sloppy oilers, but an investigation revealed the real cause was oil pouring from the tanks. In Philadelphia the crew had gone aboard a German U-boat that had been captured during World War I. They had removed a kingston valve the Germans designed to operate using a worm gear. This valve had replaced the Navy type, which required two men to throw a huge lever. One man could open the big 34-inch U-boat valve with ease. Divers discovered that—possibly when she hit the bottom—*Nautilus* had lost the big German-made kingston valve. The oil was being forced out the bottom of the combination fuel-ballast tank as fast as the Texaco oilers fed it in from the top.

The loss of the valve would not be a serious diving problem, since normal procedure was to "ride the vents." When the sub was ready to submerge, the vent valves were opened, releasing the "bubble," and the boat would slowly disappear beneath the waves. *Nautilus*'s sudden plunge to the bottom, they discovered, was caused by a piece of waste material stuck in the vent valve of one tank. The uncontrolled dive into the mud under 240 feet of water that nearly brought disaster was explained.

> *4 June: 1100—Left New London, Connecticut, for Provincetown with full crew. 1500—Sir Hubert talked with Lady Wilkins aboard the United States Coast Guard Cutter* Hunt. *2145—Underway Provincetown for London.*

Nautilus started across the Atlantic with a happy crew, escorted the first few miles by the Coast Guard, first by the *Hunt* and then later by the *Pontchartrain.*

"We're going to leave you," radioed the *Pontchartrain.* "Bon voyage. We're going north."

"So long!" Meyer radioed. "We are going east."

Sir Hubert started sending his news reports to the Hearst newspapers:

> The tiny 172-foot submarine began pushing her way across the first leg of our voyage. Cruising on the surface, the bow rose and fell with the huge waves lashing the low deck, keeping them awash most of the time. Bracing himself in the temporary canvas-rigged bridge, Captain Danenhower directed the ship.

It was not long before most of the crew became deathly sick. No one could understand the cause. After arriving in England weeks later the crew discovered that the painters at the private Camden shipyard had used red lead paint instead of nonpoisonous bituminous paint to coat the fresh-water tanks. They were being poisoned by the drinking water. Of course, the tanks were repainted in England.

In another incident, one day Meyers, as electrical officer, sent electrician Frank Blumberg aft to rig the engine room for a battery charge. Suddenly a terrific explosion rang through the boat. Meyers rushed aft to see what happened. Without careful thinking Blumberg had closed a switch connecting the generator directly to a field coil. Both generators were now turning around partly under sea water, leaking from hull fittings.

The captain ordered "All stop" on the engines and the bilges were pumped. How were they going to get salt water out of the generators? Both measured almost a short circuit.

Sir Hubert, sick but determined, joined the work crew with a monkey wrench in one hand and a bucket in the other. Fumes from the carbon tetrachloride, used to clean the salt-damaged wiring, added to everyone's discomfort.

Meyers's log read:

> 11 June: 1400—Got wx [weather] reports from ships in vicinity. Not able to use my xmtr [transmitter] since 2400 due to low battery. Now both engines stopped. Motor room full of gas. Riggs fainted. Shaw and Zoeller just about out. 1700 . . . port engine running on shaft. 15 KW runs now and then on battery charge.

After long hours the generators were finally cleaned up.

"What do you think?" asked Sir Hubert.

"I think it will work," Meyers answered confidently.

What they didn't know at the time was that the starboard engine poppit valve was below the water line. The valve hadn't been working very well, and salt water had seeped into the engine's cylinders. When the engine started, number 3 cylinder cracked. Now both the port generator and starboard engine were out of commission.

Ike Schlossbach, the executive officer, suggested starting the engine on compressed air.

With the good engine started, dragging the dead generator, away they went.

Meyers wrote in his log:

> 15 June: 1700. . . . Now our troubles begin, with load taking 100 amps, and a charge of 75 amps going in about three out of twenty-four hours . . . pretty rough it seems now.

"We better send a message for help," Meyers suggested to the captain. "We have a chance. We have two transmitters on board. One is short-wave. The only station I can work now is Germany. But on this marine set that is normally good for 50 miles, I can try to call the Coast Guard cutter and have them come out to help."

"There's no need for that." replied Danenhower emphatically. "I'll let you know."

Three days later, when the battery was nearly gone, Danenhower ordered, "Send a message for help."

"Are you a spiritualist?" Meyers replied.

"What's that got to do with it?"

"That's the only way I can think of to get a radio message off."

"That's your problem! You're the engineer!"

Suddenly Meyers remembered the old radio broadcast days. When he had tuned in on his favorite program, "Sam and Henry," which later became "Amos 'n Andy," he could also hear his next-door neighbor by his receiver's heterodyne whistle, tuning in the same station. Heterodyne whistle? It might work!

Handicapped by one dim light in each compartment, and with the aid of a flashlight, radioman Meyers went to work. *Nautilus* was pitching and rolling. One roll took the submarine 47 degrees to port.

By connecting his speed key in series with the antenna, Meyers keyed the old heterodyne receiver and got along fine. For 18 hours, he tapped out, "SOS, SOS, SOS," for the first three minutes starting at a quarter to the hour and a quarter past the hour. Those were the international silent periods of each hour when ships at sea listen for calls of distress.

"Who are you?" Finally came a reply from the SS *Independence Hall.*

Meyers tensed with excitement. Long hours of keying his jury-rigged receiver-turned-transmitter had finally paid off.

THIS IS THE SUBMARINE *NAUTILUS.*

He hoped his weak dots and dashes could be understood.

WE PASSED YOU ABOUT 1900 BUT NOBODY WAS ON DECK.

THERE'S GOOD REASON. WE CAN'T GET UP ON DECK WITH SAFETY, AND WE'RE JUST ABOUT TO START WALKING.

14 JUNE: 0822—WSEA [*Nautilus*] KDCG [*Independence Hall*] . . .
PRESENT POSITION LATITUDE 46.12 N, LONGITUDE 31.40 W AT
8:30 GMT. OUR COURSE 066 TRUE. WE ARE BOUND BORDEAUX,
FRANCE. ARE YOU IN IMMEDIATE NEED ASSISTANCE?

Meyers replied,

KDCG WSEA, RUNNING ON PORT ENGINE UNTIL BATTERY
EXHAUSTED. PORT MOTOR DISABLED. CANNOT CHARGE
BATTERY.

On board the battleship *Wyoming* en route to Sweden on a midshipman cruise, Chief Radio Operator Charles Propster was delivering the morning press. A pale-faced messenger came running down the passageway. "Hey, Chief! There's an SOS!"

Propster made a dash for the radio direction-finder room several decks above to get a bearing on Meyers's weak signals. The distress frequency was already filled with messages from other ships that had joined the *Independence Hall,* offering to help.

KDCG FROM NITR [*Wyoming*]: WHAT IS POSITION OF WSEA?

NITR KDCG, OUR POSN 46.12N, 31.40 W.ALONGSIDE

On board the *Independence Hall,* Radio Operator Marschall transmitted dots and dashes and thus was able to guide the *Wyoming* and the second battleship *Arkansas* directly to their position. This proved important because Danenhower found later his plotted position was off considerably due to the *Nautilus* drifting off course. With the submarine closed up against high seas they had been unable to make navigational fixes. It had been foggy and hazy at the time, making for poor visibility. Had it not been for the *Independence Hall* providing radio signals for the battleships to home in on they might never have been found.

Wyoming continued to take radio bearings while steaming at full speed toward the small submarine that was being tossed helplessly in heavy swells. *Wyoming* was soon forced to broadcast a message to all ships:

CONTACT NOW DEPENDS UPON RADIO BEARINGS. PLEASE GIVE
BEARINGS ALL PRECEDENCE!

Meyers logged:

> *1455—Terrific roll to port . . . bottle of ammonia carried away in FWD battery. Unable to hear my weak signals, the* Independence Hall *relayed:*
> *KDCG NACT—ARE YOU GOING TO* NAUTILUS? *HAVE YOU ANY INFORMATION AS TO WHETHER REPAIRS CAN BE EFFECTED, OR ANY EXACT KNOWLEDGE AS TO HER TOWING FACILITIES? SIGNED, REAR ADMIRAL BLOCH.*

Within two hours the *Wyoming* and *Arkansas,* with a second group of midshipmen on board, had agreed to help.

> 1618—WSEA FROM NACT—ONE BATTLESHIP WILL STAND BY. IF YOU CANNOT EFFECT REPAIRS YOU SHOULD BE TAKEN IN TOW BEFORE DARK. ELECTRICAL POWER SHOULD BE CONSERVED TO HANDLE LINES. INFORM ME AS TO POSSIBILITY OF REPAIRS, TOWING FACILITIES AND WHETHER *INDEPENDENCE HALL* WILL TOW. BLOCH.

> NACT FROM WSEA [relayed by *Independence Hall*]— CANNOT EFFECT REPAIRS UNDERWAY. BATTERY ALMOST FLAT. GOOD FOR ABOUT THREE HOURS MORE. PLEASE STAND BY UNTIL WEATHER MODERATES AND THEN TAKE US IN TOW AND WE WILL TRY BAKE OUT PORT MOTOR WHILE ON TOW LINE. HAV-ING TOWING PENNANT RIGGED. *INDEPENDENCE HALL* BOUND BORDEAUX.

On 18 June the Navy Department in Washington released to the press their version of the situation:

> The submarine *Nautilus* was struggling under her own power tonight in a rough sea without running lights or a periscope. Rear Adm. Claude C. Bloch, commander of the *Wyoming* and *Arkansas* training squadron, with midshipmen aboard, radioed to the Navy Department the submarine was being piloted blind, its bridge and periscope having been washed away.
>   Sir Hubert Wilkins, who hopes to reach the North Pole in the craft, had it sealed up. It was being directed on its course by the battleship *Wyoming.* The warship had a strong searchlight trained on the submersible, which Admiral Bloch said was rolling heavily. He added, "The *Nautilus* can see nothing!"

With final arrangements made to have the *Wyoming* tow *Nautilus* to England, the *Independence Hall* continued on her way.

KDCG FROM WSEA—MSG CAPT. MCKENZIE: ALL HANDS
ABOARD THE *NAUTILUS* ARE VERY GRATEFUL FOR THE TIMELY
ASSISTANCE RENDERED BY *INDEPENDENCE HALL*. MANY
THANKS TO YOU, SIR, AND OPERATOR MARSCHALL.
DANENHOWER.

On board *Nautilus,* the crew had had nothing to eat for several hours. No cooking without electricity. Meyers tapped out a message to the *Wyoming:*

HOW ABOUT SENDING US SOME FOOD?

Wyoming sent a big salt ham and a dozen oranges. The ham went over the side. They couldn't cook. The oranges they ate. A request was sent over for a lifeboat breaker of drinking water which was floated back at the end of the line. The water was stale, but welcomed.

Wyoming notified *Nautilus* they were going to shoot over a line and tow the boat to Ireland. A former Navy signalman, Meyers stood on the narrow, slippery sled-runner deck and semaphored instructions.

Over came a big lead sash weight flying through the air at the end of a heaving line. While midshipmen fed out the four-inch hawser that followed, three men began pulling it in. Frank Crilley was knocked overboard by Ike Schlossbach, who was struggling to show how to get the hawser over in a hurry.

Crilley went over the side with a splash. A moment later a huge wave carried him thrashing back on deck. *Nautilus* was lifted high by the wave's crest, then her bow dropped plunging into the trough, her nose cutting into the next wave. Meyers put a foot on Crilley, holding him firmly on deck as the water poured over. The bow raised again and Meyers helped Crilley to his feet.

"You darn Dutchman! Are you trying to drown me?"

"If we were over by Greenland," Meyers replied, "you wouldn't have had a chance!"

One evening during the long tow, the line broke. For a few hours *Nautilus* and her crew were on their own again. *Wyoming* turned on her searchlights as darkness fell, playing the beam across the waters to keep tabs on the submarine and her crew while submariners watched through the quartz eye-ports installed in the hull.

During the night the White Star Line *Homeric,* inquisitive about the searchlight display in mid-ocean, headed for the area. Unaware of *Nautilus*'s presence, she missed hitting the submarine by 50 to 75 yards.

The *Wyoming* finally towed *Nautilus* into Queenstown, Ireland. Her arrival was greeted by the bells of a church tower playing "The Star Spangled Banner." What a welcome! The memory of an event-filled Atlantic crossing soon faded as *Nautilus* was again taken in tow by the Dutch tub *Humber,* arriving at Cork on 22 June for a badly needed battery charge.

While the crew put up in the Queen's Hotel and looked the town over, all the submarine's bedding was sent to the cleaners. The following day Meyers and Crilley journeyed to Blarney Castle where each kissed the old Blarney Stone. Meyers remembered their wish: bring about a change for better luck.

On 24 June, *Nautilus* sailed under her own power for the first time in 10 days. Three days later, with the good wishes of the *Humber*'s captain and crew who had served as escort, the arctic submarine arrived at the Devonport dockyard for repairs. The following morning *Nautilus,* lying in dry dock, was honored by a visit from His Royal Highness, the Prince of Wales. Lady Astor, who accompanied the prince, told them they had a "one-way trip to Hades."

"We have a round-trip ticket," Meyers assured her.

"If you come back alive," she replied, "I will take you to places where even the king is not allowed to go."

"Just a minute, while I get the address," Meyers countered.

Meyer logged:

28 July 1931: 0615—Left Devonport, England, for Bergen, Norway.

29 July: 1620—Chain on steering engine carried away. Both engines stopped to repair the broken link.

Now Sir Hubert was able to send regular reports to the Hearst newspapers:

Table 1.
Members of the *Nautilus* Arctic Expedition

Sir Hubert George Wilkins, KB	Expedition leader
Dr. Harald U. Sverdrup	Leader of scientific staff
Dr. B. Villinger	Scientist and physician
Dr. Floyd M. Soule	Scientist
Emile Dorea	Pathé News photographer
Lt. Comdr. Sloan Danenhower	U.S. Naval Reserve, *Nautilus* Commanding Officer
Ike Schlossbach, USNR	Executive officer
Raymond E. Meyers[a]	Electrical and radio officer
Ralph Shaw	Chief engineer
Eddie Clarke	Quartermaster
Frank Crilley	Master diver
Carl Schnetter	Assistant engineer
Frank Blumberg	Electrician
Clarence Holland	Electrician
Ollie Riggs	Oiler
Harry Zoeller	Oiler
Raymond Drakio	Oiler
Emile Stamnes	Cook
Jacob Fleutch	Cook helper

[a]Raymond E. Meyers became a telegraph and cable operator at age 15. He was awarded the International Gold Medal by the Veteran Wireless Operator's Association for his part in the mid-Atlantic rescue of the *Nautilus* and her crew, using a jury-rigged radio transmitter. Over the years he was awarded numerous medals and citations. After retirement from the Navy he devoted many years to the International Net of Handicapped, teaching disabled persons from all over the world how to operate amateur radio stations.

Meyers, in special ceremonies in Genoa and as a guest of the Institute Internazionale delle Communicazioni, was presented by President of the Italian Republic, Guiseppi Saragat, with the 1966 Columbus award for Humanitarian Services. He was the first American to receive that gold medal.

By 0800 Monday morning we were passing through fog and hazy weather. A pilot, sent back by Commandant Moe of the Royal Norwegian Naval Base at Bergen, came aboard to pilot us into the Navy Yard.

Through the courtesy of the Norwegian government, we will prepare for our trip into the arctic waters. By 1000 hours we sighted the Norwegian coast, which was to be our final jumping off place for the ice pack—56 days out of Provincetown, Massachusetts.

The following morning *Nautilus* docked at the Royal Norwegian Navy Yard for final outfitting, and we began immediately to make preparations for our trip into the cold northern latitudes. The crew carried ashore our light clothing for storage in the warehouse until we returned. Henceforth, we would live in the submarine dress until the time came to don the heavy woolens that would be needed above the Arctic Circle.

It was late afternoon when friends and Norwegian naval officers bid us farewell on the narrow deck of the *Nautilus,* and were then put ashore. Captain Danenhower gave the order to cast off, and *Nautilus* moved away from the wharf while the crowd lining the shore gave us a rousing send-off with loud cheers.

Last minute changes in the crew had reduced our numbers by one.

The crew numbered 19.

2

NAUTILUS'S FINAL TRIP

The submarine's log read:

5 August: 1620 GMT—Left Bergen, Norway, for Tromso. Pilot on board. New members of the expedition: Dr. Harald Sverdrup; Dr. B. Villinger, the German scientist; and Dr. Floyd M. Soule. Also, a new cook, Emil Stamnes, a Norwegian, and Emile Dorea, Pathé News photographer from Paris.

Wilkins reported to the Hearst newspaper,

Electrician Rothschild, our cook, was replaced by Stamnes. Jack Lundbeck, another electrician, left us at Bergen, joining Sigruid Johnson, our carpenter, who had been engaged for the Atlantic trip only.

Dr. Sverdrup, a scientist and later director of Scripps Institution of Oceanography in San Diego, California, was the leader of the scientific staff. The Carnegie Institution of Washington, D.C., had assigned Dr. Soule to the expedition as magnetician and oceanographic assistant. He had had extensive experience taking echo-soundings to measure ocean depths and collecting deep-sea water samples.

As the third scientist, Dr. Sverdrup had secured the assistance of Dr. Villinger, a German scientist, who was also to serve as the physician of the expedition. Dr. Villinger knew the arctic conditions well from previous expeditions to Spitzbergen and Greenland. He had experiences as a physician, and had done a great deal of research work. Well qualified for an expedition such as ours.

The crew, heartened by fine weather and cheery Norwegian hospitality, departed, hopeful that, if things went well, we would have plenty of time to accomplish much work after leaving Tromso.

In the evening of 11 August, *Nautilus* slipped out of Tromso, leaving Pilot Breitvold, who had guided us along 800 miles of treacherous coastline. By 1900 the *Nautilus* was in Skjervoley—about 60 miles north of Tromso. The engineers adjusted the fuel injection valves, although there was no trouble with the fuel itself.

By Friday we were further north than any submarine had ever been and at 1900 were rounding the northwest corner of Bear Island. Then with two engines we would complete the run to Spitzbergen.

Nautilus soon ran into a storm which forced the deck watch below and we had to navigate by means of the periscope. Green seas swept broadside over the narrow deck, carrying away the light canvas bridge, as happened during the Atlantic crossing.

By 14 August *Nautilus* was cruising along the north of Spitzbergen on both engines at a speed that should bring us into Advent Bay early Saturday morning. We raised the Spitzbergen coast at 1445 GMT, when *Nautilus* came abreast of the southern tip of the gigantic Arctic Island.

Occasional rain squalls lashed the deck and the effects of the water's low temperature were beginning to appear. Dense moisture collected on every bare metal spot and water dripped almost continuously. Soon everything was sopping wet.

The thermometer registered the air inside the ship at 8 degrees centigrade; the hull of the ship and the water above was at 5 degrees centigrade. We didn't complain about the cold. When we reached the ice regions we expected to have temperatures about 0 degrees, both inside and out.

The 17th of August found us lying in Snug Harbor at Longyear City, Advent Bay, Spitzbergen. Eddie Clarke, our quartermaster who had been slightly ill during the passage from Tromso, was sent ashore. We expected him to be well enough to accompany us northward.

The following day, again to rousing cheers from the hospitable Longyear City miners, we left Advent Bay at 1500. All were well, except Clarke, who was back on board cheerfully recovering in his bunk. By 1900, using the troublesome port engine which had been put back in good condition, we rounded Dead Man's Island.

The superstructure compartments were cleared for action and everyone was eagerly awaiting our chance to try their skill with the ice. Already the Aurora Borealis painted the northern sky. At 0400 we passed Prins Karls Forland, and the northern coast of Spitzbergen disappeared from the southern horizon. Seven hours later we passed Amsterdam Island, the last land between us and the ice pack.

Cruising at eight knots with the starboard engine, *Nautilus* turned her nose north at 11 degrees west longitude where we hoped to encounter the fringe of the pack. All through the day we kept our course against heavy snow and intermittent squalls that occasionally smothered the horizon. The wind turned a little easterly as we continued northward and the temperature continued to fall. Soon the snow turned to ice pellets which peppered the deck

The season was so far advanced that the original plan to cross the Polar Sea from Spitzbergen to Bering Strait could not be carried out. Even an attempt to reach the North Pole by submarine could not be undertaken. The available time of the summer season remaining only permitted extensive trials in the area to the north and northwest of Spitzbergen, and perhaps a shorter cruise to the north under the ice.

We had two tasks before us: first, to test whether the lanes and openings in the ice could be seen from underneath; and, second, the scientists had to learn whether our scientific program could be carried out under unfavorable conditions on board a submarine. Especially, if the oceanographic work could be undertaken from the diving compartment.

The deep-sea oceanographic observations were to be taken from a diving compartment which had been arranged in the forward compartment. Originally it had been designed as the submarine's torpedo room. The diving compartment was connected by an air-lock with the spaces occupied by Dr. Sverdrup and the other scientists.

When the doors had been closed, compressed air could be bled into the diving compartment, until the air pressure was equal to the sea pressure at the bottom of the ship. When the pressure inside and outside were equal, a trap-door in the bottom of the diving compartment could be opened without water entering the room. Through this bottom door a wire cable, to which the deep-sea instruments could be attached, could be lowered.

Thanks to this arrangement, it was possible to obtain deep water and bottom samples, even if the submarine did not reach the surface.

Here the scientists could work in a closed room much more conveniently and comfortably than on the narrow deck lashed by wind and snow. A hydraulic winch, driven by a motor in the scientific compartment, lowered and raised hundreds of feet of steel wire.

The scientists had eagerly joined the expedition in spite of many deficiencies. The region to the north and northwest of Spitzbergen was for many reasons of great interest to science.

The 22nd of August found us already deep in the ice field, maneuvering to avoid colliding with drifting floes. We prepared for our first dive. With her bow whipped by a strong northwest wind *Nautilus* alternately drifted and dodged ice throughout the day. We cleared the deck and readied the ice drills. However, we soon found that the rapid drifting and heavy swells made conditions unsuitable. Within a few hours, we had drifted far south, finally being brought to a standstill by the tightly packed ice.

We continued a constant watch with drifting ice our greatest danger, twisting and turning to keep clear of fragments that menaced our propellers and diving rudder. Despite our best efforts the ship's stern and bow received many hard knocks.

When it was necessary, we flooded down aft to drop the stern until it was well under water. Then we could safely back the boat. Moving forward we went very slowly.

At last, we prepared to submerge. With the ice drifting rapidly it would be difficult to go under. While waiting for more favorable conditions for the first trials, the crew checked everything carefully, while the scientists adjusted their spectrograph, an instrument for measuring light filtering through the ice, and other gear.

Our first dives would be short. If these proved successful we would make many more. It was fortunate that we decided to conduct preliminary tests. When we came to the horizontal rudder, which normally spins easily as if it were free-wheeling, it took two men to move it.

"That's not right!" All agreed.

Crilley and Meyers went up on deck for a dive over the side to locate the trouble. Crilley tossed a quarter to see who would go into the freezing water. Crilley won the toss and slipped into the diving suit. Meyers would serve as line tender.

Crilley was doing fine. Suddenly Meyers noticed the ice had

started to move in. Fearful for the diver's safety, he gave the diving signal to come back up. Back came the answer. He was all right. Still worried, Meyers gave him a second signal. This time Crilley yanked the line hard, indicating firmly everything was okay.

Finally came the signal: "Pull me up!"

"What were you doing down there?"

"It's a wonderful sight, Ray. I was sitting on the propeller shaft on the underside of the ice. It was beautiful."

"How about the diving plane?"

"It's gone."

Recalling what they had been through all day, Meyers felt sure the plane had been broken off by a huge ice floe that earlier had struck a glancing blow with terrific force. The evidence had been recorded on film. Meyers had been taking motion pictures and photographed the huge chunk of ice as it moved rapidly in.

That ended the expedition as far as the nonscientific personnel were concerned. They did not, however, reckon with the Pennsylvania Dutchman they had for a skipper.

"We've come 10,000 miles to make a dive! Let's make it!" Danenhower decided firmly. "We'll flood the forward trim tank. We'll push her under the ice, and we'll slide along underneath it! Prepare to dive!"

In the forward compartment Crilley slipped the sound-powered telephones over his ears while Meyers waited for him to relay orders.

"Flood forward!"

Meyers opened the valves, and the bow slowly took on a down angle. Satisfied, he closed the valves and waited.

"What did he say, Frank?"

"He didn't say anything. Keep flooding."

Meyers opened the valves again for a few minutes, and stopped. He turned anxiously.

"Anything?"

"No!" Crilley repeated. "I'll give you a kick in the backside when he says stop flooding."

Meyers was really beginning to worry. All of the fresh-water tanks had already frozen, which meant the air line might also have frozen.

If that was the case, they couldn't blow the tanks in a hurry. *Nautilus*'s nose was now pointing dangerously toward the bottom.

All of a sudden the skipper gave the engine room orders to go ahead full. *Nautilus* hit the ice about the same time Crilley kicked Meyers. Perspiration beads poured from both their foreheads.

"This is a heck of an expedition," said Crilley.

"What do you mean?"

"We brought spare radio tubes, spare flashlight batteries, and spare ice drills. We have spare elements for the stove . . . but there's one spare we didn't bring, Ray."

"What is that?"

"A spare set of rosary beads. I just pulled mine all apart."

(Crilley always had a sense of humor. Years before, out of Honolulu, he made a dive on the *F-4* and faced great danger. The captain of the German cruiser *Eider,* visiting in port, was watching salvage operations. "What do you mean? You was down there?" he asked.

"Sure I was down there," Crilley replied.

"Impossible. One hundred fifty feet, ya. Three hundred fifteen feet, nein!"

Crilley turned back to Mr. Tibbles, the diving master. "Put the hat back on. Give me a wrench."

Down he went, removed the ship's bell, which was engraved USS *F-4,* brought it back to the surface and threw it on deck. The bell is now in the Navy Department as a souvenir.)

Finally, the *Nautilus* slid under the ice. Meyers quickly grabbed a movie camera and started photographing through one of the two quartz portholes. In spite of the handicaps it was a historic occasion for each member of the expedition.

Meyers's log read:

22 August: 2000—In lat. 81.20 north. Our farthest point north. Frank and I dropped in the water the VFW plaque, BPOE plaque, and a flag from Wilmington Post American Legion. Antenna up again, steaming for an open lead to get out of ice jam.

The loss of the diving plane made it impossible to cruise very far under the ice. Without diving control any submerged run would be dangerous—perhaps even disastrous. It still remained, however, to try out the scientific equipment and make such observations as conditions would permit.

Even though the expedition could not fulfill its original goal, the scientists had already shown that an extensive scientific program could be carried out under the difficult conditions on board the submarine. Wilkins had proven himself a most persistent scientist and dedicated explorer, no matter what the hardship or danger to get good information on the sea. The interest that he took in the scientific work was well illustrated when they discovered the loss of the diving plane.

Everyone on board, except Wilkins, would have been willing to return immediately—acknowledging complete defeat—but he did not for one moment consider the possibility of returning before every opportunity for scientific work had been taken.

Meyers was beginning to have difficulty maintaining radio contact with the outside world, especially sending Wilkins's reports to the Hearst newspapers.

24 AUGUST: 0127—WSEA WRH—MEYERS WSEA ... RESULTS
VOICE TESTS TODAY ZERO. ONLY HEARD ON TWO TESTS,
BOTH TIMES TOO WEAK TO USE.

By 1900 Monday *Nautilus* was less than 500 miles from the North Pole. The sun shone coldly on the horizon with high winds from the east. Danenhower picked a course through scattered ice. Choppy waves rode high above the deck, carrying with them great chunks of ice. Now *Nautilus* was in the spawn of the pack. Solid ice lay three miles north.

Nautilus moved slowly under both motor and engine power along its edge. Danenhower turned north at every opportunity, looking for an opening or a sheltered area where he might yet push under the floes and use the drills, taking soundings and bottom samples. But the winds continued, furiously lashing the decks.

Wave crests poured over the deck from stem to stern. It was impossible for men to remain on deck. Danenhower and Schlossbach took turns at the watch, with Clarke and Crilley assisting in the conning tower, keeping a sharp lookout through the periscope.

At 2214 Meyers made contact by radio with station LGS at Svalbard, Norway, and sent the first message in days:

ALL OKAY ON BOARD. LATITUDE 84.04 DEGREES NORTH,
LONGITUDE 10 DEGREES EAST, BOUND FOR THE NORTH POLE.

Meyers learned weeks later that Ronald Martin, the operator for the *San Francisco Examiner*'s radio station KUP, had picked up his message. Newspapers reported *Nautilus*'s position as approximately 256 miles from the North Pole.

26 AUGUST: WORK IN DIVING COMPARTMENT BETWEEN
1100–1630. AWAITING BETTER CONDITIONS TO WORK.

Sir Hubert reported,

For one full week we played hide and seek among the ice floes, pushing as far north as possible, seeking and gaining information, and sensing the drills. Captain Danenhower frequently shoved the submarine's slim nose beneath the ice floes that slithered from her metal sides like twin avalanches. At every opportunity Emile Dorea or I grabbed the movie camera and photographed the underside of the ice through one of the quartz windows.

On Tuesday, the diving locker crew recovered a 17-inch long and 1-inch thick column of sea bottom mud, brown in color for the first 15 inches then pale blue, representing deposits in polar waters for perhaps hundreds of thousands of years.

The first sample was taken from the bottom at a depth of 5,220 feet, through the open door of the diving chamber where the sea water was three degrees above freezing. This was the result of an operation with a new type of bottom sampler designed and operated by Dr. Sverdrup. The sampler was a glass tube, four inches long, encased in steel, and topped by heavy weights of 100 pounds. A sliding messenger of brass capped the tube after it was brought in from the bottom. The sampler was lowered at the end of a special one-eighth inch wire. Many more samples were taken during the following days.

We became locked in the ice, and decided to abandon ship. We set up our equipment in a natural ice cave. Dr. Sverdrup and Dr. Soule fixed our position—294 miles from the Pole.

Meyers had lost contact with the outside world. He tried to operate a small portable radio set to report where they were, but couldn't get the transmitter to work. It was so cold they couldn't get the gasoline engine-generator started. On the receiver, he could hear some South Sea islanders playing red-hot music. Here, they were freezing.

Wilkins later radioed,

On 31 August we again tried to push the *Nautilus* under the ice far enough to use the ice drill without success. The following day, I made radio contact with an amateur radio operator in Tromso and reported we were back on the air. The operator told Meyers reception was poor and he was just able to distinguish the signals.

Wednesday, 2 September, *Nautilus* had reached the shallow waters of the continental shelf off Spitzbergen. After fixing our position by the sun and sextant and theodolite, we decided to turn back to the western area. Stopping briefly for a few minutes to thaw out the frozen microphones of the sonic depth finder we headed west.

During the previous week, while submerged, we had for the first time in history gained a seal's eye view of the arctic ice pack. We knew what it felt like to be entirely surrounded by water two degrees below the freezing point of fresh water and capped by many tons of amethyst-tinted icicles.

The crunching of the uneven ice floes above was a fearful ungodly sound, unlike anything we had heard before. With our depth gauge reading 33 feet, we were able to look out through the *Nautilus*'s quartz portholes to view the steel-like fangs of ice moving steadily through the water as it changed in color under the influence of light and thickness, ranging throughout the entire range of blues.

These fangs leave behind showers of pearl-like bubbles. The lesser ice cakes and the small pieces glitter in bright balls of sparkling light which rival all the imagined brilliance of Aladdin's cave.

Startled small black fish about six inches long dashed through the ice holes making lightning speed for a few feet and then turning to face us. We watched their gills fluttering, their tails lashing furiously as they gazed back at us through the portholes. Shrimp and prawn-like creatures scaling down in size to almost nothing showed an active interest and concern. One species, with 18 legs, beat wildly and it appeared to spring off its tail like a miniature kangaroo conceived in a nightmare. Sea fleas and curious cockroach-shaped creatures waved their horns and steered themselves away from what must have seemed to them a double-ended whale.

Our ice drill, forward, until it was smashed, kept up a rumbling eccentric motion in keeping with the *Nautilus* twin propellers. As we pushed through the waters beneath the ice, jellyfish were the only living things that drifted seemingly unconcerned. Some of them were tiny airships in the distance. Others were of various shapes.

Even the ice appeared to live and die and, due to our forward motion, seemed to try avoiding us. It would have been well for us to keep our stern down, because the hull often came in contact with the rugged clumps of ice drawn down under the ship's quarter by suction of the propeller blades. The result was that the edge of each propeller blade on the port side soon became saw-toothed. It threw froth and bubbles far astern as we proceeded.

On the starboard side, one blade was bent over like a half-closed hand, but we were still afloat and progressing along the ice field edges toward Greenland.

Wilkins continued his lengthy report to the Hearst newspapers:

Living conditions were not comfortable, but we had some variety. At times when the submarine came to the surface in air colder than the surrounding waters the inside bulkheads would crystallize with feather-like ice. The solid ice would melt in weird—often beautiful— patterns on the bare metal surfaces. Most of the laboratory and diving compartment was adequately protected by a thin lining of spun glass. This was an experiment installed by a painter at Sears in New York, and it proved ideal.

On sunny days, when the sun's rays warmed the metal hull, the ice would melt. The bare overhead dripped and the deck was soon deep under water. Dampness even permeated all the ship's interior. Clothing became clammy and even instruments became soaked with moisture. I was kept busy rewinding several coils from the radio set, which normally would not have required repair.

On the afternoon of 4 September, her hull battered and scarred by biting tusks of ice, the forward part of the ice runner crumpled, the drill mechanism shattered, and with a leak sprung in two places, the

Nautilus pushed her way out of the arctic ice pack to comparative safety. The gallant old submarine reached clear water at 1600 Greenwich Meridian Time, at latitude 81.40 north, longitude 11 east, almost at the point just north of Amsterdam Island where we first shoved into the grinding arctic ice pack on our voyage of exploration and scientific observation.

The radio masts were upright once more and I soon established almost constant communications with the civilized world. Two days later we received a message that, in addition to the approaching winter, decided our next course of action:

"My Dear Sir Hubert:

I am exceedingly happy to hear good news from you, but I feel continued concern about the welfare of yourself and crew.

I most urgently beg of you to return promptly to safety and to defer any further adventure until another and more favorable time and a better boat.

The season is late, the ice is coming in, the *Nautilus* has been injured according to your own report. We are all alarmed about the dangers you are incurring which seem to be needless.

Will you please come back now and devote your energies to preparation for another expedition at a better time and a better vessel."

Signed
William Randolph Hearst

On 6 September, after more scientific observations of the ocean from the diving compartment, Wilkins decided to return to Spitzbergen. The ice was getting more tightly packed. On the following afternoon, *Nautilus* reached Cross Bay, where the last gravity observations were taken, and *Nautilus* sailed into Advent Bay on 8 September, after an absence of exactly three weeks.

Sir Hubert planned to sail from there, via Iceland, to New York if possible, and suggested that the scientists leave the *Nautilus* and return to Norway by a ship that was sailing that same night with a load of coal. They arrived in Bergen on 17 September.

The plan to cross the Atlantic again with *Nautilus* had to be abandoned, and the submarine turned back to Bergen, arriving on 20 September.

To fulfill the terms of his agreement with the U.S. government, Wilkins was responsible for disposing of the submarine in such a way that she could never be used again for war.

"We searched for a place to sink the gallant old ship," wrote Wilkins. "It took us six days to find 200 fathoms of water near the harbor of Bergen."

Meyers opened up the diving compartment doors, ran to the open hatch, and got out. *Nautilus* went down slowly, as if reluctant to give up. The submarine failed to sink. A ground swell, or some other force, had closed the bottom door of the diving compartment in the torpedo room.

Danenhower and the crew stayed around for a few hours until it grew dark. With her bow deep in the water and the propellers lifted high above the surface, *Nautilus* was a menace to navigation. A line was attached to prevent the boat from drifting into the path of passing ships, and they steamed around her all night with a searchlight playing on the floundering old derelict.

The following morning men went aboard and opened the kingston valves. With escaping air forming a white cloud in the cold atmosphere, water poured into the ballast tanks, sending her down on the last dive. The submarine that had made her place in history went to her glory into a watery grave—scuttled in a Norwegian fjord. The *O-12* was stricken from Navy records 9 May 1930. As the *Nautilus,* the submarine sank 20 November 1931.

3

EVALUATING THE EXPEDITION

A board of inquiry was appointed by the secretary of the Navy after World War II to evaluate for military purposes the *Nautilus* expedition to the Arctic, and its use of a U.S. Navy submarine. From the personal testimony of Sir Hubert Wilkins before the board, the reports of Sverdrup, Wilkins, and Danenhower, Wilkins's book *Under the North Pole,* and other sources, the board assembled an impressive documentation that might be valuable to any military operations into the polar regions.

Contrary to the general opinion that Wilkins had planned only to reach the North Pole, the board found that his primary mission of the *Nautilus* expedition had been to conduct geophysical research in the arctic regions that were previously inaccessible to surface ships.

This research was to include investigations in the fields of meteorology, oceanography, and earth science. It was hoped that following a comprehensive meteorology study of the Arctic, polar meteorological stations would be established to forecast seasonal conditions several years in advance. Such stations eventually might lead to the collection of scientific information that would be instrumental in developing long-distance air transportation over the North Pole area.

The experiences of past expeditions to the Arctic on foot and through the air had proved those methods of travel were not satisfactory for collecting and evaluating the various scientific data because suitable scientific apparatus could not be carried along. Survival was also critical, because a human and an airplane could operate from a base for only a short period of time exposed to the various arctic elements.

The board's report read,

Very little is known about the real arctic, and in view of its strategic military importance, it is necessary that basic information and scientific data be collected upon which to formulate future plans in all phases of global warfare.

Such data cannot be sufficiently obtained over a large unknown area like the arctic under the conditions mentioned above. It is evident then that observations must be taken over a year-round period from a vehicle or station which will afford the maximum protection to the observers from atmospheric conditions and ice. It is vital that such a vehicle or station must be capable of covering large areas inaccessible to other modes of travel and operate at a minimum cost with minimum upkeep.

Testimony from Wilkins and statements in his personal journal confirmed that Wilkins planned from the beginning to carry out the *Nautilus* expedition with the main purpose of collecting the desired scientific data while taking advantage of the various characteristics of the submersible.

This could not be accomplished by other means. To indicate the potential characteristics of a submersible operating inside the arctic ice cap and to present an exact picture of what the *Nautilus* proposed to accomplish during the arctic expedition, the following is quoted directly from the Wilkins report:

Plans of the *Nautilus* Expedition

It was realized that it would not be feasible even with a submersible in the summer months to solve the riddles of the arctic; the plans for the expedition were mainly as follows:

1. To determine whether it would be safe to establish a permanent base for scientists upon the ice somewhere between the North Pole and Point Barrow, Alaska. Which base would be

particularly valuable in connection with a plan for a meteorological investigation with relation to long distance seasonal
forecasting and for the collection of data of great value to air-
planes and airships flying in high northern latitudes.

2. To sound the depths of the Arctic Ocean with both sonic and
   manual sounding machines.

3. To collect samples of arctic sea water at various depths and
   determine the animal and mineral content.

4. To determine the velocity and direction of ocean currents
   within the Arctic Ocean for navigational purposes.

5. To observe the summer temperatures of the arctic water, ice,
   and air at various depths and altitudes.

6. To determine the magnetic variations and horizontal and vertical intensities in high northern latitudes.

7. To conduct physical experiments with the gyro compass at
   the North Pole.

8. To carry out geophysical investigations by means of a gravity
   machine.

9. To conduct wireless telegraph and telephone experiments
   from high latitudes.

10. To determine the influence of light on the development of
    surface and deep sea animal and vegetable matter within the
    arctic region.

11. To determine solar light values beneath the arctic pack ice.

12. To collect surface and upper meteorological observations
    throughout the mid-summer months in high northern latitudes.

13. To study the formation and disintegration of ice masses
    beneath the surface of polar waters.

14. To determine the influence of low temperatures on the oper-
    ation of submarines, their batteries and auxiliary equipment.

15. To determine, if possible, whether submarines may be used
    as transports for crossing the Arctic Ocean.

16. To survey the underwater surface of the ice and measure ice
    thickness in various locations.

The submarine will make possible the examination of an area hitherto
unapproached by a scientific staff equipped with a scientific laboratory and facilities for carrying out their investigation in comfort.

The board's notes on the handicaps confronting the *Nautilus* and resultant bearing on the arctic edition were:

It is the opinion of the Examining Board that the *Nautilus* expedition to the arctic had considerable merit but was seriously handicapped by the following, which directly and/or indirectly affected the successful accomplishment of the expedition.

(a) Poor material condition of submarine *Nautilus;* the submarine *Nautilus* (Navy *O-12*) as delivered to Wilkins had already seen 13 years' service in the Navy and was considered to be obsolete and in a run-down condition.

    The *Nautilus* could not be favorably compared to the present fleet-type submarine. In addition to its run-down condition and obsolescence, it was further handicapped by its thin hull, shallow test depth, riveted seams, and other weak design features.

    It was not designed to operate in and around the arctic ice pack on the surface nor was it designed to slide under the ice like a "sled" with a slight positive buoyancy.

    The engines were in need of a good overhaul and did not perform satisfactorily throughout the entire expedition. Frequently the personnel were forced to put one engine on battery charge and overhaul the other remaining engine and generator while drifting in the open sea.

    While en route from New London, Connecticut, to Bergen, Norway, the vertical steering rudder failed and a diver had to go over-the-side to repair same. The bow planes had been removed during overhaul as it was believed they would be useless for sliding under the ice. The stern planes were maintained but these dropped off after two days of operating in the pack ice northwest of Spitzbergen.

    The ice drills (engine supply and exhaust and the access drill) which had been ill-conceived from the beginning failed to operate normally even in and around the New London–New York areas. The jackknife type of periscope designed by Mr. Lake also proved unsatisfactory due to excess fogging.

(b) Difficulties concerning technical cognizance of converting the *O-12* to an arctic submarine: from the beginning and throughout the conversion job, Lake had requested and maintained final decision and determination as to the type and quality of special equipment installed. It is apparent that Lake insisted on and did install considerable equipment on the *Nautilus* which was inadequate and unnecessary, according to Wilkins who had had previous valuable experience in the Arctic and Antarctic Oceans.

Some of the major differences in selection of special equipment which developed between Wilkins and Lake included type of ice drills, type of auxiliary superstructure, type of periscope, type of conning tower, questionable need of a cushioned guide arm, and the need for cushioned bowsprit.

The most important item which caused considerable differences of opinion and which eventually affected the under-ice travel of the *Nautilus* was the selection of a satisfactory type of ice drill. Simon Lake wanted to use an elevated conning tower with drilling attachment located at the top section.

The entire drill was to be rotated by toothed gears and elevated by hydraulic rams. A peripherical nine-inch drill independently rotated at high speed and located at the top of the main tube was to do the main cutting.

According to Wilkins, the entire device incorporated many mechanical weaknesses and was further hampered by failure of the eccentric shaft which extended more than half the length of the ship and supplied power to the drill through three separate bevel gears.

In addition, the drill was impractical because of having to rotate it through four foot-long stuffing boxes which, in the low temperatures encountered, caused it to be "bound" and inoperable. It is the opinion of the Board that Wilkins' attempts to travel under the ice successfully were handicapped by the complete failure of the ice drills and loss of stern planes.

(c) Wilkins states in his report that the ship's personnel were reluctant to conduct the experimental submerged runs under the ice floes, particularly when the *Nautilus* departed from Spitzbergen and headed northwest for the "ice pack." He believed this to be due to the many material failures which had been experienced on board since the *Nautilus* left the United States and particularly in view of the non-operating ice drills and lack of stern planes.

The crew apparently were justified in their attitudes and lack of enthusiasm and interest for further operations in and under the ice fields and appeared well satisfied with their collection of scientific and operational data.

It is the opinion of the Board that had the *Nautilus* been in satisfactory material condition while in the vicinity of ice field—stern planes and ice drills in working order—perhaps Wilkins would have been able to penetrate far into the ice floes by means of hedge-hopping from one opening to another and may even have been able to reach the North Pole.

Wilkins's Plans and Operations of the *Nautilus* in the Arctic Ice Fields

The primary purpose of the *Nautilus* edition was to carry out geophysical research in the arctic regions in areas previously inaccessible to surface ships. A secondary investigation was to experiment with the *Nautilus* so as to prove or disprove the feasibility of operating a submarine under the ice fields and to investigate the possibility of reaching the North Pole by means of a series of up-and-down operations from one ice lake to another.

Wilkins planned to thread his way up through the loose ice pack on the surface and then push on toward the Pole by submerged hopping from one ice lake to another. It was his intention to conduct submerged operations by trimming the *Nautilus* with a very slight positive buoyancy and sliding under the ice floes like a sled until he reached open water, at which time he would surface, run on the engines, and then submerge again on reaching another ice floe.

If he was trapped under the solid ice floe at any time with the battery completely discharged, it was his intention to stop, anchor up against the ice, and bore up through the ice by means of special ice drills. There were three such drills on the *Nautilus:* one for engine air supply, one for engine gas exhaust, and one for access to the surface. These were probably the forerunner of the German snorkel.

Wilkins believed that there were sufficient "lakes" and open water throughout the Arctic during the summer which would not necessitate his having to use the ice drills except for an emergency. He had no sonar equipment on board the *Nautilus.* He relied on glass eye ports in the conning tower for observing the ice and for navigating while submerged.

Simon Lake had installed a jackknife type of periscope which, if struck by an ice floe, would collapse. This was poorly designed and did not function satisfactorily during the entire cruise.

The bow planes were purposely removed in the Navy yard so as to avoid entanglement in the ice floes. The stern planes were not altered but were mysteriously sheared off immediately after the *Nautilus* reached the ice pack.

Wilkins stated that this, coupled with the failure of the ice drills, discouraged the ship's crew and resulted in his not conducting an extensive and conclusive under-the-ice operation.

The *Nautilus* did succeed in running under the ice like a sled for short distances, but not without considerable difficulty. To undertake such submerged operations under the ice without sonar equipment, ice drills for emergency use, diving planes, and satisfactory buoyancy controls was not only dangerous but also was considered impractical and unnecessary.

Wilkins did prove, however, that an obsolete submarine like the *Nautilus* could sustain a severe pounding from ice floes as experienced northwest of Spitzbergen and, if thrust up against the underside of solid ice with a high degree of positive buoyancy, could be so maintained without adversely affecting the safety and stability of the ship.

Wilkins stated that the *Nautilus* was trimmed with a 30-ton positive buoyancy when it conducted its short runs sliding under the ice. He further stated that much difficulty was experienced in getting the boat completely submerged while in this condition and that the propellers "raced" above the water.

The minor damage that resulted from these submerged operations was not serious and could be blamed on the excessive buoyant trim of the ship.

What the *Nautilus* Accomplished on the Arctic Cruise

The *Nautilus,* lacking bow and stern planes, did make several short runs under the ice floes by trimming "down by the bow," pushing her way down under the ice, and sliding along under-surface like a sled. The *Nautilus* did not run submerged at a given depth under the ice floes because it had no diving controls.

Dr. Sverdrup and F. M. Soule collected and recorded observations relating to physical oceanography and meteorology and these were published in a Massachusetts Institute of Technology publication.

Recommendations and conclusions of the board, after interviewing Sir Hubert Wilkins and studying the pertinent records and reports, were, in their opinion, that operating submarines in and under the arctic ice floes "is not only feasible but also desirable in view of certain characteristics which the submarine enjoys over other modes of transportation."

4

OPERATION NANOOK

On 6 March 1944, the 2,030-ton submarine *Atule* slid down the building way at the Portsmouth Naval Shipyard in New Hampshire. The war with Japan was in its third year and the next few weeks were busy ones as yard workers swarmed over the decks readying the new boat for combat. On 21 June, the *Atule* was formally placed in commission under command of Lt. Comdr. John H. Maurer.

With a large number of Irishmen in her first crew the new fighting ship was soon given the nickname "O'Toole," and it carried a shamrock insignia designed by Walt Disney. Packed into a busy schedule of training dives and war rehearsals, the crew prepared the *Atule* for duty in the western Pacific. Many had already been through combat operations on previous war patrols. Jack Maurer himself had been through several hair-raising battles with Japanese destroyers while serving as executive officer of the *Harder* under Medal of Honor winner Comdr. Sam Dealey.

By the time they reached the war zone in late fall, all crew members were ready for action. It was not long in coming. *Atule* was ordered to join the *Pintado* and *Jallao*. The three boats formed a "wolf pack" whose objective was to coordinate and carry out search and attack.

On the night of 1 November, the *Atule* saw her first action. In poor visibility, Commander Maurer fired two torpedoes at the first target, later identified as the 16,975-ton *Asuma Maru*. The Japanese ship was torn apart by both warheads and quickly sank. Before that first patrol was finished the "O'Toole" lived up to her fighting name by sending three more ships to the bottom: two escorts and another 7,000-ton *Maru.*

In January 1945, the *Atule* joined the *Spadefish* and *Pompon* to form another wolf pack. The group roamed the Yellow Sea searching for more targets. On 25 January, *Atule* sent the fifth ship to the bottom, a 6,880-ton freighter.

A day or so before cessation of hostilities, Maurer was patrolling off the south coast of Hokkaido, the northern Japanese island. Here *Atule* was credited with her last war victim, a new escort type, which added the sixth Japanese flag to the conning tower.

"We knew it sank," said Maurer later, "because it blew up in our faces."

Her war service completed, the *Atule,* commanded by Maurer, the senior captain, led nine other submarines on the long trek back across the Pacific and through the Panama Canal for peace-time assignments along the East Coast.

Leaving the other submarines scattered at different ports along the way, the *Atule* ended her long voyage in New London, Connecticut. She was assigned to Submarine Squadron Two, to serve as a submarine school boat for training volunteers entering the Navy's silent service.

Within a few months, however, that peaceful duty was terminated by orders to an unusual type of submarine operation. "It was a welcome change," recalled Maurer. "After combat duty it was boring to operate a school boat."

In 1946, 15 years after Wilkins's *Nautilus* expedition, the Navy organized its first arctic expedition. Its mission: cold-water research, high-latitude sailing, and exploration of the iceberg-choked waters as far north as the Kane Basin, a relatively uncharted body of water separating Greenland and Ellesmere Island.

Early explorers had fought their way along the rugged coasts searching for open-water passage, but in recent years few ships except icebreakers and supply ships had ventured that far north.

Given the code name Operation Nanook, the expedition embraced a six-ship task force under command of Capt. Richard H. Cruzen.

Captain Cruzen was an officer with wide polar experience. As a lieutenant commander, he had served as skipper of Rear Adm. Richard
E. Byrd's flagship *Bear* during Byrd's 1940–41 antarctic expedition.

The task force consisted of the *Pine Island,* destroyer *Whitehead,*
the Coast Guard icebreaker *Northwind,* borrowed from the International Ice Patrol, and two other Navy ships.

One of those was to be *Atule.* Her job was to carry out submerged
operations within the ice field, and, it was hoped, take a look under
the ice pack in Baffin Bay and to the north. The gyro compass had
always been troublesome in high latitudes and here was an opportunity to test its improved design features and fire a few torpedoes to learn
how to make them more effective in the cold-water environment.

Workers began immediately to prepare the boat for under-ice
operations. Special watertight cargo lights were rigged on the forward deck, focused upward to illuminate the underside of the ice.
Using a periscope-mounted camera, developed to record combat
operations, they hoped to learn something of the ice cover, including icebergs.

Much had already been learned about icebergs and their origin
since the establishment of the International Ice Patrol in 1913 after
the tragic sinking of the oceanliner *Titanic.* The high pressure due to
the immense thickness of the Greenland ice cap resulted in the formation of numerous tongues of glacier ice that protruded from valleys and emerged into the sea. The buoyant effect of sea water with
wave and swell action resulted in the calving of icebergs.

Bergs calved on the west Greenland coast were carried northward
and westward by the west Greenland current. From there they came
under the influence of the cold Labrador current, which conveyed
them southward to the vicinity of the Grand Banks of Newfoundland
where, after entering the warm Gulf Stream, they melted.

Atule was fitted out in a fashion similar to Wilkins's *Nautilus,* but
superstructure modifications were fairly modest by comparison. Two
sled-type runners fashioned from bar steel ran from the forward end
of the sail back to the trailing edge. It was believed that if the sail
struck the ice the runners would prevent the ship from sustaining
serious damage.

An experimental echo sounder was mounted in an inverted position on the forward deck to measure the clearance between the boat and ice. Working in concert with the submarine's depth gauge they could measure both the thickness of the ice pack and keel depth of icebergs. The echo sounder was an ordinary fathometer, eventually used even on pleasure boats, to measure the depth of waters.

In late July, loaded with equipment strange to the men who manned her, the *Atule* sailed down the Thames River and entered Long Island Sound. Once clear of the coast, Commander Maurer turned his boat northward. A few days later they entered the Gulf of Saint Lawrence and passed through the Strait of Belle Isle into the North Atlantic.

When he reached the first waters of Baffin Bay, Maurer became disturbed when floating ice started to appear in their path.

"There was very little twilight that time of year," he later recalled.

We had the visibility that permitted us to see and detour around ice floes, growlers, and bergy bits, but in transit we were much perturbed on the way up. The radar didn't detect them because the ice lay low in the water and we were making routine day and night dives. We had a few occasions where we very nearly stove in our bow with icebergs. Surprisingly enough we soon gained confidence. We found we could edge our way in and force the brash ice apart to penetrate the field to considerable depth.

Jack Maurer did not hesitate for long in attempting a major objective of his mission. Sighting a bergy bit he eased his boat up to the edge, looked it over carefully, and took the submarine under. Slowly he followed the rough contour of the berg's sloping keel. The sled runners struck the ice, pushing the boat clear. Surfacing, they found the runners had proven effective. The superstructure had suffered no structural damage.

In the early hours of 28 July, *Northwind* ran aground while exploring uncharted waters near Dundas Harbor, on the southeast coast of Devon Island. The destroyer *Whitehead,* which served as escort and sonar communications link to the submarine while it was carrying out under-ice exploring, rushed to the icebreaker's assistance. *Atule*

continued skirting the southern edge of the solid ice pack, searching for a suitable place to go under.

By 0900 *Whitehead* was sighted returning from her rescue mission. *Northwind*'s skipper, an experienced Coast Guard ice pilot, had
been able to free his ship from the rocks without help.

A low overcast sky pressed down on the cold sea, causing visibility to open one moment and close the next. By 1000 snow began to
fall, reducing visibility to a few hundred yards. It was a dismal scene.
The temperature stood at 34 degrees Fahrenheit. A 15-knot wind
from the southwest whipped the snowflakes swirling about the bridge.
Wrapped in heavy woolen GI cold-weather clothing, the bridge watch
maneuvered *Atule* carefully along the edge of the pack.

"We didn't have a commitment to go very far," Maurer later
remembered.

> We didn't have a need to. What we wanted to do was to go under the
> pack and see just what the characteristics were and while submerged
> get some sort of feeling for it. We got a feeling in a hurry! We were in
> the wrong location of Kane Basin and the pack was loaded with cap-
> tive bergs!

At 1200 the navigator fixed their position at latitude 79 degrees
11.5 minutes north, longitude 73 degrees 15 minutes west. Maurer
radioed his position report to Captain Cruzen on *Pine Island* and
ordered, "Prepare to dive."

To the south, occasional icebergs and bergy bits drifted on a mean-
dering course toward Smith Sound, pushed by opposing currents and
shifting winds.

The destroyer stood by while *Atule* was taken down for a trim
dive. Satisfied, Maurer brought his boat back to the surface. Three
hours later he found the spot he was looking for.

Maurer later reported,

> Before we went under, we edged our way up to the limits of a floe and
> viewed the scene from the surface. We could see that pressure ridges
> and trapped icebergs extended up to considerable heights. It made us a
> little apprehensive to start with because we knew that if they were that
> high above the surface their keels would be four or five times as deep.

Commander Maurer's log records what they found:

1529—Dived for experimental photography under the edge of the ice field. USS Whitehead *maintaining position parallel to ice at 2 knots in sonar communications with Atule, and echo ranging on her during dive.* Whitehead *300 to 500 yards from ice on easterly headings. Atule submerged between* Whitehead *and ice on parallel course, then angled under the edge of ice on divergent 30-degree course at depth of 65 feet, checking operations of secure echo sounding machine, submerged camera and floodlight circuit. All tests proved satisfactory with echo sounding machine establishing ice thickness within 2 feet. Changed to southerly heading, after proceeding about 500 feet under ice, passed under* Whitehead *and surfaced after establishing that area clear of growlers, using smoke bomb and word from* Whitehead *on sonar.*

1643—Dived. At 65 feet diverged from Whitehead *course by 70 degrees and headed under ice, checking position with respect of ice and* Whitehead *on DRT.*

1645—Under brash ice on edge of consolidated pack. Secure sounding machine indicating 1 to 2 feet of field ice below surface. Ice thickness commenced increasing rapidly and the 15-foot clearance between shears and underside of ice rapidly changed to 8 feet. Stopped and ordered 70-foot depth. Distance under ice 1,000 yards. Readings changed rapidly from 5 fathoms 4 feet, to 3 fathoms 2 feet as we passed 70 feet, going to 80. A reading of 3 fathoms meant zero clearance between top of shears and underside of ice.

"As we addressed it," Maurer recalled, "the ice got thicker and thicker, forcing us down. We were forced down to where we were beginning to get a little worried about the clearance between the ship's keel and the bottom of Kane Basin!"

Simultaneously, with readings of 2 fathoms 5 feet we struck the underside of the ice with a plainly audible grinding, and a belated order to 100 feet. Keel depth 73 feet, indicating the ice thickness of 23 feet below the surface. Struck ice again and started for 150 feet, 47 feet of ice below the surface, and at 150 feet, 62 feet of ice—up to 87 feet.

Pictures were taken at the time of striking ice, and during changes in depth. Echo ranging was not satisfactory for searching ahead because of multiple reverberations from all ice projections. Reversing course, passed under Whitehead *and surfaced. We had thoroughly scouted the field ice from the surface prior to submerging, and had chosen a stretch that presented the most uniform flat surface free of pressure ridges and captive ice bergs. Yet, ice extended down to 87 feet maximum, and varied from 25 feet to that thickness.*

The *Atule* had successfully penetrated the ice pack nearly a mile. Maurer had gone far enough to learn that a rugged ceiling faced a submarine that dared to go under the frozen canopy.

One periscope had been wrecked when it struck the ice while photographing. Two rolls of film had been exposed before it was knocked out and these were sent to the destroyer for developing. By 2000 that night the film had been processed with disappointing results. The high-intensity cargo lights had blown early in the dive and the sun's rays that reached the surface through low clouds and snow had penetrated the ice with only enough illumination to merely change the shading of the negatives.

Early the following morning, the wind shifted to the southwest, increasing to gale force. Forced to remain on the surface in a sea of churning, scattered ice, the *Atule*'s deck was lashed with a mixture of rain and wet snow. Visibility was almost zero. Further under-ice exploring had to be abandoned.

Leaving the destroyer to continue her own work, the *Atule* was put on a course for Thule, Greenland. By mid-morning the wind dropped, snow and rain ceased, and with increased visibility Maurer ordered standard speed on all four engines.

Outside Wolnetenholme Bay the waters were again filled with icebergs. Maurer reduced to two engines to slow speed and maneuvered carefully into the bay littered with growlers. As a representative of the U.S. government, Commander Maurer paid the customary courtesy call on Danish diplomatic officials stationed at Thule and made plans to move farther north for more work.

Up to this time the crew had an unusually good record of perfect health. Suddenly a young crewman became seriously ill with a lung hemorrhage. Hoisting anchor, *Atule* raced south to the *Pine Island* where a doctor went to work. It was thought that the hemorrhaging had been brought under control, but later that night it began again. The young sailor literally bled to death.

With a crew saddened by the loss of a shipmate, the *Atule* worked her way up the coast to Etah, the scene visited by many early explorers. Sir Allen Young of the *Pandora* erected a cairn on the bleak coast recording his visit in 1875 while searching for the *Alert* of the Sir George Nares expedition. The *Fram* had stopped there in August 1898.

A short distance to the north in Lifeboat Cove the American steamer *Polaris* with members of Capt. Charles Hall's expedition was abandoned in a sinking condition in 1872.

Maurer anchored *Atule* in the great Foulkes Fjord. From the deck, men could see what they thought were small mountain goats picking their way along the barren rocky cliffs. Climbing into a small wooden dory built especially for their arctic cruise and powered by an Evinrude outboard motor, Commander Maurer and a few men went ashore to investigate. The "mountain goats" were found to be huge snowshoe rabbits wandering over the rocks searching for food. The country's short summer welcomed only the hardiest of animals.

A small cabin sat perched above the great fjord's cold waters, the only remaining evidence of a World War II weather and radio station. On the walls someone had scrawled "Kilroy was here."

Maurer later related,

Back out in open water, we went under good-sized bergy bits with the idea of getting some measurements. We wanted to learn just how deep they did go. We did get measurements at times, but it was tricky. There was that unknown element. When you stick your nose up into an iceberg while submerged you are never quite sure just what you will find. We visualized all sorts of things. We might get trapped in there. How deep does the ice extend?

We knew from our own studies above water that there were huge cavities and caves. If we accidentally stuck the submarine into a cave, could we get back out? Did we have enough power to do it? We couldn't always come back to the surface and with our battery-powered submarine we were a little bit more careful. The runners occasionally struck ice. The sub bounced clear, preventing serious damage to the sail.

After several more weeks *Atule* and *Northwind* began working their way south past Devon Island. They hoped to follow a new course along the western side of Baffin Bay.

Maurer recalled,

> We came down the west side of the bay and entered the middle pack. We went under the ice again, coming up in a huge polynya, trying to work our way through. The route was ice-choked and impassable. We were forced back up the Baffin Island coast and eventually forced to move back across to the east side of Davis Strait, retracing the route we had taken north weeks before.

The *Atule* fired a dozen torpedoes to test their operation in cold water and to determine if there was a degradation of torpedo speed.

"We did test them," said Maurer. "We tried to chop some icebergs down to size but weren't very successful. We made practically no impression on them whatsoever!"

Sir Hubert Wilkins's theory of using explosives to blow an escape route to the surface from deep inside the polar ice pack did not appear too promising.

On 14 August, during the time when Commander Maurer was slamming torpedoes into icebergs floating in Baffin Bay, the Air Force made an important discovery of its own far to the west. Crewmen of a weather plane, while making a flight from Ladd Air Force Base, Fairbanks, Alaska, to the North Pole, passed over a huge glacial fragment 300 miles north of Point Barrow. It was an unusual sight to find a huge piece of fresh-water ice several square miles in area amidst the arctic ice pack so far from the Canadian archipelago where the nearest glaciers of great size form.

Its drift course was watched with considerable interest. Beginning with the *Fram* expedition, observers had found that in the Northern Hemisphere ice usually drifted to the right of the surface-wind direction. According to scientists, that phenomenon was caused by Coriolis force, the deflecting force of the earth's rotation. Month after month, "Target X," later identified as "Ice Island T-1," followed a slow circle course westward, drifting from its place of birth, which was believed to be the west coast of Ellesmere Island. Years later another submarine and other ice islands would meet under other circumstances.

The *Atule*'s part in the Navy's probe of the Arctic Ocean drew to an end. Leaving the Arctic Circle behind, Maurer retraced his route back through the Strait of Belle Isle. At a brief stop at Magdalen Islands crewmen found lobster fishermen still living in a relatively primitive environment using Coleman lanterns to light their homes.

After a last stop at Halifax, Nova Scotia, the Navy's first arctic submarine returned to New London. Commander Maurer had taken his first command through a brief, spectacular period of combat and an arctic expedition. He continued as her skipper until *Atule* was placed out of commission, excess to the Navy's peacetime needs.

Although the *Atule*'s patrol was a great experience, the operation lacked the necessary team of naval officer (to operate the submarine) and Navy scientist (to provide technical assistance). The combination was needed to gain important knowledge in a step toward achieving a submarine under-ice capability. Collection of environmental data and correlation of the data of under-ice operational technique proved essential to the evolution of under-ice equipment developed in the years following *Atule*'s independent effort.

5

THE *SENNET* IN THE ANTARCTIC

Operation Nanook was a relatively small beginning in polar operations by the Navy, but it stirred interest for a much greater effort. While the task force was still exploring the cold waters of Baffin Bay, Fleet Adm. Chester W. Nimitz, Chief of Naval Operations, signed a directive in 1946 to set up a second polar expedition in 1947.

Given the code name Operation Highjump, this antarctic expedition was the largest ever organized by any nation in the history of geographic exploration. It was to be conducted as a part of the research and training program of the Navy Department, under the direction of Rear Adm. Richard E. Byrd who, as a Navy pilot, had conquered both the North and South Poles by air.

A short time after Admiral Nimitz issued his directive, the Navy Electronics Laboratory in San Diego, California, received a letter from the Chief of Naval Operations. It described the forthcoming expedition to be carried out during the approaching antarctic summer. Did the scientists in the Experimental Submarine Group at the laboratory have any ideas they wanted to test or experiments they wanted to conduct in the South Polar region?

"We realized immediately," remembered Dr. Waldo K. Lyon, at that time a young physicist who headed the group, "that this would give us an excellent opportunity to further study sound transmission conditions. Also, we could study some oceanography in an area where the waters are very cold."

Dr. Lyon promptly suggested that a submarine be added to the task force and volunteered to join the crew. The idea met with immediate approval.

Operation Highjump consisted of 4,000 officers and men manning 13 ships in three groups. One group consisted of two cargo transports loaded with Admiral Byrd's sledge dogs, men, and supplies, a command ship, two icebreakers, and one submarine. That group was to operate in the Ross Sea. Its destination was Little America, riding the great Ross Glacier on the shore of the Bay of Whales, Admiral Byrd's base on his three previous antarctic expeditions.

The *Sennet,* also a war veteran with four sunken Japanese ships to her credit, was the fleet submarine selected. Stationed at the Navy's Balboa operating base at the northern end of the Panama Canal, she was closest to the jumping-off point for the long 7,000-mile cruise to the Scott Island rendezvous point. While the group waited for several units of the expedition to arrive from East Coast ports, extensive preparations began.

Under command of Comdr. Joseph B. Icenhower, *Sennet* had just returned with Submarine Squadron Six from a visit to Callao, Peru, and immediately commenced a scheduled upkeep period to ready the boat for the long trip ahead. To streamline the superstructure, the plastic windshield was removed from the open bridge cockpit. A K-25 underwater camera was installed on the bridge with four 1,000-watt diving lamps mounted on the shears for underwater illumination.

A protective ice shield was added to the radar antennas that extended above the shears that were vulnerable to floating ice. A small boat stowage was rigged aft of the conning tower just forward of the five-inch gun. Another camera for 35mm motion pictures was mounted on a special stand forward of the periscope shears with a clear view for underwater photography.

After a final check of all machinery, *Sennet* headed into the Gulf of Mexico for an overnight full-power trial run and one deep dive.

On 1 December 1946, Commander Icenhower made his report to Richard H. Cruzen, now a rear admiral and Task Force 68 commander: "*Sennet* ready for duty!"

All hands formed a human chain, cramming storage lockers with tons of fresh and dry provisions. Two war-shot torpedoes were loaded into torpedo racks, one forward and one aft, for experiments on icebergs.

On the fifth anniversary of the Japanese attack on Pearl Harbor, the task force flagship *Mount Olympus,* with Admiral Cruzen's two-star flag flying at the masthead, arrived at the Balboa Naval Base. With her were the Coast Guard icebreaker *Northwind,* the *Pine Island,* a seaplane tender, and the destroyer *Brownston.*

More supplies, including winter clothing, came aboard the *Sennet* for the 82-man crew, overflowing storage lockers onto the decks, reaching into every compartment corner.

At precisely 0950, Tuesday, 10 December, *Sennet* backed away from her pier and moved toward the first locks of the Panama Canal. All ships had cleared the last lock by 1400 and entered the waters of the Pacific Ocean. A course was set for the Antarctic with *Mount Olympus* leading the column.

While the flagship set the pace, *Sennet* carried out daily training dives, dropping behind, then racing to catch up to her position nearly a mile astern of the column.

Within a few days Dr. Lyon, Icenhower, and the crew would go to work on the first phase of oceanographic studies. Beginning on 15 December, as a part of the expedition's continuing plans to chart the ocean floor, *Sennet* slowed her engines once each hour for slow-speed depth measurements.

The operation paid off. At 0900 the following morning they discovered a great uncharted submerged mountain, with two huge peaks, rising from the ocean floor. One peak rose to within 1200 feet of the surface and the second, 12 miles farther south, peaked just 1,170 feet below the submarine's keel. *Sennet* again lost a great deal of distance and spent the next day at full power, catching up.

It was 2200 in the evening of 20 December when the group crossed into a zone known to seamen as the "Roaring Forties." Here the cold easterly winds from the polar region meet the warm humid opposing winds of the middle latitudes where gale follows gale in endless succession.

With Admiral Cruzen setting his speed for surface ships, Commander Icenhower was forced to spend less time taking soundings.

Regaining position was increasingly difficult in high seas. During the many hours of high-speed cruising, the boat's huge diesel engines had depleted the submarine's fuel supply. Fueling at sea while under way even in good weather demanded a high degree of skillful maneuvering. Now stormy weather tossed the submarine and tanker *Canisteo* about as if they were toys.

The first line from the tanker came over at noon. Twenty-five-foot waves crashed over the small boat's bow while crewmen struggled for a foothold to make connections. The heavy drag on the fuel hose was too much. Within 20 minutes the hose parted, pouring oil into the sea. Men on deck had to be relieved often. Finally, after nearly six hours, all lines were clear. The oil tanker had pumped 39,000 gallons of diesel fuel into *Sennet*'s tanks.

Icenhower wrote in his log,

> *For our first time fueling at sea, we were initiated properly. All hands in the fueling party were given a hot toddy and put to bed, much bruised and battered and very cold. Station keeping was a problem and we were mighty glad when the last line went back to the tanker.*

On 24 December, Commander Icenhower wrote in his ship's log, "It was the night before Christmas—all was quiet!"

But on Christmas Day, the entry was different:

> *Our pride and joy, the small boat upon which so much loving care had been lavished by the Sub Base, Balboa, was swept overboard. A section of the life line went with it. Holding down rods snapped like matchsticks. We have Atule's boat aboard the Mount Olympus.*
>
> *During the day we had a songfest, big dinner, and eggnog party. Had a small Xmas tree in the control room and tried to capture the spirit of Christmas. Sent a summary of day's activities to CTF 68 for broadcast to the States.*

Also on Christmas Day, all hands had their turn on the small bridge for a look at their first iceberg. The huge glacial fragments came from the 160,000-square-mile Ross Ice Shelf, which moved down the continent's northern slope about four feet each day. From his many years of studies in the Antarctic, Admiral Byrd had determined that it was possible for a single cake of ice as much as 800 square miles in area to be broken from the Ross Shelf. It was a formidable opponent that lay between the task group and the Bay of Whales. It was a welcome sight when at 2300 the veteran icebreaker *Northwind* came into view.

At 2000 on 28 December, *Sennet* crossed the Antarctic Circle. During the night while steaming at the rear of the column, Icenhower followed the movements of the two ships ahead, careful to avoid loose ice and more bergs.

Another fueling maneuver was scheduled. By 30 December the four hungry diesels had consumed 85,700 gallons of oil. Another 40,000 gallons were pumped into the tanks while *Canisteo* and *Sennet* dodged ice by changing course several times.

As the old year neared its end, Scott Island hove into view. Commander Icenhower's log showed 7,020 miles from the Panama Canal Zone to the lone sentinel that marked the arrival of ships to the Antarctic. Named after Capt. Robert F. Scott by Captain Colback of the *Morning* who first discovered it in 1902, the white-capped black rock rose out of the sea among hundreds of blue and white icebergs. The island was the only land above water within a radius of more than 300 miles.

An Adelie penguin suddenly appeared on the stern. *Sennet* had not passed close enough to an ice floe for the first visitor to get aboard and it was assumed that the penguin had washed from the water onto the low deck of its own volition. "The penguin," recalled Commander Icenhower, "was named Cosmo. When frozen fish failed to tempt him (or her) the ship's cook baked a cake. When Cosmo failed to eat that, the cook took a razzing from his shipmates."

Refusing to make friends, Cosmo remained alone, standing on the turtle back, aft of the wooden deck. Thirty-five hours later it disappeared, just as suddenly as it had arrived.

At 0830 on the last day of the year, Dr. Lyon reported aboard for duty. He had transferred from the USS *Merrick,* which he had joined at Port Hueneme. That night the icebreaker investigated the ice pack to the south for a distance of 100 miles. Her HOC-4 helicopter, piloted by Lt. James Cornish and accompanied by Captain Thomas of the *Northwind,* flew some 50 miles beyond.

No end of the pack was seen, but Thomas, a veteran polar ice-breaker skipper, reported the pack as old and in the process of disintegration in the antarctic summer. After a conference on board *Mount Olympus,* Admiral Cruzen made his decision: proceed to their destination, Little America.

It was soon necessary for the icebreaker to force a channel through close-packed floes of young ice. The *Mount Olympus* was a great help to the submarine. Her broad beam widened the newly formed channel, but Icenhower was still forced to keep his boat close astern to take advantage of the cleared path before growlers and pack ice closed in.

Careful piloting demanded constant vigilance by the submarine officers. Commander Icenhower had organized his officer watch list so that he himself, his executive officer, and the third officer acted as ice pilots during two-hour watches. Having been thoroughly schooled by accounts of early ships fighting their way through the churning ice field long before, the skipper laid down two basic ground rules. First, "never to hit ice of any size that you don't have to, and take it at a glancing blow if you have to hit it!" And second, "that not being possible, put the bow against the ice at a dead slow speed, then push it away!"

"The first of these two instructions," Icenhower said later, "became very foolish within the hour." His entry in the ship's log explained:

> 1 *January 1947: Entered New Year and progressively heavier pack. Temperature 25 degrees Fahrenheit and seemed like 25 degrees below. Pack conditions not too bad until 0330 when* Merrick *beset, and* Yancey *almost immediately there. She was followed in turn by the* Mount Olympus. *Leads closed in around* Sennet. *We flooded down aft to put propellers deeper. Had prop guards about a foot under water.*

> 0400—Northwind *to rescue of all hands. She roared up the port side, out across our bow to cut us out, then went on ahead to cut* Mount Olympus.

As soon as the submarine was broken out, Commander Icenhower shouted jokingly across the icebreaker's bridge, "Those guys up ahead are all that's holding us back!"

The crew watched. "It's a rare sight," he wrote, "to see *Northwind* cut a ship out of the ice. She rocks, rolls, twists, and rides up on the ice to break through. *Sennet* cleared the patch, then, by easing ahead slowly, forced a crack with her bow."

Within two and one-half hours the column was moving ahead slowly, forcing its way through increasingly heavy pack ice. *Sennet* tried desperately to keep up to within 75 to 100 yards astern of the larger ship. By 1000 the wind freshened considerably and the ships ahead were having an increasingly difficult time. The icebreaker again roared to the rescue. In Captain Thomas's words, the icebreaker really "earned her salt." All ships were soon in the clear and heading slowly south.

The column eventually broke into a small lake. It was 1500 when Cruzen ordered his charges to halt. Leaving the group in their temporary haven, he took the *Northwind* ahead to investigate ice conditions further south. The radio flashed a storm warning. Snow began to fall. Winds whipped across the bridge.

The strain of the past few hours left the submarine's three ice pilots exhausted. The passage thus far had been tough on the antarctic novices. The lake where *Sennet* lay, scant miles from the edge, was surrounded by bergs and heavy pack, creating a breathtakingly beautiful scene that fascinated many early explorers and often caused them to risk their lives in search of the unknown. Their lake also held several large bergs and a six-foot ice pan floating around, but there was ample sea room to maneuver and avoid danger for the moment. The task force commander ordered the ships' captains to get some rest while a plane from the carrier made another reconnaissance flight south.

"I have said nothing about the beauty of the pack today," wrote Icenhower, "but early in the day when the sun was out it was really awe inspiring. So ends the first day of the New Year."

The early morning hours found the submarine still maneuvering to remain in clear lanes, avoiding the constantly changing surface pattern. While the submarine waited for a review of plans, the plane headed south, passing overhead at 0730. The icebreaker continued short trips to test the ice. For nearly five miles she broke her way through heavy pack, circling a large iceberg, and returned to the lake. The plane pilot's report was even less encouraging. As far south as he could see, the endless field of white broken stratum of heavy floes towered as high as a ship's bridge. Here and there a berg reached its jagged peak above the ice field. It seemed endless.

It was 1900 when the *Northwind* returned to the lake and Admiral Cruzen summoned the four commanding officers aboard for a conference. The plane had discovered a large polynya about 40 miles south which the admiral considered a much safer spot than the one they were in. In case of a blow, the approaching storm could play havoc with the ice against the thin-skinned ships. Nearly 700 miles of hard going still lay between them and the Bay of Whales. At 2230, the five ships again formed a column, left the small lake, and entered the pack.

On 3 January, while passing through a gap in a great pressure ridge, *Sennet* became beset a second time. *Yancey* had stopped ahead, forcing the remaining ships to halt. All were soon locked tight. When the command ship was finally able to move her propeller, wash piled up more chunks around the submarine. By working hard, Icenhower forced his way through and triumphantly reported to the icebreaker that they didn't need help.

His elation was short-lived. Within 1,000 yards *Sennet* was again beset. This time Icenhower had to use every ounce of power available to break free. Another mile and the boat was again beset. *Northwind* came crashing through to the rescue, relieving the pressure and cutting the submarine free.

By 0530 the following morning, the group reached a small open lake. It was the third day of fighting ice and the storm. Still only about 65 miles inside the pack, Cruzen evaluated their progress as far from satisfactory. He decided to take all ships back to the nearest open water some four miles north.

Each ship would be returned to safety individually, aided by *Northwind*. *Sennet* was to be taken first. After 500 yards of slow progress the submarine again became beset—locked tight, unable to move.

Northwind cleared the sub's bow and passed a tow line. It took two hours to make just three miles, during which the tow line broke twice. Finally, *Northwind* was forced to shorten the tow, snugging the submarine's bow right up into the crotch of the icebreaker's stern.

By 0800 the next morning they reached a small polynya surrounded by icebergs and heavy pack ice. Leaving Icenhower to his own devices, the rescue ship headed back south for the other three charges. When Captain Thomas arrived, Cruzen decided to keep the ships where they were, about three miles from pack and four icebergs south of the submarine.

Sennet's safety did not last long. By 1800 that night a pressure ridge pushed by the pack to the north broke loose, closing the polynya and squeezing the small boat against constantly shifting ice. Answering her call for immediate help, the icebreaker came charging to the rescue, an hour and a half later.

"At this point," recalled Icenhower, "all hands on the *Sennet* murmured 'God bless 'em' when the *Northwind* came into view."

Ice had built up over the bulging tanks, crowding onto the submarine's low deck in the way of the after capstan.

"It was a tight situation," remembered Dr. Lyon.

"The *Northwind* broke us out by relieving pressure on the starboard," recalled Icenhower, "where the ice was only about four feet thick and then took *Sennet* in tow."

Within one hour the tow cable parted under the heavy strain. The icebreaker's crew attempted to prevent that from happening again. "This time," said Icenhower, "they passed us a cable that I believed would pull the bow off before the cable would part. She again was towing us with the bow up against her stern in a padded crotch."

Admiral Cruzen decided that after three days they had made a maximum effort. *Sennet* should be sent back to Scott Island, while he continued on to McMurdo Sound with Byrd's men and supplies. For the submarine's captain and his crew, it was a hard decision to accept. "Although we knew it had to be," said Icenhower, "almost every member of the crew expressed his disappointment that we could not see Little America after coming as far as we had."

During the night of 3 January, *Sennet*'s bow had suffered greatly while riding up on *Northwind*'s stern. The icebreaker's huge propellers churned broken ice that crashed against the sub's bow with considerable pounding. By 0800 the other three ships began calling for help. Reluctantly, *Sennet* was left to fend for herself. Her log records the trying hours that followed:

0820—Cast loose in more loose pack because Mount Olympus, Merrick, *and* Yancey *need help and we can make more time following 100 to 150 yards astern of* Northwind.

*0920—*Northwind *forced to leave us in small lake to return to other three ships whose condition is critical. As* Northwind *left us in a snow flurry, we had a feeling of aloneness akin to desolation. After snow cleared, our position was roughly as follows:* Sennet *was 35 miles north of the other three ships. Our lake was about one mile by three-fourths mile in extent with wind from 270 degrees true.*

We stayed on the windward side of the lake and as ice broke loose from the side we would maneuver to let it pass clear of us. The wind freshened to force 6 in the afternoon with frequent snow squalls. The closest berg was about 2 miles but tracked clear. One big berg was in the east, tracked as a possible threat but was 10,000 yards away, so tracked it closing slowly toward us, but with a good possibility of its passing us to the north. As the day progressed the lake remained about the same with the weather improving slightly.

Pack around us was of varying thickness but the major portion of it was 4–5 feet thick. Large blocks forming north of the lake were about 30 feet thick, and moved with current to northeast, as did the berg. Pack ice moving to east with wind making an ever changing picture.

2400—Berg bearing tracked. Has moved in to 1500 yards on northern side of pond.

5 January: 0000–0300—Berg shifted direction. Broke into our lake and made it look plenty crowded. It moved across to southerly side closing off our originally small lake. Wind died down and berg started moving 280 degrees true again—toward us! When the range got to 550 yards it broke loose from southerly side and we moved between pack and berg to easterly side of lake.

0400—Berg now well clear and moving away. "Hearts resumed normal anatomical position." It had so much underwater body it would have taken another berg to stop it!

Icenhower had been sending hourly reports on their shaky situation. By 0415 Cruzen reported the other ships were in comparative safety and that *Northwind* was returning. *Sennet*'s radio operator immediately began sending a series of long dashes with his Morse code key to give the icebreaker a signal to home in on. While the icebreaker's direction-finder held a steady bearing, Captain Thomas pushed, smashing floe after floe, twisting and turning in search of weaker points.

At 0600 the wind shifted 90 degrees in a five-minute period, bringing more snow and a changing picture of the sub's pond. Ice began to break off the southern edge. Their once-free area kept growing smaller and smaller.

Starting at 0800, at Thomas's request, Icenhower commenced firing flares with their Buck Rogers pistol to guide the rescue ship the last few miles. By 0915 men on the bridge and the radarman made contact. With the aid of radar bearings, the submarine officers began tracking the approaching ship, although the radar screen had solid pack and bergs all over it. Coached by the radar operator, the vessel was tracked the last few miles with no strain.

By 1045 the submarine had taken station astern once again. They were making excellent time when at 1520 Scott Island's black form came into view. Before bidding a sad farewell to the icebreaker's crew, Icenhower moved alongside to starboard. "We gave 500 gallons of lube oil to *Northwind*," said Icenhower. "A submarine's reserve of lube oil was considerable." When the job was finished *Sennet* moved on to open water, while Captain Thomas took his ship back into the ice pack.

Little could be done to repair the damage sustained during those trying days early in the new year, but for the record the crew inspected and took underwater photographs of the propellers, shaft, and battered superstructure. The boat vibrated badly, especially at speeds above five knots. The outer edge of one blade on the port propeller was bent aft 8 to 10 inches. Elsewhere the rock-hard ice had left its mark. A crack was found in the hull plating close to number 7 torpedo tube. Superstructure plating was dimpled and cracked in several places along the boat's side.

In spite of *Sennet*'s injuries, there was much work to be done. While the main body of the central group fought its way to Little America, Icenhower scouted the ice edge and surveyed the area within a 30-mile radius of Scott Island.

On 7 January the seaplane tender *Currituck* began trying to get planes into the air for scouting. Icenhower sent Admiral Cruzen hourly weather reports while standing by as an auxiliary seadrome and acting as radio relay for the eastern and western groups.

Dr. Lyon recalled,

> For the next couple of weeks we worked with *Sennet,* making tests and experiments with the operation of the submarine on the surface near the ice. We made some submerged runs, but stayed in open water simply to learn what sonar ranges we could get on icebergs.
>
> We did not make any attempts to go under the ice at that time. We studied the situation and realized that what we needed was a good reliable sonar system to tell the story of the ice we might be cruising under. It was the first experience I had ever had with sea ice or icebergs or with knowledge of working in sea water at the freezing point.

Sennet also began extensive tests with the sonar to establish the feasibility of ice navigation in reduced visibility. The experiment proved effective and, using sonar alone, scientists developed a contour of the pack's edge and ice fingers extending up to 1,000 feet from the pack. The results were excellent. Growlers and loose ice along the edge showed up clearly from 500 yards as Icenhower made his approaches.

On 9 January, the *Sennet* was ordered to a new station 200 miles east to act as weather station, auxiliary seadrome, and lifeguard for any pilots forced down. Numerous icebergs and brash dotted the open water. An average of 60 ice monsters crowded in white dots on the radar scope at all times.

On 12 January the barometer started dropping rapidly. In the early morning hours, winds increased to gale force. They were in for another blow. The day was spent avoiding bergs when the storm hit, bringing both snow and rough seas. Icenhower was forced to move his boat still farther north to avoid loose ice. High seas poured over the low deck. By late evening the barometer had dropped to 29:00. *Sennet* could barely hold a course in the storm.

Two days later the storm eased and Admiral Cruzen ordered the boat back to Scott Island. While the submarine maneuvered through still-treacherous seas, Dr. Lyon and the sonarmen worked to improve the sonar's performance.

During the weeks that followed, while the icebreaker hammered its way through shelf ice toward the Bay of Whales with tons of supplies, sledge dogs, and heavy equipment for the base at Little America, *Sennet* continued her work.

The ship's log recorded:

21 January—We were to the west of Scott Island and sea moderate because of protection of pack east of Scott.

23 January—Asked Northwind *for rendezvous point in order to proceed in company with her to rendezvous with* Philippine Sea. *Spent entire day trying to find her in dense fog.*

When *Sennet* joined up with the *Philippine Sea,* Dr. Lyon, his work completed, was transferred to the carrier. "It was with regret we saw him leave," wrote Commander Icenhower. "He has been an excellent shipmate and a great help. Our sound department is especially improved by his help and guidance."

Icenhower moved close to the tanker *Capacon* for another fueling and transferred a packet of pay receipts signed by his crew. An hour later he put the sub's bow close under the tanker's stern to receive a bag of money. "Great interest in safe transfer shown by all hands!" he wrote in his log.

At 0800 4 February *Sennet*'s part in the Navy's antarctic expedition ended. Commander Icenhower set a course for Wellington, New Zealand. While making turns for 12 knots and fighting high seas with damaged propellers, the boat barely made 7 or 8 knots.

On 9 February, they sighted Banks Peninsula, South Island, still 36 miles away as it rose over the horizon. At 0715 the following morning the submarine entered Port Nicholson, Wellington, and moored to the dock at the Royal New Zealand Air Force Base in Shelly Bay.

The excitement for the small submarine and her crew was not over. A hurricane was approaching. On Friday, 14 February, *Sennet* shifted berth to the Burnham Wharf to take on more fuel for the homeward journey. The storm struck with all its fury. The already battered boat was thrown against the fuel dock, denting a ballast tank, adding to her many bruises of the Antarctic.

Their departure home, set for 15 February, was postponed. The full force of the hurricane came roaring in from the South Pole. Winds increased to 93 knots. Shore telephones went out. Railroads ceased to operate. Other ships in port canceled sailing schedules to remain in the safety of the port.

By Saturday morning, when *Sennet* left Wellington for Tahiti, winds were still blowing at gale force. The submarine barely made three knots before it cleared the entrance buoys.

After committing himself to the open sea, Icenhower could not have returned to port safely if he had chosen to do so. All day and through the night *Sennet* fought high seas just trying to get clear of the New Zealand coast. By 0600 the weather improved and a course was set for the Society Islands, where they arrived the following day.

During the next week the battered boat and her tired crew rested in the tropical beauty of Papeete, the first real rest since leaving Panama more than two months before.

Sennet sailed into the Panama Canal on 13 March, having traveled a total of 18,606 miles. Her hungry engines had consumed more than 130,000 gallons of fuel oil.

An interesting geographic fact was becoming evident: namely, the Antarctic is a continent surrounded by water. The Arctic Ocean is a body of water surrounded by land. The submarine's environment is under the sea, even if it meant learning new methods of doing that.

6

INTO THE CHUKCHI SEA

During the war while serving as commanding officer of the battle-ship *Iowa,* and beginning in the fall of 1943 as chief of staff to Adm. Ernest J. King, commander of the Tenth Fleet, Rear Adm. Allan R. McCann had had close contact with antisubmarine warfare.

When the Germans capitulated, Admiral McCann was assigned to take President Harry S Truman to the Potsdam Conference. Then, fol-lowing a brief period of duty with the Chief of Naval Operations, the admiral was ordered back to submarine duty.

In December 1945, McCann took over as Commander, Submarine Force, Pacific Fleet. From his desk at Pearl Harbor, he looked to the Aleutian Islands and beyond with increasing interest. He saw the Russians as the next submarine enemy. The Aleutian area was no more hospitable to ships than the Antarctic. With the relatively warm Aleutian current flowing along the island chain under cold arctic winds, dense fog often blanketed the water. A submariner, whose environment is the area beneath the sea, is naturally concerned about the physical properties of the sea floor.

The Aleutian Islands north to the Bering Strait were charted in great detail after the United States recovered the westernmost island from Japanese occupation during the war. The floor of the 270,000-square-mile sea was found to be divided into two physical provinces of approximately equal areas by a precipitous continental northwest-southeast slope.

The Bering Sea was virtually land-locked by the Aleutian Island chain. However, deep water lay along most of the chain and along the western part of the sea, and was a part of the Pacific Ocean. Depth profiles from echo soundings showed a deep, flat-bottomed basin.

The northern half of the Bering Sea and the Chukchi Sea to the north were very shallow.

Submarine operations off Alaska during the war had never been very successful. The old S-boats, given the job of attacking Japanese landings on the western islands, had a tough time. The *S-27*, on her first war patrol, ran aground on the coast of Amchitka Island and on 19 June 1942 had to be destroyed.

Determined to investigate the submarine's potential in the North Pacific more fully, in 1946 McCann directed his planning chief, Capt. Lucius H. Chappell, and operations officer Capt. Albert L. Becker to plan an operation to see just how feasible it would be to operate in the Bering Sea.

Comdr. Lawson P. Ramage, commanding Submarine Division 52, was selected to carry out the mission riding on the *Boarfish.* During late July and August 1946, while Maurer was probing Kane Basin, Ramage's division spent more than a month working in the eastern part of the sea. *Boarfish* reached further north on what was described by the *Nome Nuggett* as "probing the arctic ice pack between Alaska and Siberia, gathering data for 'Operation Iceberg' to explore the hazards of arctic maneuvers." They were also to determine the extent and nature of the ice fields and investigate diving conditions.

To gain firsthand knowledge, McCann flew up to join the group during a stop at Dutch Harbor, the Unalaska Naval Base. His personal interest in the north reached back to 1930 when, as liaison officer at the Philadelphia Navy Yard, he had played a part in the transfer of the *O-12* to Wilkins.

Meanwhile, when Dr. Lyon returned home from the Antarctic in 1947, he realized that an entirely new area of study in sonar conditions lay ahead. Exploration in and around sea ice was badly needed.

At his suggestion, the Navy Electronics Laboratory made a request to the commander, Submarine Force, Pacific Fleet, for another submarine to be used that summer into the Chukchi Sea.

The request met with instant approval. McCann and Lyon had been close friends for many years. Both had similar ideas. Over the years both realized Wilkins's idea of sliding under the ice would never prove successful. Sonar could, however, provide the tool to see where the ice was, thereby allowing the submarine simply to move in its normal manner in free water.

Admiral McCann organized a small task unit consisting of a submarine tender and four submarines. *Nereus* would serve as mothership and research center. *Boarfish,* commanded by Comdr. John H. Turner, was selected as the boat to make close-in surveillance of the ice field. The boat was first sent to San Diego to be installed with special equipment.

The Bering Strait and waters north had never been seen by members of the San Diego research group. As advisors to submarine officers, the scientists needed as much knowledge of the area as possible. "An important personality on whom we leaned heavily," recalled Dr. Lyon, "was Dr. Harald U. Sverdrup," the *Nautilus–O-12* expedition veteran. Also Dr. Sverdrup was able to provide first-hand knowledge from his personal records and vivid personal recollections of two years' work on the Raold Amundsen *Maud* expedition beginning in July 1918.

Boarfish returned to Pearl Harbor and the task unit sailed for Adak. Admiral McCann again decided to go along.

"I knew Jack Turner as an outstanding skipper and an extremely capable seaman," McCann related.

My presence aboard was only in part to relieve Chappell and Turner of responsibility for anything that might occur. I had, and still have, an innate curiosity to see for myself what conditions might be and what improvements could be made in instrumentation for under-ice navigation in the future. It was necessary not only to see ahead but to know what was overhead in order to be able to surface in open lakes for battery charging.

One of the problems Commander Ramage and his men had faced

the year before was the need for good cold-weather clothing for submarine bridge crewmen. The clothing the Navy stocked was too bulky. Commander Icenhower had reported the same problem following *Sennet*'s return from the Antarctic. At Adak McCann's group picked up a supply of Army GI clothing that was much more suitable above the Arctic Circle.

Leaving the Fox Islands behind, the task unit entered the Bering Sea. North of the Bering Strait the submarines reconnoitered at the edge of the pack ice. Brash ice soon appeared and crews took to small boats to penetrate briefly into the face of the ice field. Snow flurries added to an unfamiliar midsummer environment.

Nereus and the undersea craft pushed north, fanning out on a 100-mile line toward Siberia as far as the international date line with a 40-mile gap between each submersible.

Dr. Lyon recently recalled the preliminary visual survey of the ice field before committing the submarine to unknown dangers, an important first in arctic submarining.

At this point, we took the *Nereus*'s motor whale boat and worked our way into the pack ice, twisting and turning between the ice floes for a distance of 8,000 yards. McCann, Chappel, Turner, LaFond, Roshon, Lyon (and probably others) were in the boat.

We observed the ice floes, noting their shape, size, height above water, and estimating the size, shape, and draft of the ice mass underwater. This gave an impression, a mental picture of what the under-ice field should look like and helped greatly in interpreting the images shown on the scanning sonar screen when we dove under this ice field.

This was the first dive and "look" underneath. This "look-see" in the small boat was the smart way to approach the problem of the first dive.

Nearby lay the *Boarfish,* ready for her special assignment. All motor whale boat passengers got aboard. An entry in the ship's log, recorded later in the day, read:

1 August 1405: Rear Adm. A. R. McCann, Capt. L. C. Chappell, Capt. D. C. White, and Lt. Comdr. A. B. Catlin came aboard for a trip under the ice.

The *Boarfish* moved up. The pack ice looked solid. Only Dr. Lyon had viewed such a scene as this from water level. It appeared one solid mass of jumbled ice reaching 5 to 10 feet high. It was a formidable sight.

Boarfish nosed in and around small brash. Gaining confidence, McCann suggested, "We ought to take the boat a little closer." Jack Turner did not hesitate. He moved in. When they had no difficulty maneuvering the boat in and around a few floes, Turner backed his boat off for a wardroom conference. Should they go under? It was unanimously agreed they should. The submarine was again backed off several hundred yards farther for a good trim dive. With only a few feet to spare beneath the ice and the bottom, considerable time was taken to make it good.

The ship's log read:

1439—Made stationary dive . . . then planed down to 110 feet. Depth of water is 31 fathoms and bottom flat according to echogram.

Boarfish moved ahead, slowly cruising at three knots. The diving officer was visibly anxious. Other than holding the boat on an even keel and at the prescribed depth, he knew little of what was taking place in the forward torpedo room. Crammed into a small corner, recorders drew thin black lines on a continuously moving roll of white paper. With their eyes glued to the instruments, Dr. Lyon, research engineer Art Roshon, and Admiral McCann appeared impassive. Behind, others strained for a look. "Like watching a crap game," recalled Lt. Comdr. Allen B. "Buck" Catlin. "Fifteen people hovering around two little dice."

Commander Turner beat a path between the diving station and the torpedo room snapping orders. The boat had not gone far when a malfunction rendered the sonar scanner useless. Without its searching beam *Boarfish* was blind, unable to see the track ahead.

Quickly the sonar engineers shifted to the keel-mounted projector. This compromise gave them a strong beam from beneath the boat, bouncing echoes off ice projections up to several hundred yards and good enough for navigation. *Boarfish* was still left comparatively blind by the shadow effect caused by the bow.

However, the inverted echo sounder on the deck did its work, registering thickness of ice floes passing overhead, now averaging 18 feet. By 1500 *Boarfish* was passing under a deep ice ridge 53 feet below the water's surface and plotted as 200 feet long. Soon the traces recording from the sea floor and ice overhead began to converge. Another ridge was sloping downward. McCann knew the captain was becoming concerned for the safety of his boat and indicated it was entirely up to him how long they wanted to continue northward.

"It looks like we're going to be the ham in the sandwich between these traces," he observed quietly.

"Well," added Chappell, the division commander, "I guess we better go back."

Shortly thereafter, Turner ordered the course reversed and going to 140 feet for added safety. Clearing the ridge, he brought his boat back to 110 feet. With motors stopped Turner hoisted the periscope to scan the area:

The log read:

1616—Hovering at 80 feet. Can see nothing. Water is a light jade green overhead. Can see no ice.

1617—Hovering at 60 feet. Ice all around. Closest piece about 10 feet from periscope and is small. Larger pieces all around but are all flat.

1624—Commenced pumping ballast to come up slowly. Put a small bubble in safety and came up very slowly. At 30 feet blew main ballast and surfaced remainder of the way.

As *Boarfish* broke surface, one floe skidded off the bow. Another slid off the stern. A third fell off the port side of the cigarette deck, crashing into the water after bending the antenna stanchion. The latter was estimated to weigh about 7 1/2 tons.

"This procedure is not recommended," wrote Turner in his report, "if one is desirous of keeping his periscope!"

In two days, the minor damage was repaired. Fifteen minutes with a blow torch straightened the antenna stanchion.

Looking into the future, Admiral McCann wanted answers to many questions. How far could they go under the ice with the battery they had? What damage would a submarine sustain in the present super-structure configuration?

He also wanted Jack Turner and his crew to gain more confidence. On 4 August they were ready for another run. The ice at the edge of the field was mostly brash—small chunks mixed with finely ground slush. At first this gave a very poor picture on the recorder. Soon *Boarfish* passed under solid ice and echoes began coming back strong when floe keels reached six feet below water level. They had not gone very far before Turner was again forced to take his boat deeper. Ahead a pressure ridge loomed up with its keel at 40 feet. After cruising about, gaining confidence, Turner returned to open water.

The last run was made 5 August, and since they could go no farther north, *Nereus* and the boats turned back to the Bering Strait. While *Boarfish* continued on to Pearl Harbor, the others put into Juneau for a chance to stretch sea legs and engage in a bit of recreation. Long hours on deck in cold northern waters had been far from comfortable. With their blood thinned by duty in the warm Hawaiian climate, the crew found that even the Army clothing was inadequate protection along the ice field. One evening Admiral McCann joined a group of his officers.

"How are things going, Art?" he asked the submarine *Caiman*'s executive officer.

"Admiral, please sit down. I want to tell you a story," replied Art Rawson, an experienced submariner. "It's cold out there! Do you have any idea how cold it is, Admiral?" Rawson was firm, respectful, but very frank.

"Well, I think I have an idea, Art," said McCann, understandingly.

On the plane while returning to Pearl Harbor the admiral, who had been comfortably billeted in a warm stateroom on board the *Nereus*, did not forget those words. "You know," he said to Lieutenant Commander Catlin, his flag lieutenant, "I didn't appreciate that those men were standing out there in the cold."

"Well," replied Catlin, "from what I've heard, it is pretty brisk up there on the bridge, and they are running with fewer watch standers than during the war."

"You know, I'd forgotten about that."

Rawson had made his point. The Navy's own foul weather gear must be improved.

Reaching Pearl Harbor, Admiral McCann was very enthusiastic. He felt his submarines, especially *Boarfish,* had made a giant step. He was determined to continue. These operations, however, took personnel. They took submarines. The Navy was in a postwar depression atmosphere and, even with a successful operation completed, few people agreed with the importance the admiral placed on the operation. *Boarfish* had returned undamaged, and McCann's enthusiasm was difficult to stifle.

7

DIVING IN THE ICE PACK

In March 1948, Dr. Sverdrup left his post as director of Scripps Institution of Oceanography in La Jolla to return to his native land, where he had been asked to take over as director of Norway's Polar Institute. By now Sverdrup and Lyon held little doubt of the submarine's future role in the Arctic. With the addition of a few instruments and design changes to standard Navy equipment, it could easily become a working platform from which they could explore the long-hidden aspects of the sea.

Lyon vividly recalled their last conversation following a farewell luncheon—an optimistic verbal exchange that clearly predicted events of the future. "We agreed to again meet when I crossed the Arctic Ocean by submarine." Their optimism was well founded.

That summer preparations began for the next step. On Tuesday, 17 August 1948, Lt. Comdr. James M. "Skip" Palmer backed his submarine *Carp* clear of the Navy Electronics Laboratory dock, cleared the harbor, and headed north. The date of departure had been selected with great care. Dr. Lyon had recommended the timing of the sub's penetration to coincide with the maximum withdrawal of the pack in order to obtain oceanographic data as far north as possible.

Lyon knew that in late September the consolidated ice pack stopped shedding its winter coat. Between the pack's edge and open water to the south stretched an ice field for miles, filled with shining, churning floes, battling each other under force of wind and currents. It was the time for the final phase of the summer melt period.

Melt water ran off the floes and into cracks and leads. As the old pack ice was composed almost entirely of fresh water, the runoff formed a layer on the denser salt water. This layer varied in thickness with the size of the watershed, the intensity of melt, floe movement, wind mixing, and extent of leads. During some years, even in late August the polynya surfaces froze, the leads began to freeze, and the entire area would soon be covered with fresh snow.

The water temperature dropped to the freezing point of seawater, about minus 1 degree centigrade. Topped by a layer of slightly lighter fresh water, slush ice began to appear, the first evidence of approaching winter. A balance in time.

Commander Palmer's boat was selected for a deep probe of the ice field for good reason. *Carp*'s springtime overhaul and operating schedule was the one best fitted to the time set for operations. Forewarned, workers at the Mare Island Navy Yard had ample opportunity to squeeze a multitude of gear into the already cluttered maze of cables and pipes.

Beyond the limit of the *Boarfish* probe still lay a great many miles to the main arctic ice pack. Although the northern Chukchi Sea was relatively uncharted, logic dictated the continental shelf should start dropping away as it neared the main arctic basin. To operate beyond the fringes littered with loose drift ice, the undersea boat needed to learn to hedge-hop from polynya to polynya, as Wilkins had planned to take the *Nautilus,* and surface periodically for a navigational fix and battery charge.

Operationally, the necessity for vertical ascents and descents in the confines of small ice-bound water areas presented a new and untried problem. The speed of advance would be slow, with many hours spent on the surface.

Training for such dives had been put into high gear at the earliest possible time. Commander Palmer spent many days submerged off San Diego, diving under another ship to simulate an ice floe and to test the effectiveness of his instruments. Weekends in port found laboratory technicians swarming through the boat installing more equipment.

While *Carp* was plunging north off the California coast, her crew intensified its training efforts. Submariners, by the nature of their job, training, and specialized talents, are a close-knit team. Palmer wasted no time putting his six officers and 71-man crew through their paces. Their safety demanded no less than excellence in each man's performance.

Three section dives were made daily, going deep on a predawn dive. In preparation for the under-ice excursions, each dive included one or more stationary dives and ascents.

After three days' rest in Vancouver, British Columbia, during which time Palmer paid courtesy calls on several Canadian officials, Dr. Lyon joined the boat and *Carp* headed for Nome, Alaska. Once clear of the Strait of Juan de Fuca, *Carp*'s sharp bow plowed a furrow through the North Pacific on course for the Aleutians. Except for a fishing boat and one lone freighter picked up by radar during the night, they were alone.

The first day out, a cyclonic storm struck. Hour after hour, winds pushed mountainous waves over the low deck, throwing cold spray over the bridge as Palmer pushed his boat toward Unimak Pass. Within a few days, however, they entered the calmer waters of the Bering Sea.

Nineteen days out of the Canadian port, *Carp* entered the Nome roadstead. The submarine *Blower,* assigned to be available for help if needed and relay information while Palmer was inside the pack, had already arrived. The two boats moored alongside each other and officers and scientists gathered in *Carp*'s wardroom to go over plans.

Meanwhile, an aircraft arrived and the pilot was asked to locate and survey the edge of the ice. The pilot reported ice to the north.

On the morning of 3 September all was in readiness. The two boats headed north. It was 1930 when the fringes of the Chukchi ice field came into view six miles ahead. To these submariners the view was breathtaking. Spreading across the water in either direction the thin white line formed a rim marking the end of open water.

Even from a distance of four miles the ice still appeared as one solid mass. No drift ice was seen. Fresh southerly winds had pushed scattered pieces into a loose-packed state.

"After sighting and entering the ice," recalled Palmer, "we found it so calm and peaceful that we pulled up alongside a large ice floe and rested for the night."

In the early morning hours the weather was fine and clear, with visibility a good 20 miles. Palmer's plan was first to penetrate the ice field as far north as possible. Beyond the limit *Boarfish* had reached still lay a great distance to the consolidated pack. No one knew just where the main Arctic Basin started. Under partly cloudy skies *Carp* got under way at 0500.

"It was a deceptively peaceful place," recalled Palmer. "There was no swell, even though a stiff breeze rippled patches of water between floes. Leads were clearly defined. Occasionally, we had to push through ice two to three feet thick to reach leads leading north. Actually, we had one easy time!"

For the first time in days the submarine rode on even keel while moving slowly through a scene of rugged beauty. Cruising at a cautious five knots, Palmer wound his way through the field, stopping briefly every four to five miles to allow the scientists to obtain seawater samples. The submarine was making steady progress when suddenly the ice became so dense, the floes so close-packed, it was more and more difficult to find passage. Snow flurries again dimmed his view, but Palmer continued forcing the sub's sharp bow through cracks and leads. At times, openings could be seen ahead, but to reach them required pushing through ice that often reached 15 feet thick.

"That evening," Palmer remembered, "*Carp* lay in a polynya one mile wide and four miles long. We knew beforehand that the arctic ice area had clear lakes which appeared usable for a submarine, if we could move from one lake to another." This one, however, was surprisingly large. Ice lakes are often found in the lee of heavy floes. The wind could separate the ice because it swept light floes along at a more rapid pace. Here they found a temporary haven. It had been a hard day's work and Palmer ordered the boat halted for the night.

"At this point," he recalled, "we estimated we had penetrated the ice field about 62 miles." He could have easily ordered the anchor dropped in the still-shallow waters had it not been for a continuously changing surface pattern. During the night the officer of the deck was forced to constantly maneuver the boat, avoiding floes and blocks drifting haphazardly on all sides. Increasing winds suddenly shifted to the north. The temperature dropped to freezing. The contour of the lake began changing, closing and opening at various points. All southerly paths soon closed. Clearly a change of plans was necessary.

Palmer said,

> The experience during the night convinced me I could not survive continuous operations on the surface that close to the consolidated ice pack. Also, fleet boats had only about 70 miles battery endurance while cruising submerged—excluding current effect. Consequently, after finding ourselves nearly boxed in by ice, we decided to move south to a safer distance. Hopefully, we could run submerged at any time to open and safe water. Later, when I learned that a Coast Guard icebreaker had left the Alaskan area, the decision to move to less distance inside the ice field proved wise.

When they were ready to start breaking their way out, two polar bears were sighted riding a large floe on the lookout for food. Such an opportunity rarely presented itself to the arctic novices.

> I had a hard time convincing my men I shouldn't land a party to bring back the hides for trophies. Even though this was a tense time in the cruise, the bears did brighten the situation.
>
> We found to the south a section of ice barring our way. Fortunately it had two deep cracks. After ordering number six and seven main ballast tanks flooded to protect the propeller while breaking through thick ice, I nudged *Carp*'s nose up to one of the cracks and poured on all the power our four main engines could muster. *Carp*'s bow rose up to a steep angle before the ice gave way at both weak points. The boat slipped through with the ice bounded by the two cracks rotating and just missed the screws, even in a flooded condition.

Continuing south while locating and pushing through weaker points kept everyone on their toes. Their experience of the first day had shown that ice three or four feet thick, or less, could be penetrated by *Carp*'s bow without difficulty. Thicker chunks had to be pushed aside or crowded into adjacent weak points—or avoided! At one point it took two hours of close maneuvering to reach a position where leads and open areas could be found without forcing passage.

During the afternoon they continued to make slow progress to the south with the bridge watch constantly on the lookout for a passable route. When a point 25 miles from the pack's edge was reached, Palmer became anxious to find an open area large enough to conduct submerged operations. Three miles further, the aircraft pilot spotted them struggling.

Circling overhead, the pilot radioed Palmer with a description of the contour of some brash on a general bearing to the southwest. With a clear picture formed in his mind, Palmer pushed the submarine through. "The aircraft was actually of little use throughout the operation. I spent more time worrying about its safety than getting useful information," Palmer recalled.

The lake was finally located. About 90 percent was open water littered with numerous pieces of rotten ice and brash. Each piece was drifting at various speeds and directions, pushed by opposing wind and current.

Carp made three stationary dives and Palmer took his boat on one short trip under the ice. While surfacing from a second dive, *Carp* had a four- to six-ton ice cake land on deck just aft of the five-inch gun, breaking the lifeline stanchion. It was quickly disposed of and *Carp* lay to for the night. Small brash, broken loose from surrounding floes by the wind's action, again closed their parking area. By early morning Palmer was able to move clear and began searching for another open area. He finally located a suitable polynya large enough to maneuver safely and took the submarine down for the fourth time, making a second excursion under the ice. That evening, Commander Palmer drafted a message to the *Blower:*

SATURDAY DEPARTURE DATE DEFINITE. ARRIVING NOME
MORNING OF 13 SEPTEMBER. MAKE RECONNAISSANCE SWEEP
ON WEDNESDAY. OPERATE AT DISCRETION OTHER DAYS. HAVE
SCHEDULED COMBINED OPERATIONS WITH YOU SATURDAY.

At 0700 on a Sunday morning the wind returned to the south, bringing heavy fog. Within two hours visibility began increasing.

Carp was taken down for two more dives while Palmer snapped periscope pictures before surfacing the last time. During the afternoon, with experience gained by numerous dives, Palmer took his submarine confidently on the first extended trip under solid ice enclosing the area.

On Monday morning, overcast skies shadowed the ice field. A gentle 10-knot wind soon cleared patches of fog and operations continued. *Carp* was taken back north while Palmer searched for a more favorable spot. They made a last stationary dive but found the space too narrow for comfort and maneuvered to a larger polynya. For the next two days they remained on the surface while Dr. Lyon and his two laboratory technicians made seawater studies.

On Wednesday morning, 10 September, *Carp* started maneuvering to reach open water. Progress was rapid as they neared the edge. By 1600 the submarine pulled clear of the ice field. Commander Palmer was convinced his submarine did as much, if not more, than could be expected of a conventional submarine by penetrating 62 miles of pack ice. Only superb ice seamanship and good fortune enabled them to return with the boat undamaged. With the operation order carried out in every detail, the two undersea craft headed south.

The commanding officer's report read,

Entered the Bering Sea at 0000, 13 September, and anchored in the roadstead at Nome, Alaska, about 1,000 yards southwest of the cement jetty. Dr. Waldo K. Lyon, Mr. L. L. Morse, and Mr. F. Baltzly disembarked. Liberty was granted for those who could fit into the Coast Guard motor whale boat, which was made available for transporting passengers and liberty party ashore. The boat was of a type known as self-bailing, but was promptly reclassified by those few who ventured ashore as one of the "free-flooding" type, and a menace to navigation.

Carp and *Blower* left Nome at 2100 that night and sailed for St. Paul Island. It was almost midnight the following day when they arrived off the Village Cove amid a violent storm. "We were very happy to seek shelter of that island," Palmer said, "but could not land. We did want to exchange greetings with the local inhabitants before leaving." A searchlight was brought to the bridge and aimed ashore in an effort to arouse interest in their presence, but was without success.

The next afternoon the radio operator on the *Carp* picked up a dispatch from Commander, Submarine Force. Rear Admiral Colclough directed them to Kodiak to pick up a passenger. The storm was still raging. Even though they had protection from the high seas, the anchors fought to maintain a hold on the bottom.

That evening, with winds subsiding, they made their way south once more to Kodiak Island to pick up the passenger. The warm reception and excellent service the submarines received, Palmer reported, was a "most welcome experience" after what they had been through.

Blower turned toward Pearl Harbor while *Carp* headed for San Diego, her home port.

"Arctic patrols should be continued," wrote Commander Palmer in his final report, "if only for the experience gained. It appears, however, that further penetration of field ice should not be attempted without a specially constructed submarine."

8

REDFISH REACHES MCCLURE STRAIT

Through the window of a circling Air Force weather reconnaissance plane, Lt. Comdr. Robert D. McWethy studied the broken pattern of the arctic ice pack. Patches of open water amidst the ice created a green and white maze as far as his eyes could see. It was 25 August 1948. Eighteen thousand feet below lay the top of the world. The North Geographic Pole.

"Why not?" he later said it flashed through his mind. "Why couldn't a submarine reach the Pole by surfacing when necessary for a battery charge, navigational fix, and a breath of fresh air?"

For years, submariner McWethy had studied the polar region with growing interest. Many facts were already known. The sort of solid ice cap that covers land at the South Pole does not exist at the North Pole. Only a relatively thin canopy is spread like a huge, white patchwork quilt across the northern sea. Exploration of this vast sea, which influenced circulation of northern waters and, in turn, the daily weather, had thus far been restrained only by lack of know-how. Not even the best constructed ship could move easily inside the ice pack. There was little doubt the ocean would never be thoroughly explored except by a vehicle that could move freely across the huge polar basin.

From a naval standpoint it was obvious that if submarines proved practical in under-ice operations, the United States, could, at least for a while, dominate an increasingly important strategic area. By now enough information had been gleaned from experience to provide concrete design for a true arctic submarine. A great many changes and improvements had been made to fleet boats during the 30 years after the *O-12* was launched.

In early 1949, after his flight to the North Pole, Bob McWethy was serving as liaison officer with the U.S. Coast Guard, the service that was to eventually operate all icebreakers. With growing national interest in the ice pack and arctic environment McWethy was determined to learn more at close range. He requested and—after consideration of his background—gained the unprecedented position as executive officer of the icebreaker *Burton Island.*

It was not an easy decision for a family man to leave the submarine force to go into another area just because he was sincerely interested. It meant giving up extra submarine pay. But duty aboard *Burton Island* from 1949 to 1951 was a rewarding experience. He was heading into unexplored territory. And for good reason.

In the fall of 1949 the American submarine *Baya* joined a Canadian-U.S. scientific operation along the Canadian arctic coast. The submarine made still another probe of the Chukchi Sea ice field and proved herself a good icebreaker, but remained to the west. Submariners were afraid to go east of Point Barrow because there was no information on the bathymetry, the depth of the sea.

From July to September 1950, and the following summer, the icebreaker fought her way through the ice pack miles offshore until she could go no farther. When cartographers transferred depth readings to new charts, a new sea valley appeared. It was named Barrow Sea Valley. With increasing depth the huge polar valley plunged downward and disappeared under the ice, leading into the deep Arctic Basin.

Like a dedicated evangelist, Commander McWethy promoted the undersea boat's return north by giving talks at every opportunity and showing very good filmstrips he had taken during his icebreaker duty.

The man with the power to act on continued submarine operations in the Arctic was Rear Adm. Charles B. "Swede" Momsen, who was on duty in the office of the Chief of Naval Operations. Admiral Momsen was an experimentalist who had developed the Momsen lung, an underwater breathing device for individual escape from a disabled submarine. As such, he was sympathetic to McWethy's ideas and to those of the Navy Electronics Laboratory for more arctic submarine experiments.

In 1952, just prior to leaving his Washington post, Admiral Momsen initiated a request to the Pacific submarine command. The timing was deliberate. Upon his arrival at Pearl Harbor to take charge of the submarine force, Momsen answered his own request: Affirmative! The next submarine expedition to the Arctic thus became a personal project of two men—Momsen and Capt. Lawrence Daspit, his chief of staff.

The *Redfish* was chosen to join the *Burton Island* on the icebreaker's next trip north. Commander McWethy was offered command of the submarine on the operation he had worked so hard to promote. It was a tough decision. "I turned down an offer to command *Redfish* and elected to remain on the East Coast." The assignment was given to Lt. Comdr. John F. Bienia, an equally experienced submariner. McWethy's influence in arctic operations was not over, however.

While the *Redfish* was being outfitted for her task, another historic event took place that summer which was to begin a new era in undersea history. On 14 June 1952, President Harry S Truman officiated at the keel-laying ceremonies for another *Nautilus,* the world's first nuclear-powered submarine. The true submarine perhaps envisioned by Jules Verne was almost here. It had a submerged cruising range limited only by the physical endurance of her crew. The need to employ a limited-storage battery power while submerged was eliminated. Into *Nautilus* went a nuclear reactor, powered by a small core of fissionable uranium weighing less than 10 pounds. It was expected to be capable of propelling the 3,150 tons of steel at high speed thousands of miles under water.

Meanwhile, although Bienia was embarked on a peaceful mission, the influence of the Korean War still reached across the Pacific and placed a blanket on his radio communications. Bienia's orders were to maintain radio silence. Even while cruising on the surface during transit from San Diego to the Arctic he had to follow a course to avoid populated areas except in emergency. Oil and fresh-water tanks were filled to the brim, and lockers were jammed with food supplies for at least three months at sea.

Bienia chose a course that led through the Aleutians far to the west, then northward to the Bering Strait. Hugging the Alaskan coast he made his way toward Point Barrow. *Redfish* stopped briefly off Icy Cape for the crew to view a 12-foot concrete monument, a memorial to one of the most famous plane crashes of the century: Will Rogers and Wiley Post, flying in Post's small Lockheed seaplane, were killed when it crashed on 18 August 1935.

Bienia resumed his course east. Waiting at Point Barrow was the *Burton Island,* commanded by Navy Comdr. E. H. "Pat" Maher, an experienced icebreaker skipper.

Two days later, after picking up Dr. Waldo Lyon, Eric Baltzly, and Leighton Morse, *Redfish* hoisted anchor and followed the icebreaker on an eastward course, skirting the fringes of the ice pack. There had been years when ice conditions were so favorable as to permit a straight course from Barrow to Cape Bathurst. This year the ice was too close to the Alaskan coast.

Few ships had ever ventured into the area. Daylight spread across the expanse 24 hours each day as the sun never dropped lower than 15 to 18 degrees above the horizon. Turning north with the icebreaker, Bienia pushed his boat deeper into the ice pack than any submarine had gone before, as he hedgehopped from polynya to polynya. He was forced to recharge the batteries more often than usual. Near-freezing temperatures penetrated the hull, lowering the battery water temperature and making it difficult to bring the battery temperature high enough to get a good charging rate. Daily recharging of the two huge groups—each made up to 126 cells—required large quantities of distilled water. Fortunately, the two distilling plants produced almost 2,000 gallons of fresh water per day.

To break the monotony Bienia occasionally tied up alongside the icebreaker to let his men stretch their legs, make new friends, buy needed supplies from the ship's store, and take showers in more spacious quarters.

At the end of five days *Redfish* had ice close aboard on all sides.

The wind had shifted and the ice had closed in tight against the boat's hull. *Burton Island* was working 100 miles away. Without any assistance from ice reconnaissance or communications with surface ship or aircraft, Bienia had to take his boat out under the sea ice margin to reach open water.

This was the first time an American submarine had been placed deep within the ice field without external assistance to determine which way to go. The crew had to depend entirely on sonar and navigate by dead reckoning. They hoped that with oceanographic knowledge of the area they could dive, proceed under the ice, surface to recharge batteries, and proceed again until they reached open water. "It was the acid test," remembered Dr. Lyon, "of our beliefs, doctrine, and equipment."

"No one aboard was sure just where open water lay," recalled the *Redfish* skipper. "However, a course was chosen that led toward where we knew open water had been." It was to the southwest off Point Barrow where the water flowed northward. It was expected the warmer current that moved out of the Bering Sea would melt small brash between big floes, thus creating open water lakes.

At 1230, 23 August, taking the boat down in a vertical dive, Bienia headed south. *Redfish* carried a battery supply for a maximum of 30 to 40 hours, depending upon how well it was conserved. Only then, if they cruised very slowly—two to three knots—would the power last up to nearly 100 miles.

"During this dive," said Bienia,

the conning tower was notified through the intercom that the after-torpedo room was flooding. Periscope observations on the way down showed me that ice had quickly closed the space *Redfish*'s hull had occupied while on the surface. To surface now would have damaged the topside sonars. So if we could, we would continue to dive.

Upon further questioning, the after-torpedo room notified me that the pumps would probably handle the leakage, so the dive continued.

The water in the area was amazingly clear.

We had the conventional submarine upward beamed lights, one forward and one aft. These were standard on submarines and were turned on during night practices off San Diego to show our location to destroyers making practice attacks on us. We also used our periscopes while submerged beneath the ice almost constantly, in conjunction with the topside sonars.

Hour after hour *Redfish* crept slowly along, dodging deep ridges picked up by the sonar scanner, looking ahead. The boat was held at slow speed to conserve power and the upward-looking echo sounder bounced signals off the bottom of the ice canopy.

"Lt. Arthur Battson was an excellent navigator," recalled Bienia, "and we knew where we were at all times."

Outside, the sea flowing past the hull was below the freezing point of fresh water. Ice formed in the engine-room bilges. Space heaters that were used to keep living and control-room spaces at a cold 35 to 40 degrees Fahrenheit added to the load on the battery supply.

After 8 hours and 22 minutes the topside echo sounder located a small opening. It was too small for comfort, but Bienia decided to bring his boat up while the opportunity was at hand. "*Redfish* used the periscope for maneuvering into a good position after open water was detected by sonar. The sea current, as noted by suspended plant and animal life in the water, showed ice and water were not moving at the same speed."

Maneuvering carefully to keep the escape hole in sight, Bienia eased the 311-foot submarine through the opening. Throwing open the conning tower hatch, the crew was greeted by a welcome and yet depressing scene. The ice pack still stretched into the distance through a blinding snowstorm. "There was a little water on either side of the hull," said Bienia, "but after we surfaced winds pushed us against the ice on one side."

Nearby a pressure ridge reached above the bridge level, forming a jagged mass. The diesel engines were started in order to purge compartments of foul air. *Redfish* remained on the surface overnight, recharging batteries while crewmen replaced the gasket that had failed on the after-torpedo room hatch.

At noon the next day they made one stationary dive to get out of the tiny polynya and cruised under the ice cover all afternoon, finding it necessary to make one course change from southeast to east when the water temperature began dropping. It was an indication they had moved away from the Point Barrow outflow. Bienia hoped to find small lakes free of brash. The change of course corrected the trouble, and finally small one-foot waves appeared on the black trace indicating open sea—the margin's edge. Surfacing, Bienia headed east for a rendezvous with *Burton Island.*

"*Redfish* did no more under-ice cruising" said the commander. Dr. Lyon added,

After we got out from under the ice cover, we decided to remain on the surface while continuing survey and oceanographic work. One point was brought home to us clearly. The submarine has such an excellent cover overhead no one could possibly be aware it was around! Even if the submarine surfaced inside the ice, there was no way another ship or submarine could be aware we were there. The ice was a perfect camouflage to the approach of another ship.

During a conference on the icebreaker, it was agreed *Burton Island* should move on to other work. While the icebreaker was busy with its task, *Redfish* continued eastward alone, skirting the edge of the ice pack to remain in shallow but clear waters along the coast. When Bienia reached the Mackenzie River outflow, he turned northeast and soon found himself in open sea.

Moving on toward Cape Kellett, he turned north, paralleling Banks Island's west coast while remaining 20 to 30 miles off shore. It was the first time for a submarine in this area and their view of the part of the Beaufort Sea was equal to the occasion. The ice was very heavy. Massive pressure ridges appeared everywhere.

Moving around the Gore Islands, off Cape Prince Alfred—the southern end of the gateway to McClure Strait—Bienia stopped his boat briefly 28 August for one deep sounding, which was carried out in raw wind and snow.

The position of Cape Prince Alfred did not check out. Who was right? The crew or the chart? One purpose of the expedition was to provide more accurate data of an area where few ships ventured. Those that had sailed through the area, more often than not, hugged the coastline to avoid the ice. *Redfish* continued north until stopped by great ice floes, miles in extent.

This penetration to Cape Prince Alfred was the farthest point north yet reached by any submarine on the Pacific side of the Arctic Ocean. *Redfish* had set a new record. For the next eight days *Burton Island* and *Redfish* surveyed new waters, wandering back and forth, covering a wide area west of Banks Island. On one occasion the icebreaker tried to reach too far north off McClure Strait and suffered broken blades on the starboard propeller for her effort.

Wind, snow, and 19-degree temperature added to unfavorable weather reports and indicated it was time to return south—15 September was fast approaching. The coast pilot for the area warned: "Off Icy Cape new ice forms in the middle of September and forms about six inches thick. The ice pack starts drifting south after that date and ships are recommended to start south before that date."

Those published instructions for all ships along the north coast were very clear. It was time to get out of the Arctic. It was a long way back along the Canadian-Alaska coast to escape around Point Barrow.

Then it was homeward bound after the most successful arctic expedition yet made. South of the Arctic Circle, the approach to Juneau was anything but friendly. The submarine's scheduled arrival was supposed to have been given to proper authorities. For some unexplained reason, the U.S. Coast Guard had not received the word. An Alaskan bush pilot circling over the coast sighted the boat moving toward the sound and quickly notified Coast Guard headquarters.

Operating under wartime conditions the Coast Guard prepared for action. Hardly a match for a combat submarine with a full complement of torpedoes and a five-inch gun, a cutter suddenly appeared, ready for battle. On the forward deck was a gun manned by determined Guardsmen. Recognition signals were quickly exchanged and with some amusement the ice-scarred boat made her way into port for the first shore leave since leaving San Diego. It was a real good liberty at the Red Dog Saloon.

Redfish arrived in San Diego 7 October, where the special gear was removed and she returned to more conventional duties.

9

REDFISH MAKES A SECOND TRIP

Encouraged, Admiral Momsen issued orders for *Redfish* to undertake a second cruise north in 1953. Her primary assignment was to gain follow-on experience and more training as a fleet submarine. After a brief stop at Adak, 2 August, to pick up Dr. Lyon, Baltzly, and Edward Howick, Commander Bienia headed for Point Barrow.

An ominous warning for what lay ahead soon appeared. Barely clear of Bering Strait the submarine was forced shoreward, skirting rocks and shoals close to the beach while avoiding heavy ice that had been pushed far south by northerly winds.

The *Redfish*'s partner this year was *Northwind,* commanded by Coast Guard Capt. Richard Morell, reputed to be one of the most successful icebreaker pilots of any decade. *Burton Island* was also back on the job, under command of Comdr. Pat Maher, bound for the waters of the eastern Beaufort Sea.

The day after Bienia arrived at the northern outpost, *Northwind* moored alongside the submarine to more easily transfer numerous instruments. While crewmen carried out that task, plans were made to begin work deep inside the pack. Again, the mission was handicapped by the need to operate under a blanket of radio silence.

To survey farther out in areas of the continental shelf not covered by previous efforts, Bienia set a course to the northwest, pushing his boat directly into the pack. Within a few miles the crystal-clear air disappeared. Northerly winds dropped and a cold, wet fog closed in. The submarine soon became caught in the ice pushed north by the Barrow current. In the heavy ice *Redfish* could not maneuver toward open water except by diving. The position they were in was too shallow.

"We were, in fact, beset," recalled Bienia.

> However, there was no immediate danger even though the ice hemmed us in and shifted position constantly. This made us list moderately several times as ice crawled over our ballast tanks on one side. The particular floes we were in acted like a huge merry-go-round, with *Redfish* at its circumference. We would swing northwards in a great circle and lose sight of *Northwind.* Then sweep around southward and regain visual sight. We had *Northwind* in visual contact several times.

At the end of the second day, Morell was becoming seriously concerned. He had noted that position reports showed Bienia moving further into the pack. This was not good. He was aware that the currents move north from Point Barrow. A local helicopter reconnaissance flight in that direction, although limited by poor visibility, found what Bienia already had learned—there was extreme ice coverage.

In a coded radio message sent to *Redfish,* Morell clearly indicated his concern and requested that if the submarine was beset Bienia should reply by giving his position as an affirmative reply. The beset signal was not long in coming and placed the helpless boat 20 miles almost due north from the Point. With no chance for the submarine to escape under her own power, the icebreaker headed into the pack.

"Visibility was poor," wrote Captain Morell later.

> Considerable maneuvering in the ice was required to get close. The submarine was surrounded by heavy block and hummocked floes on all sides. *Redfish* was the first to make contact and flashed her light on *Northwind*'s bearing. This we spotted about 50 degrees on the starboard bow during a short period of fair visibility. Fog again closed in. Progress was made in the direction of the last visual contact. If visibility had not previously improved temporarily the *Northwind* might have missed *Redfish* entirely as the icebreaker had poor results trying to locate the submarine by radar. This is probably due to the relative heights and size of the hulls in relation to ice targets.

The icebreaker eventually passed close aboard and signaled Bienia to follow in her wake. Pushing through close and shifting ice was slow work. It was soon decided the only recourse was to take the submarine in tow.

A heavy line was passed to the submarine at the end of a heaving line. Progress was a little faster, perhaps two knots, until the submarine's bow caught on a floe. Her stern swung sideways. Both captains soon learned even a tow with a shortened scope of line was impractical as floes constantly wedged between the two vessels. In short order the hawser snapped.

The icebreaker's two-inch steel towing cable was passed through her stern chock, run through the submarine's bull-nose, and made fast to the towing pad. With the towing cable set tautly the submarine was pulled up into the stern notch by the powerful towing winch. The *Northwind*'s Antarctic experience with the *Sennet* was repeated.

Northwind moved out. Slowed to a snail's pace with her heavy load, the icebreaker pushed her blunt nose into floes but was unable to back down or maneuver. The ice was a mixture of close block, brash, and large floes. Corners were sharp. *Redfish* was often dragged through crooked leads at an angle of 45 degrees from *Northwind*'s heading, threatening serious damage.

On the morning of 12 August the ice concentration decreased. A course was set to the south to avoid heading into the strong northerly current off Point Barrow. It took 12 hours to cover the 20 miles back to Point Barrow. The icebreaker's distance returning was twice as long as going out. Propeller turns were four times as great.

Redfish was left in relative safety near the Point, though often forced to shift position closer to the beach to avoid the constantly moving pack. *Northwind* returned briefly to her work escorting empty cargo ships south from Point Barrow to Icy Cape where they were safely free and could return to the States.

On 15 August Morell was finished with his escort mission and headed back to join up with the submarine. When the icebreaker approached Barrow, the course he had taken ended abruptly. Her passage was blocked by a huge floe three miles wide and six miles long, lying in shallow water at the beach and surrounded by nine-tenths concentration at its seaward side.

There would be 16 miles of heavy going to get around it. Morell chose to work his way through, backing and ramming, finally getting his ship wedged tight. Backing at full speed with full use of the rudder, and ahead speeds, had no effect. The heeling tanks were full of reserve fuel oil and could not be used. The trim tanks were used with no effect. The vessel was locked tight in a vice-like grip. The ice breaker took on a list of several degrees to port.

There appeared for a moment no choice other than to blast his way loose. Morell called his underwater demolition officer to prepare dynamite charges. In the meantime the experienced ice pilot continued working his ship. He ordered full speed astern, hoping the propeller blades could wash water around the ice wedging the broad hull. The blasting became unnecessary. After considerable working and eroding, the ship forced the ice to lose its grip and *Northwind* rolled back to her upright position. Morell ordered full reverse power from the 2,000-horsepower engines and the icebreaker backed free.

Morell decided to try another route. The *Northwind* began working to the westward. After two miles he decided to stop for a more careful study. For three hours Morell examined the shifting white mass. A northwesterly drift was apparent, indicating perhaps a wide lead was developing near the beach.

The helicopter was dispatched and its pilot sounded waters along the coastal side of the huge floe. His observations showed the vessel could possibly pass safely on the shore side. Eventually, *Northwind* reached a point northeast of Point Barrow and made rendezvous with *Redfish*. In contrast to the struggle that had been taking place, Dr. Lyon's journal read:

> *This 16 August was sunny day, white clouds drifting by. We on* Redfish *waited in fairly open water 5 miles NE from Point Barrow—at one time about 500 gulls were sitting in the water around us, unconcerned about* Redfish *and not even looking for handouts. Ed Howick and I, for want of exercise, borrowed five potatoes from the cook and played catch on deck, using cold weather gloves for fielder mitts.*

When *Northwind* and *Redfish* joined up at about 2000 the two ships immediately started off to the east, heading for Barter Island. During the early morning hours and through most of the day they worked their way through ice, finally breaking into open water and increasing their speed to 12 knots.

Shortly after sunset they were off Pitt Point where ice began showing up ahead and to port for a brief period. This was followed alternately by clear sailing and more ice. The course tended toward the southeast. At midnight soundings suddenly shoaled off the Jones Islands. All ice to port was grounded. Since poor visibility prevented effective observation ahead, they were forced to back clear and Bienia and Morell decided to anchor to rest for a few hours.

Early the next morning they were again under way. Reversing direction the two felt their way along the edge of grounded ice. From the particular distribution of the floes both men believed that instead of attempting to find a route outside the shoals they would try remaining inside near the beach. There they might find a clear passage.

Throughout the day icebreaker and submarine struggled just trying to get by Jones Islands. With poor visibility standing at about 2,000 yards, fog made it difficult to even see what lay ahead and prevented any kind of observation to obtain a navigational fix. Soundings were useless if they could not be plotted with accuracy. However, by watching soundings carefully, the two men finally managed to maneuver around the last shoal, where they headed northeast for several miles and then turned east.

With *Redfish* having constant trouble with the ice, progress was slow. They came upon great numbers of dirty floes, covered with soil, rocks, and mud that appeared grounded on shoal areas that acted as anchors to hold brash and block ice in tight masses.

Working their way east, after covering 18 to 20 miles, by 2000 they were again forced to a stop. Drifting during the night and morning of 19 August, their visibility again became poor. During the afternoon ice conditions seemed to improve and at 1900 they again headed eastward, recovering 20 miles of ground lost by hours of westward drift back past the Jones Islands.

By 0400 the ice was too heavy for *Redfish* to proceed any further. Although fog and icing made flying condition hazardous, at 1000 one of the icebreaker's three helicopters took to the air for a scouting mission. The pilot found open water to the south only behind the Jones Island shoals. To the north the ice was heavier. To the east, no change.

When the pilot reached seven miles to the eastward he reported his carburetor had begun icing. Visibility was poor and the ship advised him that radar contact was lost. Setting a course in the general direction of the icebreaker, the pilot asked for high-altitude flares, which are normally visible for up to eight miles. With the craft flying above the fog layer, the flare rose through the solid ceiling to an altitude of 1,000 feet.

The pilot spotted the flare as it exploded with a brilliant flash in the distance. About halfway back, he requested another flare to verify the final heading. Radar contact was regained and although ice on the rotors made maneuvering difficult the helicopter landed safely.

That night *Northwind* took the submarine in a tight tow in the notch for a ride few men have experienced. "It was an indescribably jarring rough ride," recalled Dr. Lyon. "Like a careening railroad car at high speed, continually running through track crossings and switches with occasional screams of ice on steel right at one's head level. The most awful noise I have ever experienced in a submarine. It recalled my same experience on the *Sennet* in the Antarctic!"

The tow was continued until 0100. Sighting a heavy floe, the icebreaker halted with her charge to watch its drift. The floe was grounded in 10 fathoms of water, with anchored ice all around. Between 0200 and 0400, pushing on a southwesterly course, they made a good half mile, then lay to in the darkness.

Bienia and Morell decided to remain where they were among grounded floes until morning. At 0900 they were underway again, breaking through about 500 yards of grounded ice to reach open water. They then dropped anchor.

They had reached longitude 149 degrees west, at the eastern end of Jones Islands at last, but the going had been rough. It had taken until the afternoon of 23 August just to get by the islands. It was just 35 miles.

During the afternoon the icebreaker's underwater demolition team divers slipped over the side into freezing water to inspect the submarine's propellers and torpedo-tube shutters. The bow and stern had taken the brunt of punishment and the result of the battle was clearly evident. Five forward shutters were found severely damaged and one propeller blade was slightly bent.

The icebreaker and submarine remained at anchor while Bienia and Morell studied their position, hoping for favorable winds. Some grounded floes appeared to have movement. None threatened their position.

At 1000 the next morning they headed for the east. Captain Morell instructed Bienia to explore the area at his discretion while he continued along toward Barter Island.

Commander Bienia moved inshore seeking open water between the beach and ice pack for survey work and soon located a sizable lead just offshore. The echo sounder's transducer, located in the forward trim tank, was okay for deep-water cruising but not accurate enough for his needs in shallow waters. Just as in the old river boats in the days of Mark Twain, crewmen stood on the bow heaving a lead-weighted sounding line into the waters ahead, calling depth readings to the bridge. Mile after mile, painfully slowly, the track was charted.

"Few *Redfish* men were qualified to read all the marks on the sounding lead," recalled Bienia.

> However, we were in shallow water and soundings did not and would not change radically enough for the lead men to have to know all marks on the line. Several of us took turns heaving the lead for exercise but it was hard to pull the job away from the quartermasters. They wanted to do it all. It was a break in the monotony.

"We successfully slipped by Midway and Cross Islands," remembered Dr. Lyon, "and ran into darkness and more large floes at Stockton Islands." By 0400 in the morning the weather had cleared. Hugging the beach, *Redfish* worked her way past Brownlow Point, which jutted to seaward, but not without being pinched between floes again. East of the Point, *Redfish* broke into open water and made an easy rendezvous at sunset with *Northwind*. The icebreaker had completed her scouting mission and arrived at the meeting place eight hours earlier. Morell had found conditions to the east somewhat more favorable and the two headed for deep water off Herschel Islands. Forced back, they attempted to work north of Barter, looking for open water.

During a routine check on 25 August one of the submarine's torpedomen discovered sea water had entered a torpedo tube. At some point when the bow had taken a hard blow, the outer door had been forced, warping the heavy shutter. The shutter had become partially opened. Through a small opening sea water had leaked in.

Normally this would not be serious. The torpedo tube, however, contained an electric torpedo mounted with a warhead! This could arm the warhead exploder and make the warhead itself sensitive to shock of collision with ice floes.

The torpedo had to be removed. Opening the inner door while the bow was underwater would bring a flood of sea water into the torpedo room. Somehow the leak had to be stopped.

While *Northwind* was called for help, men went to work pumping trim tanks. The bow was raised slightly but the leaky door still remained under water. At 0300 the icebreaker arrived and Morell maneuvered into towing position. The towing cable was secured to the bow and the powerful winch lifted the bow higher, but the door was still under water.

Joined by the demolition team, two submariners worked feverishly. Standing knee deep in freezing water, clothed in thermal boots and working on a small stage rigged over the side, the *Redfish* crewmen struggled with a hydraulic jack trying to warp the damaged shutter back in place.

Happily, by 0830 the men were able to get a watertight seal. The tube was drained and the war-shot torpedo removed to safety.

In the next afternoon *Northwind* lay to while a helicopter took off for another scouting flight. Just clear of the ship the engine failed. Flipping upside down, the craft plunged. The trained icebreaker crew was always alert to such a possibility. The pilot and copilot were plucked from the freezing water in eight minutes flat. The fliers had been able to crawl from their broken bubble and suffered only minor abrasions and shock.

The helicopter did not fare as well. It was hauled aboard by the crane with both rotors broken and structural damage. The craft was a total loss.

The ice had increased to nearly solid. Captain Bienia decided not to proceed further east to Amundsen Gulf in hopes of meeting with *Burton Island,* primarily because of the casualties: damage to the submarine and one helicopter lost. With the advanced stage of the season, lack of open leads, and lower than normal temperatures, it was time to think of an early withdrawal from the area.

During the next two days *Redfish* worked by itself, making several dives and firing one torpedo. But diving was treacherous. The turbid waters were filled with silt, carried to sea by wind and current when the ice melted, dropping its muddy cargo.

While making the torpedo shoot, *Redfish* made a regular approach on an ice-floe target. Racing through the water the torpedo struck the ice, exploding with a roar. The afterbody continued its journey, sliding through the huge hole and coming to a stop on top of the floe.

"It was a rare opportunity to recover an exploded torpedo," recalled Commander Bienia. "We tried to retrieve it for a souvenir." Maneuvering the boat alongside, a man was put over the side to get a line secured. As he stepped on the ice, his body weight tipped the floe slightly and the torpedo remnant slid off and quickly disappeared beneath the water's surface.

At 0400, 30 August, *Redfish* and *Northwind* rendezvoused by radar in heavy fog. It was the beginning of their long journey west, homeward bound. Back opposite Cross Islands they were locked in ice and darkness, jammed tight and unable to find a clear passage. For hours they got nowhere. Heavy floes off both Cross and Jones Islands forced the submarine to a standstill. Again it was back to the tow line, finally reaching the western end of Jones Islands. The ice-breaker pulled the submarine along at a snail's pace for a day and night, but eventually reached open water.

On 3 September the radar screen showed Point Barrow a few miles ahead. With more hours at the end of the tow line they finally rounded the Point and the two captains set a course from Point Barrow to Skull Cliffs. By staying close to the beach they were able to avoid most of the ice the icebreaker had tangled with less than a month before.

At one point two Eskimos were sighted hunting from an ice floe. The depth of water and maneuvers through drifting ice, however, made it necessary to pass close by. "The ships apparently disturbed their position," reported Captain Morell. "The hunters quickly got into their boats and departed."

Off Point Franklin the *Redfish* was released from the expedition and freed to sail to Pearl Harbor for repairs. With the damaged propeller and part of one diving plane lost, the boat had a rough ride home.

When Admiral Momsen left the Submarine Force, Pacific, the new Pacific fleet staff took a new point of view: after *Redfish*'s experiences, the submarine should stay out of the arctic and ice zones.

10

THE WHITE HOUSE ENTERS THE PICTURE

A whole new set of circumstances came on stage in 1955, specifically the culmination of defense against arctic aircraft threat with the construction of the early warning radar fence stretching along the north coast of Alaska and Canada, to Greenland. The strategic thinking of this project had supported work on submarines and icebreakers during the 1950–54 period. Now the icebreakers were drawn into use to help complete more important tasks.

That tremendous effort called for every experienced man available. Dr. Lyon acted as ice pilot, shifting back and forth between the icebreakers as they shuttled between Point Barrow and Amundsen Gulf, rescuing heavily laden cargo ships and clearing the way through waters men had feared to penetrate a scant five years before. Sixty-five ships reached points along the coast to discharge their supplies during one of the most difficult ice years on record.

Even before some ships had finished unloading, the battle to escape began as increasing pressures from the fall freeze-up started early in September. Ship after ship suffered broken propellers, disabled rudders, and caved-in hulls. Many were jarred to a standstill until rescued by the icebreakers.

On 9 September, 41 ships were still to the east, icebreakers lending every available assistance by towing or breaking channels. By sheer determination and with high spirits, thousands of men brought their ships to safety without a single loss—a story equal to any written in the pages of polar history.

That operation in the Beaufort Sea during the summer of 1955 reverberated throughout fleet commands and into the offices of the Chief of Naval Operations. Many flag officers had a new awareness of what the North held. A new cold weather program was called for—but there was no mention of submarines.

The fall of 1957 was a period of agitation when in early October the Russians launched *Sputnik* on their first space success. Capt. Peter Aurand, President Eisenhower's naval aide, later described what he had learned about an under-ice ("nibbling," he called it) expedition up north a few weeks before. The purpose, he explained, was to find a good way for a submarine to cruise under the ice. The new nuclear-powered *Nautilus,* with its greater underwater capabilities, had gone several hundred miles inside the pack.

During a visit to the Pentagon late that year, Captain Aurand had a chance meeting with Comdr. William R. Anderson, who had taken over command of the *Nautilus* and made the trip. Recalling the deep interest shown in his own brief remarks, Aurand knew the White House staff would enjoy hearing more of the story. He invited the *Nautilus* skipper to attend one of the meetings and brief the group in greater detail.

The story Anderson told stirred more than just a passing interest in the mind of press secretary James Hagarty. Anderson's account, plus details Dr. Lyon later added, removed any doubt of the great boat's capability.

On 27 August 1957, Anderson had reached the vicinity of Iceland and within a few hours his boat was cruising deep in little-known waters. At 2000 in the evening of 1 September, while their companion submarine *Trigger* stood by at the edge of the pack, men of the *Nautilus* took one last look at the white mass spreading beyond the horizon and took their boat deep, soon passing beneath the edge.

Within a very short time Dr. Lyon's sonar began showing a good picture of the ice overhead, or so they thought at the time. No one had yet actually seen the shape of the deep pack from below. Previous submarines had graphs and traces describing a profile of the fringes, and even though *Redfish* had cruised some 40 miles during her 8 ½-hour trip, she had barely touched the heavily rafted, consolidated region. Wilkins's own brief views of the underside of floes through his *Nautilus*'s small quartz windows were enough to send chills down the spine of observers.

On this first trip Anderson reached 150 miles from the edge of the pack. At one point while surfacing in a small polynya, the periscope, which was not completely housed in the sail, had collided with a small ice chunk, which rendered the instrument useless.

Returning to open water, technicians climbed to the open bridge and for 15 hours, while the boat was buffeted by high seas and lashed with freezing winds, repaired the damage. With the periscope back in operation Anderson went back under the ice. This time his goal was to reach the North Pole—660 miles away. If all went well, the submarine could make it there and back in four to five days.

Traveling at a greater speed than the first cruise had done, the boat quickly dropped miles. The magnetic compass soon began to behave erratically and the old-style gyro, designed for a maximum of 70 degrees north latitude, wavered abnormally. A newer model installed especially for the trip functioned well.

Nautilus reached within 200 miles of the North Pole when both gyro compasses suddenly went out. Electricians quickly found a blown fuse had knocked out the power supply to the most critical pieces of equipment aboard ship. Without a reliable gyro to guide them the navigator quickly turned to dead reckoning—calculating speed by the pit-log and distance by clock-time.

The power was soon restored, but it would take several hours for the gyro compass to regain its stability. There was no way Anderson could be absolutely certain of their position. He dared not continue on a northerly track. Shortly after *Nautilus* passed 87 degrees north— about 180 miles from the Pole—Anderson reluctantly gave the order to execute a long, sweeping turn and the boat headed back south.

Hours later everyone became concerned about their position when bottom soundings did not check. Ice overhead did not look right. It was too thick! And there were massive ridges! *Nautilus* should have been near the area northwest of Spitzbergen traversed by Wilkins 25 years before. The tables of sea-water temperatures, salinity, currents, and sea depth measurements assembled by Sverdrup, Soule, and others were carefully studied by Lyon aboard the old submarine's successor.

"The water temperature in particular did not check with data of Harald Sverdrup's measurements," said Dr. Lyon later. "Both in regard to depth and temperature. Those data were most valuable to us on this first trial. Water temperatures indicated we were most likely in the outgoing Greenland current and hence too close to Greenland. A decision made to turn southeast proved correct."

Nautilus eventually reached open water after going farther north than any ship had ever been under power. She had covered a total distance of 1,383 miles under the arctic ice pack.

It was a stirring story the submarine officer told the White House staff. "Everyone was very interested," remembered Captain Aurand, "particularly Jim Hagarty. Jim and I were both interested in doing something that would take the curse off the Sputnik scare! We wanted some technological development that the United States could make."

In November, a few days following Anderson's visit, instructions came from the National Security Council to consider the *Nautilus* taking an around-the-world cruise via the Arctic Basin the next spring (the trip was eventually made in 1960 by the nuclear-powered *Triton* under the command of Comdr. Edward L. Beach, following a route bordering the equator). The major objective was, of course, political, but payoff in scientific information was planned and expected.

Captain Aurand explained the reasons for the final decision:

We knew the trip could be made underwater but that would take at least 30 days. That would take too long. It would be dramatic enough just to go from the Pacific to the Atlantic, crossing the North Pole enroute. With political aspects in mind, Hagarty's prescription was to get world-wide attention, both inside and outside the United States. The United States image, especially in the space program, was damaged by Sputnik all over the world. Such a cruise would have more impact and, of course, if *Nautilus* failed it would be bad. It was decided at White House request that it would be done in the deepest secrecy!

The first outlining of the route was done in Captain Aurand's White House office on a polar projection map he had hung on the wall. The *Nautilus* skipper was again called to Washington. He looked over the proposed route. The problem, Anderson knew, was getting through the Bering Sea and Strait. Too shallow, and no one knew exactly how deep the ice was before they reached the deep Arctic Basin.

Jim Hagarty, however, was encouraged. The country, particularly the administration, was getting beaten about the head on technology. He wanted to do something in a hurry to get the lead over Russia. Turning to Anderson, he asked, "Is it possible for *Nautilus* to cross the Arctic from the Pacific to the Atlantic?"

Although *Nautilus* had experienced some difficulty on her first trip, Anderson felt certain that with the addition of some new gyro compasses and other aids to navigation, with careful planning they could make it. When he left the White House both Aurand and Hagarty were smiling broadly.

"I told the President about it," said Aurand. "He thought it would be a great thing to do. He asked me to see if Admiral Burke thought it was all right. So, I went over and saw him."

Captain Aurand soon learned this was not one of those operations where everyone choruses "yes."

When he first learned about the proposal, Adm. Hyman G. Rickover, director of the Naval Reactors branch of the Bureau of Ships, was against it, and understandably so. Many submarine people thought it would risk the *Nautilus,* which was unquestionably true. Others wondered whether we were ready to do it. Adm. Arleigh Burke, Chief of Naval Operations, decided it was something we should try to do. He gave the order: "Set it up!"

Admiral Burke first issued orders for a small, select group to make a feasibility study. Their conclusion, like Anderson's, was a confident "yes!" Shortly thereafter the Navy chief proposed to the president that *Nautilus* should attempt the trip the following summer.

Subsequent to President Eisenhower's concurrence, the White House issued orders to execute what was to become Operation Sunshine, implying a cruise to southern climates.

The instruction limited the personnel knowledgeable of the operation by name only: Pres. Dwight D. Eisenhower; Adm. Arleigh Burke, Chief of Naval Operations; Capt. E. P. Aurand, naval aide to the president; Adm. Hyman G. Rickover, director, Naval Reactors branch of the Bureau of Ships; Vice Adm. Thomas S. Combs, deputy Chief of Naval Operations; Rear Adm. Lawrence R. Daspit, director of Undersea Warfare (OP-31); Capt. Frank Walker; Comdr. M. G. "Duke" Bayne, Submarines (OP-31 staff); Dr. Waldo K. Lyon, scientist, Navy Electronics Laboratory, San Diego; and Comdr. William R. Anderson, commanding officer of the *Nautilus.* As time passed, others were brought into the small circle on a "need-to-know" basis.

In January 1958, Anderson received an urgent telephone call directing him to report as soon as possible to the office of Admiral Daspit. The subject, he was told, was "too sensitive" to talk about over the telephone. Anderson quickly boarded an overnight train for Washington. Arriving at the admiral's Pentagon office, he noted that little time was lost getting to the subject:

"Anderson, what do you think about taking the *Nautilus* across the North Pole?"

Anderson was told that Admiral Burke had already made the proposal to the president, who was very enthusiastic about such a cruise. Since his own visits to the White House, Anderson himself had given a lot of thought to the idea strictly from the operational standpoint. He was the man who would have to do the job.

There was little doubt in Anderson's mind that *Nautilus* could penetrate the ice safely from the Greenland-Iceland side in deep water. He also knew that the really formidable problem lay in getting into the Chukchi Sea through the Bering Strait. Operationally, the question was: could a submarine negotiate this track in face of possible poor weather and navigational errors? That answer lay at the top of the world and would not be the result of studying charts and statistics. There would not be many feet to spare in the Chukchi's shallow water going in either direction. Where *Nautilus* had confidently maintained normal cruising speeds in deep water the summer before, here the great boat would have to creep through that relatively uncharted area, echo sounders measuring the distance to the bottom and clearance to the ice overhead. It could be done, Anderson was certain of that. His affirmative reply to Admiral Daspit reflected confidence.

June was the time selected. By that time of year the ice pack normally receded well north into the Bering Strait—shortening the distance to deeper water.

When Dr. Lyon arrived in Washington on 12 February, he was informed of the White House order. A request to include Capt. John Phelps, Lyon's San Diego boss, in the need-to-know group was denied. This might prove unfortunate in several ways. As an active participant in Operation Sunshine, Lyon would have to do some extensive traveling. Since he was an employee of the San Diego research laboratory he might have difficulty explaining his trips.

The task eventually fell on the shoulders of just three men, Comdr. Duke Bayne, Commander Anderson, and Dr. Lyon, to do all the detail planning, write the top-secret orders, and in great secrecy make all preparations for Operation Sunshine.

Although definite plans were still in a state of flux, Lyon and Anderson began seriously looking into details of the arctic crossing. It had been suggested that the route should be from west to east. This choice was contemplated in order to ensure that the difficult shallow-water portion of the crossing would be faced at the beginning of the trip. Large-scale charts from the 1950–54 expeditions were now available and the currents and water temperatures were well known in great detail. The type of ice cover and its behavior in relation to currents were also pretty well established.

The basin crossing itself was important militarily to impress capability of missile delivery.

Whatever details were written into the final operation order, the movements of *Nautilus* required a camouflage. An article by Commander Anderson and Clay Blair Jr. was published in the 28 December issue of the *Saturday Evening Post,* and the submarine's commander appeared on Arthur Godfrey's television show the following day. Because of the publicity, any new movements would quickly be spotted by Blair and many newsmen. It therefore became necessary to carry out plans under a new front.

A second nuclear-powered submarine, the *Skate,* entered the picture when the Commander-in-Chief, Atlantic Fleet, employment schedule for 1958 listed an arctic cruise from 28 July to 1 September.

During the declining winter months, work continued feverishly, especially with planning for the upcoming front operations. On 8 April, an all-day conference was held aboard the submarine tender *Fulton* docked at New London, Connecticut, bringing together representatives from commands and activities throughout the country. "Its purpose," stated the agenda, "was to brief them on the status of plans for arctic submarines, to solicit comments and recommendations, and to promote coordination through personal contact." Forty-three officers and 18 civilians outlined a concept of the program for that summer: *Nautilus, Skate,* and the conventional fleet submarine *Halfbeak* were assigned a period of 34 days commencing 28 July for cold-weather operations.

The operating area selected included Denmark Strait, the Greenland Sea, and the Arctic Ocean. It was planned that *Nautilus* and *Skate* would cruise in company most of that period, while *Halfbeak* would work considerable distance from the other boats. All three could expect to spend 10 to 13 days in and under the ice pack.

To two men, Commander Anderson and Dr. Lyon, required to sit in and contribute their own ideas to the conference, it seemed somewhat academic in view of the special mission for *Nautilus* to cross the Arctic Basin alone beforehand. "It was a most interesting, and at times ridiculous position," the scientist noted in his journal, "to argue for essentialness of a reconnaissance survey of the basin by air, knowing full well that the crossing was already scheduled, yet attempting to meet arguments of others, and to avoid 'tipping our hand.'"

After the conference adjourned, Dr. Lyon and Anderson left for dinner at the latter's home where they discussed the real mission. There was much to talk about and they continued until 0100. The most difficult question was how to conduct an aerial reconnaissance of their own off Kotzebue Sound just prior to *Nautilus*'s departure from the continental United States. Finally, after much talk, both felt it would be best to hire a bush pilot in Alaska, under Lyon's auspices, as a part of the laboratory's work to prepare more field stations along

the Alaskan coast from Cape Prince of Wales to Point Barrow and also
as a part of his continuing sea-ice study.

Anderson would go along disguised as a civilian scientist. Dr.
Lyon would prepare a false set of travel orders; it would be necessary
for him to use his correct name in case he met old friends in Alaska.
Anderson would use an assumed name.

Remembering his experience on *Nautilus*'s first trip, the senior
scientist found serious technical questions that also called for
answers: "The important thing we learned on the previous trip—
what fooled me—was the echo sounders. Moving so fast the existing upward looking units did not do the job. We had to change the
frequency and also get a very narrow beam."

The actual track also posed a tremendous problem. Diesel-boat
crews had always selected a period in the season when the ice had
cleared far north of the strait and made short slow-speed dives while
remaining on the surface most of the time. *Nautilus* was specifically
designed for submerged high-speed cruising. There were no charts
of the Bering Sea, Strait, and Chukchi Sea that could be relied upon.
As Dr. Lyon later put it:

> We were worried. We were looking for a place a little bit deeper than
> the diesel-powered boats had found. I asked the Hydrographic Office
> to send me a copy of every single ship's track it had of the area. To
> maintain secrecy imposed by the White House, I worked under cover
> of scientific work we had been doing in the Strait.

The Hydrographic Office sent a pile of ship's track charts. Putting
them together, Lyon searched for a place just a little bit deeper than
normal. The trouble was these ships had all stayed close to the
Alaskan shore. Very few wandered out to the west. The charts didn't
show much that was encouraging, but they did indicate there was
one fathom or more to the west of the line of usual surface ships'
tracks. *Nautilus* would take advantage of that.

"We didn't know anything about the thickness of the ice we could
possibly expect at that time of year," Lyon explained.

> We tried to get some story on the ice cover from Cape Prince of Wales
> field station. One of their echo sounders, mounted on the end of a long

cable stretching from the beach, lay on the bottom recording the ice as it drifted by.

Analysis of three or four months' records showed a maximum thickness of 40 to 45 feet. This gave us a false sense of safety, actually, because what we were doing was just sampling. Our equipment would sample the ice thickness for a few hours, then the instruments had other work to do measuring noise levels and water temperatures. Much bigger pieces of ice probably went by and were missed when the sounder was turned off.

The type of ice that comes around the Wales area, Lyon had learned, was frozen right on the beach where it really got packed. When summer came, the big pieces broke free and just slid off with the tidal currents until the next winter, during which time they drifted haphazardly while being carried south with the current. (Scuba divers had worked from icebreakers in 1950 and 1951, but did not join the *Redfish* crew. Those divers did not venture under the ice. They worked mainly in wet suits during those early installation periods of the Defense Early Warning [DEW] line, surveying the beach contours for laying cables.)

Dr. Lyon faced another serious technical problem:

We didn't have a QLA forward scanning sonar. Fleet submarines weren't going through mine fields any more. That equipment had been declared obsolete, removed from ship's and supply stock, and sent to the scrap pile. I looked all over for just one for the *Nautilus* since we were going to have a real problem getting through the shallow water area.

In my search for just one model QLA scanning I couldn't press the supply people too hard. To complicate matters, I couldn't search everywhere. It might give the mission away. We were under top secret orders. Someone might guess what I was trying to do!

Nautilus had been supplied with only low-frequency sonars. All that equipment could do was pick up ships, submarines, monumental submerged mountain peaks, or obstacles of that nature. They were useless for guidance in close-in work. *Boarfish, Carp,* and *Redfish* had been far better equipped for under-ice cruising than was the *Nautilus* years later.

The *Nautilus* had to go almost blind.

Meanwhile in Washington, while the chosen few at the Pentagon drafted plans, Captain Aurand was careful to avoid the planning group so that his presence would not create suspicion. The naval aide and Anderson also guarded their secret with great care during those visits to Pennsylvania Avenue. Aurand had especially noted that Clay Blair, the ex-submariner and associate editor of the *Saturday Evening Post* attached to the Washington office, was becoming suspicious.

Hoping to dispel any speculation, Admiral Burke approved the cover operation plan and with the approval of the president ordered it released to the press. The Navy announced that *Nautilus, Skate,* and *Halfbeak* were to engage in arctic operations during the approaching summer. No details were revealed. Advance preparations, however, which included installation of polar equipment, would make *Nautilus* ready before her West Coast trip for familiarization runs with the Pacific Fleet ships.

The day after the *Fulton*'s early April conference, with groundwork laid on his and Anderson's personal plans, Dr. Lyon was in Washington working with Comdr. M. G. "Duke" Bayne, the principal architect of Operation Sunshine. Both men agreed the best method to cover expenses for Dr. Lyon's travel was by personal funds. Bayne would cover the entire pseudo travel orders incognito and personal travel money by a sealed directive to be opened only after completion of the operation to ensure reimbursement.

Lyon noted in his journal: "This operation is becoming more and more like a story book—most fascinating to live through it—there is no change in the number of people who know of the operation other than the executive officer of the *Nautilus*." For obvious reasons, in addition to Lt. Comdr. Frank Adams, Anderson had cut in Lt. Paul Early, chief engineer, and Lt. Shephard Jenks, his navigator. "It is expected that the Commander-in-Chief, Pacific, will be, or by now, is informed of the real purpose of *Nautilus* to Pacific in order to assure no embarrassing requests against her—cover operation is now a 26-day habitability cruise submerged and experiment between Seattle, west and south of Panama."

Back in San Diego, Lyon attended to a minor but important detail, requesting Dr. Franz Kurie (technical director of the U.S. Navy Electronics Laboratory, which headed the Submarine Laboratory) to obtain for him a Navy Civilian Service identification card. Although Lyon intended its use for Commander Anderson's incognito during the Alaskan reconnaissance flight, he gave Kurie no reason for the request other than for a special job for Lyon himself to enter a Navy yard without his own name appearing on any list requiring entry. The card Dr. Kurie found was made out to one Charles Henderson, a former employee, dated 10 October 1955. Splitting the edge of the plastic cover with a razor, Lyon carefully covered Henderson's photo with a small photo Anderson had given him earlier, and resealed it.

A few days later came a telephone call from Dr. Tom Killian, chief scientist at the Office of Naval Research. Could Dr. Lyon serve on a committee being set up by the Canadian Defense Research Board, Esquimalt? Its purpose, he was told, was for research and development in the Arctic, with visits to Ice Island T-3, a station at Lake Hazen, and Thule, Greenland, with briefings at International Geophysical Year (IGY) stations. The committee was to include several prominent Canadians, and Allen Dulles from the United States. The committee would act 8 through 13 June.

Lyon sidestepped this request on the basis he believed he was scheduled for another task during this period, but would call back later with more details. Hurriedly he put through another call to Duke Bayne. Lyon relayed Killian's needs and asked that he call off the request somehow. During the course of conversation Lyon also inquired if Washington intended to send a letter covering his absence from San Diego. Bayne agreed to take care of the Canadian request—later confirmed—but a letter covering his real movements was denied. Daspit feared putting out a letter in the Washington office might stir up questions. Lyon would just have to cover his absence from the laboratory by local action with a "smoke screen" in lieu of a letter from the Chief of Naval Operations.

To build a smoke screen, Lyon's next step was to prepare a trip report to Captain Phelps, stating he had received verbal instructions concerning work with the Alaskan commands, with vague reference to a survey of the most northern line and consideration of Arctic Ocean and air defense—a study within commands. In the unclassified category, Dr. Lyon prepared travel orders for himself and Rex Rowray, departing about 2 June, giving the reason: "Field survey and participation in planning studies in accordance with verbal instructions from OpNav."

For his part, the stage had been set.

USS *O-12* in the Philadelphia naval shipyard to
remove deck and conning
tower superstructure and
install *Nautilus*'s ice sled
runner design. Ice drill–
crew escape shaft is visible in the center of the
deck.

The modified *O-12*, renamed *Nautilus*, with hydraulic ice ram, sled runner
deck, temporary canvas "bridge," and radio masts. *(General Dynamics)*

William Randolph Hearst, Sir Hubert Wilkins, and radioman Ray Meyers study a message in front of the ice drill before *Nautilus*'s departure for the Arctic. *(Ray Meyers)*

Sir Hubert Wilkins, Mrs. Sloan Danenhower, and Jean Jules Verne, grandson of author Jules Verne, peruse author Verne's novel *The Mysterious Island,* March 1931. *(UPI)*

Radioman Ray Meyers and Sir Hubert Wilkins attempt to use a portable radio set up on an ice pack north of Spitzbergen in 1931. *(Ray Meyers)*

Submarine *Nautilus* crew poses for a 1931 arctic expedition photograph. *(Ray Meyers)*

Atule lying off the northwest coast of Greenland during Operation Nanook. Iceberg peaks are seen off to the right of the bow. *(U.S. Navy)*

Sennet locked between two ice floes in the Ross Sea during her battle to reach Little America. *(Department of Defense)*

Second rescue of the *Sennet* by *Northwind* in the Antarctic. *(U.S. Navy)*

***Carp* returns to the surface with chunks of ice riding on its deck.** *(U.S. Navy)*

Burton Island wrapped in a coat of ice, Bering Sea, 1952. *(U.S. Navy)*

Icebreaker *Northwind* maneuvering to take the submarine *Redfish* in tow during operations in pack ice in Beaufort Sea, 1953. Years earlier, submarine crews were afraid to venture east of Point Barrow, Alaska. *(U.S. Navy)*

Nautilus, the world's first atomic submarine, slides down the building way of the Electric Boat Company. *(General Dynamics)*

Mrs. Mamie Eisenhower christens the *Nautilus* with a bottle of champagne. The age of nuclear power is born. *(General Dynamics)*

Under way on nuclear power, 17 January 1955. *(General Dynamics)*

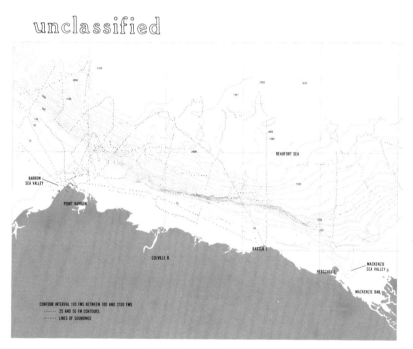

Burton Island's soundings reveal the Barrow Sea Valley off Point Barrow, Alaska, permitting *Nautilus* to enter deep water under the arctic ice pack and successfully cross the North Pole. *(Naval Electronics Laboratory Center)*

Under the arctic ice pack Dr. Waldo Lyon and Comdr. William Anderson watch upward-beamed echo sounder during the *Nautilus*'s dash across the Arctic Ocean and the North Pole. *(U.S. Navy)*

President Eisenhower congratulates Commander Anderson at the White House after the *Nautilus*'s transpolar voyage. At far left is Capt. Peter Aurand, the president's naval aide. *(National Park Service)*

Nautilus returns to New York City in 1958. Fireboats provided the water display. *(General Dynamics)*

Adm. Hyman Rickover and Dr. Waldo Lyon on the deck of the *Nautilus*. *(U.S. Navy)*

Skate's crew hold tug-of-war across a small lead with members of Drift Station Alpha during the submarine's visit. *(Dr. Nordert Untersteiner)*

Sir Hubert Wilkins visits Comdr. James Calvert aboard the *Skate* at New London, 1958. *(General Dynamics)*

Comdr. George Steele (*center*), on the *Seadragon,* discusses a proposed under-ice route through the Northwest Passage. *Left to right:* Art Roshon, Dr. Waldo Lyon, Walt Wittmann, Commo. O.C.S. Robertson, RCN, and Lt. Al Burkhalter. *(U.S. Navy)*

Sargo surfaces through a frozen polynya in the Arctic Ocean, 1960. *(U.S. Navy)*

Seadragon is welcomed home by a Navy helicopter as the boat nears Pearl Harbor after conquering the Northwest Passage. *(U.S. Navy)*

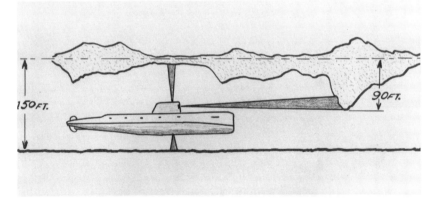

Graphic illustration shows how sonar beams guided *Sargo* 900 miles under the ice from the Bering Sea to the Arctic basin. *(Naval Electronics Laboratory Center)*

President John Kennedy congratulates Mrs. Waldo Lyon at the White House ceremony awarding Dr. Lyon the President's Award for Distinguished Federal Civilian Service. The award was presented 7 August 1962, while Dr. Lyon was on board *Skate* cruising under the arctic ice pack en route to the North Pole. *(U.S. Navy)*

Vice Admiral Rickover congratulates Comdr. Joseph Skoog Jr., commanding officer of the *Skate,* after a record-breaking cruise under the North Pole, 1962. The commander brought the admiral a block of ice from the North Pole. *(U.S. Navy)*

Mountains and valleys of the Arctic Ocean floor as plotted by American submarines. *(U.S. Navy)*

The Arctic Ocean has become the submarine's private sea. *(Naval Electronics Laboratory Center)*

Lt. Comdr. Marion D. Williams on the bridge of the carrier *Hancock*, 1956.
(U.S. Navy)

11

ACROSS THE NORTH POLE

When *Nautilus* left Groton, Connecticut, 25 April 1958, the details of the front operation had been handled so well that even her crew still remained ignorant of their real destination. Although Commander Anderson said he trusted his men completely, this was first and foremost a White House mission, fully planned to enhance the United States' image both at home and abroad. With her every movement watched with great interest by those in the Navy and in the news media, a friendly remark could easily create suspicion.

When they arrived at the Balboa Naval Base a few days later crewmen were allowed to place orders for routine supplies to be picked up on the way back. According to the published schedule the boat would be returning in early July to be ready to join *Skate* and *Halfbeak* by 28 July. Anderson readily approved the requisitions, which would add credibility to the story of a routine Pacific cruise.

With another 3,049-mile submerged run added to her growing record, *Nautilus* put into San Diego 13 May and workers began installing a Sperry depth sensor and checking out new sonar gear. The great boat was almost ready. The day before her arrival Dr. Lyon had received a personal letter from an assistant to the chairman of the Defense Research Board, Canada: Would he join a flight around the arctic area? Again placing a call to Washington, Lyon asked Duke Bayne to learn what story Admiral Daspit had given Tom Killian concerning Lyon's adventure in the weeks ahead. Both stories had to agree.

Daspit was not in his office, but Bayne agreed to call back when he learned the answer. When the call finally came, Bayne said that the admiral had told Killian that Dr. Lyon was needed for a job he—Daspit—controlled and would not be available to act on the Canadian committee.

Hoping that the matter was closed, Lyon returned to his discussion with Anderson about the reconnaissance flight plan once they reached Alaska. Anderson then took possession of the altered Charles Henderson ID card. On 14 May the two men held their final talk and agreed to catch the Pan American courier flight at the Seattle airport. Lyon would purchase round-trip tickets—Seattle-Fairbanks—and change the name on the reservations from Rowray to Henderson.

At the first party given for the crew in San Diego one speculator almost caused a disruption in *Nautilus*'s schedule. An aviator present pressed Paul Early for an explanation of the ship's "unrealistic" schedule. "Must be," said the pilot, "they are scheduled for the Arctic in August." This was the first case where outside guessing could lead to a leak.

After completing the San Diego training phase, *Nautilus* headed for San Francisco. On 20 May Dr. Lyon paid his last visit to Washington for final talks with Duke Bayne. Both men agreed it would be most difficult to free Anderson for the Alaskan flight once the boat reached Seattle. After more discussions with Admirals Daspit and Combs, many rough dispatches were written and torn up. No special secure communications would be made linking Admiral Grenfell in San Francisco. A final decision was made to bring in the commandant of the Thirteenth Naval District in Seattle. Between these two officers and Admiral Grenfell, arrangements had to be made to cancel underway operations scheduled in Seattle, and Commander, Flotilla One, would act as chief dignitary when the boat arrived. Commander Anderson could then depart immediately to catch the plane, using emergency leave as an excuse for his speedy departure and absence.

A final meeting was held on 22 May in Washington, D.C., with Admiral Daspit, Combs, Captain Walker, and Commander Bayne.

With Operation Sunshine orders in hand they reviewed proceedings and the rendezvous off Iceland. With last wishes and good luck to all, they noted a final reminder that the decision remained in the field as to whether the transit could be made. With the orders safely in his briefcase, Dr. Lyon headed for the West Coast. It had been planned that Anderson would fly down from San Francisco and meet him in Los Angeles to personally pick up the *Nautilus*'s orders. Despite a few minutes' difference in plane arrivals and the confusion of plane connections, the two men finally met at the San Diego Lindbergh Field that night and the operation orders changed hands.

When *Nautilus* docked at Pier 91 at the Naval Supply Depot, Seattle, Anderson quickly changed to civilian clothes and hurriedly left the boat on "emergency leave." Dr. Lyon was waiting at the airport and the two were soon comfortably seated on Pan American Flight 902, bound for Fairbanks. They continued their trip by commercial DC-3 to Kotzebue, where they chartered a bush flight from Wien Airlines. The reconnaissance route was from Kotzebue, around Cape Lisburne, to Icy Cape and then Point Barrow, to get a good flight in the afternoon and another in the evening, with ice conditions clearly visible during 24 hours of daylight.

The excursion was not without its drama. Running short of fuel the pilot radioed a nearby Air Force DEW line station asking permission to land. "Who do you have on board?" asked the air controller.

"Two civilians," replied the pilot.

"Permission not granted!"

With no alternative the pilot turned his craft to a small Eskimo village at Point Lay, south of Icy Cape, where he knew a gasoline cache was located. It was left there by other bush pilots for just such an emergency. After a hair-raising landing and takeoff from a sandy beach bar near the spot where Will Rogers and Wiley Post had crashed, the plane continued to Point Barrow.

When the two men returned to Seattle, they encountered no trouble clearing immigration. Not the slightest question arose with Anderson using the alias "Henderson." While the *Nautilus* skipper headed back to his boat, Lyon checked in at the Hotel Olympus in Tacoma where Rex Rowray was waiting.

By Sunday, 8 June, *Nautilus* was ready to go. Anderson received verbal orders over the telephone from Washington to execute Operation Sunshine. The *Seattle Post-Intelligencer* routinely reported, "Ship leaves Seattle today on submerged endurance cruise to Panama, first leg of ship's return to home. Scheduled to arrive in Panama July third."

When the telephone call came for Lyon and Rowray to board ship, to avoid being seen by reporters and crewmen they were told to arrive Sunday morning during a muster of the crew below deck in the crew's mess. Dr. Lyon decided to go by rented car to Seattle because the bus schedule from Tacoma would put them in town just when liberty was expiring and men came straggling back.

At Pier 91 Lieutenant Jenks was waiting with a staff car. After waiting out of view until signaled by the watch, Lyon and Rowray rushed aboard ship and were quickly locked in Jenks's stateroom until it was time to get under way—scheduled for 1500. The hour was soon extended until midnight because of an electric motor failure. "What a solitary confinement," Lyon wrote in his journal, "what a long stay with three pieces of bread and no space."

Minutes past midnight the crew cast off lines and *Nautilus* backed away from the pier and headed through the darkness for the open sea. Their orders were to remain undetected from now on. If they were detected, they were to conceal their identity. A working party was sent topside with a pot of black paint. The huge white "571" disappeared.

The moment Lyon and Rowray appeared, the crew knew without a word spoken they were not headed for Panama. Soon afterward Anderson announced over the public address system their real destination: Portland, England, via the North Pole.

At 0900 Monday, after clearing the Strait of Juan de Fuca, the diving alarm sounded twice and *Nautilus* slipped deep beneath the surface. Three days later the warm Japanese current was left behind and sea temperatures dropped sharply as the boat approached Unimak Island, 1,700 miles northwest of Seattle. By 0000, 13 June, *Nautilus* had reached the Pribilof Islands.

This was a zone familiar to Dr. Lyon from the many pioneering cruises of previous years and he was able to brief the crew with expert advice. Two possible tracks were available for entry into the deep Arctic Basin. One, Lyon had found on the track charts, lay to the west of St. Lawrence Island near the coast of Siberia. The second was closer to the Alaskan coast. Anderson decided to try the western approach first.

On Saturday, just six days out of port, the first ice was detected, still south of the Bering Strait. *Nautilus* was soon sandwiched in by ice above and the shallow flat sea bottom below. Utmost care would now be needed by the diving officer and his planners to keep from striking either. With 45 feet of water between the boat's keel and the ocean floor and less than 25 feet from the top of the sail to the bottom of the ice, the "bubble" was watched carefully, for any "porpoising" could drive the submarine's nose into the mud and sand or send it crashing into a protruding ice ridge.

At precisely 0020, near St. Lawrence Island, *Nautilus* passed beneath a huge floeberg reaching 30 feet below the surface. This had not been anticipated. The total thickness of ice that has spent its entire life in open sea is fairly predictable. But rafted ice, or chunks that break loose from the bleak, snow-capped Siberian coast, are not. Dr. Lyon knew from his own studies that huge chunks—some as thick as 60 feet—had broken loose from the Alaskan coast. But he knew nothing of the thickness of rafted ice that had torn loose from Siberia, and especially Cape Chukotski, which jutted into the sea only a few miles west of the international date line.

With even shallower stretches of water still ahead, Anderson and Lyon discussed the situation privately to avoid alarming the crew. Anderson was genuinely concerned. Lyon, calm and experienced, admitted he also was apprehensive. Ice expert that he now was, Dr. Lyon had been through many close brushes with the foe. They both had learned that ice is an enemy to be respected even at the cost of time. Reluctantly Anderson ordered the boat's course reversed. They would circle south of St. Lawrence and try the eastern route. The chance of detection by some on the Alaskan shore might be increased if the sail broke water in shallow places but there was no other choice.

Nautilus followed a huge circular route to the east and again turned north. Forced to expose the sail occasionally, the boat passed

King Island just south of Bering Strait on 17 June at periscope depth, dodging scattered ice floes. Deep water was somewhere around 400 miles north and they were still in water of known depth varying between 150 and 170 feet.

Eight days out of Seattle *Nautilus* crossed the Arctic Circle north of Cape Prince of Wales, and by 2300 that night they were deep under the ice in the Chukchi Sea, cruising through water barely 160 feet deep. It still seemed unlikely that the ice would reach down to them. The sonar echoes traced the contour, revealing underwater ridges averaging only 10 feet below water level. Soon the control room grew tense as the recorder drew a profile of a jagged ridge directly overhead reaching a depth of 62 feet.

Without hesitation, Anderson ordered the boat turned around and her depth increased to 140 feet. With just 20 feet clearance the keel barely cleared the bottom. The helmsman was still making his turn when the black line showed a massive ridge blocking their return track. It was too close to dodge and Anderson ordered speed slackened to dead slow. The recording pen continued downward. *Nautilus* slipped under the 85-foot-deep point with just five feet clearance. Only by his sudden decision to take the boat deeper was the great boat saved from serious damage and possible disaster.

Operation Sunshine for the present was a failure. Without charts showing deeper water, if it did exist, there was no doubt in the *Nautilus* commander's mind that the 300 miles remaining to the deep Arctic Basin was impassable. "It took a lot of moral courage," said Peter Aurand later. "Here was a presidential-directed project. Turning around was probably just as tough as going ahead. But he used good judgment."

Anderson drafted his message to Admiral Burke. The operation would probably be feasible later on, he was almost certain, after the ice boundary had receded north, closer to deep water. Back in open water, still remaining submerged to avoid detection, the radio antenna was raised above the surface to wait for the coded reply from the Chief of Naval Operations. It soon appeared on a scheduled broadcast by Navy Radio Honolulu:

I CONCUR ENTIRELY WITH YOUR PRUDENT ACTION WITHDRAW-
ING FROM THE ICE PACK. IT IS OBVIOUS THAT YOU HAVE MADE
A MAXIMUM EFFORT. I TENTATIVELY CONCUR WITH YOUR
RECOMMENDATION TO LAY OVER AT PEARL HARBOR UNTIL
CONDITIONS IMPROVE. SET COURSE AND STAND BY FOR FUR-
THER INSTRUCTIONS. REMAIN UNDETECTED. ARLEIGH BURKE.

Next came a two-part message, initiated by the Chief of Naval
Operations. The first part was the Pacific Command:

DIVERT *NAUTILUS* TO PEARL FOR INDOCTRINATION IN
NUCLEAR POWER FOR PERSONNEL OF SUBPAC AND EVALUA-
TION OF FIRST PHASE OF ENDURANCE CRUISE X SCHEDULE 4
WEEKS UNINTERRUPTED LEAVE AND UPK (UPKEEP) PERIOD.

And for the Atlantic Commander:

CANCEL PARTICIPATION ARCTIC OPERATIONS SCHEDULED JULY
AND AUGUST.

Nautilus approached Pearl Harbor cruising at a depth of 250 feet,
only occasionally coming up to loop depth to receive radio schedules. Soon a message appeared stating that Adm. H. G. Hopwood,
Commander-in-Chief, Pacific Fleet, and Rear Admiral Grenfell would
meet the boat at the sea buoy entrance to the harbor for a conference.
Also, a plane would be available for a flight to Washington. Dr. Lyon
decided to go along to learn the next move and what was expected
for *Skate* operations scheduled for August and to take part in any
decision making.

Nautilus arrived off the entrance to Pearl Harbor at 1000. After the
party boarded, the boat moved into the harbor amid a big, noisy welcome by all ships and helicopters. The traditional Hawaiian flowers
were abundant. All these pleasures were missed by the two stow-
aways, again safely hidden from view below decks. Almost bumping
into an old friend from New London, Dr. Lyon ducked into a stateroom just in time.

When the boat was tied to the pier at the submarine base, the two
men slipped into the backseat of an automobile and were rushed to the

waiting plane. To get the scientist on board, Anderson listed Lyon on the manifest of Admiral Hopwood's staff DC-6 as Charles Henderson. Anderson had also listed him in the log at the MATS (Military Air Transport System) office so he would not have to appear personally.

A few happy crewmen were granted leave to visit families left behind on the East Coast. As the huge plane took to the air newspapers again carried a routine news item: "Ship arrives at Pearl Harbor after underwater cruise from Seattle."

When Dr. Lyon finally returned to San Diego a few days later, one of the first and most difficult tasks he faced was to prepare a false travel voucher to verify and record actual travel and personal expenses. The recently completed "trip to carry out special study assignment made by Chief of Naval Operations by instruction of 22 May in connection with NEL problem L6-1" was made for the most part by government aircraft, he wrote for the record, with only meals at "Barter Island" and "Resolute Bay, Canada" being required at own expense. Total cost, including taxi fares: $28.41. Even the trip to Washington was explained as by government aircraft from Sand Point Naval Air Station, near Seattle.

Undaunted by the fact that the second attempt to reach the North Pole was a failure, Navy planners quietly went to work for a third try. August would be the earliest it could be made. Since *Nautilus* was now in the Pacific and would remain there for a few weeks, Jim Hagarty had his doubts that the secret could be kept that long.

"They won't be able to protect the story," he told Aurand. "Now everyone in that crew knows what they are trying to do, and it's going to leak out!"

"Jim," replied the president's naval aide, "you don't know the Navy. Particularly men in the submarine service. They know how to keep their mouths shut!"

"I'll bet you a dollar it'll leak!"

"I'll bet you it won't!"

That small wager against the integrity of the *Nautilus* crew was to become very important within a few weeks.

Anderson was well aware of the public interest in *Nautilus* and he and his crew had taken care to safeguard the operation. Anderson

gave written instructions detailing precautions necessary to guaran-
tee no leaks from *Nautilus* and her crew:

> The Chief of Naval Operations has directed in the national interest
> of the United States that all information regarding Operation Sun-
> shine be retained in the category of Top Secret, sensitive information.
>
> I cannot impress on you too strongly the grave responsibility
> which rests on each of you individually to carry out this order. Not
> only is it necessary for each of you to "forget" entirely everything that
> has happened or been divulged to you regarding this operation, but
> you must each also actively participate in maintaining a plausible
> cover story for what we have been or will be doing. I cannot imagine
> a situation requiring greater discretion, common sense, and alertness
> and loyalty.
>
> Remember that the strength of the chain depends on the weakest
> link. Neither rank or rate, nor the lack of it; nor time on board, nor
> years of service, nor any other factor, changes the degree to which you
> are personally responsible.
>
> You may come in contact with those who conjecture that *Nautilus*
> has done this or that or plans to do this or that. Do not let conjecture
> on the part of others cause you to lower your guard.
>
> From this moment forward do not discuss any facet of Operation
> Sunshine with any person on board or ashore by either verbal or writ-
> ten means. In privacy it is permissible to consult the commanding
> officer or executive officer on factors relating to the subject.

Anderson directed the crew to search for and seal all letters,
papers, and documents that might reveal any information. Special
arctic equipment, navigation equipment, charts, cold-weather clothing, and identifiable items were locked up by the top secret control
officer, Lieutenant White.

As a cover story, an operation plan was drawn up including an
endurance run by *Nautilus,* arctic operations with submarines *Skate*
and *Halfbeak,* and elaborate plans to cross the equator, a first by a
nuclear-powered submarine.

During the weeks of waiting at Pearl Harbor, *Nautilus* was being
equipped with another unconventional piece of equipment, a closed-
circuit television. The camera itself was installed in such a manner

that its lens could be trained upward and forward. The view through murky, dark waters might be limited in range but it would eliminate the need to raise a periscope.

To back up the gyro compass, an inertial navigator, called the SINS, had been installed at New London.

During the weeks that followed, a second operation was being planned. At the submarine base in New London, the 2,360-ton *Skate* was undergoing final preparations for another attempt to reach the North Pole. As far as the *Skate*'s crew and the public knew, the *Nautilus* was presently concerned with normal fleet operations in the Pacific. *Nautilus* had made one attempt to reach the Pole the year before. That they had learned through the Navy's scuttlebutt channels. Now it was their driving ambition to succeed where the first attempt had failed. Only Comdr. James F. Calvert, *Skate*'s commanding officer, was told of *Nautilus*'s real mission again that summer.

Skate's primary mission was to improve vertical ascents through holes in the ice pack, thereby permitting the wider range of exploration. Reaching the North Pole was of secondary importance.

At the time Calvert was going through final preparations, Anderson was well on his way. At 0625, 29 July, *Nautilus* crossed latitude 66 degrees 33 minutes north, the Arctic Circle, and was entering the Chukchi Sea, when Calvert backed his boat from her berth alongside the *Seawolf* and headed for the sea.

As expected, Anderson and Lyon found the edge of the pack had receded back north of the Bering Strait. *Nautilus* continued northward, following the 165 meridian to where solid ice lay ahead. Sonar echoes bounced off the bottom, showing the depth still a shallow 180 feet. A course was set to the east toward Point Barrow, searching for a deep-water channel leading into the Arctic Basin.

In the early morning hours of 1 August *Nautilus* was cruising on the surface, with Point Barrow hidden from view by the curvature of the earth, when the water started gradually increasing in depth. Things looked promising. Suddenly the trace dipped to 220 feet. This was what they had been looking for. *Nautilus* had reached the southwest end of the deep Barrow Sea Valley discovered by *Burton Island* during Lyon and McWethy's tour in 1950. It had been plotted in great detail far enough to seaward that there was no question they could use it to reach the deep Arctic Basin.

Anderson gave the order: "When you are ready, clear the bridge and submerge!"

In minutes *Nautilus* disappeared under the ice. The bottom increased—300 feet and deeper, as the sloping canyon plunged deeper in a northerly direction toward the main basin. The boat was safe at last, far below even the deepest pressure ridges. It picked up speed, turned north, her low-frequency sonar probing the waters ahead for any submerged mountain peaks that might loom suddenly from the uncharted sea floor.

The following day *Nautilus* had reached latitude 76 degrees and soundings soon measured 2,000 fathoms—12,000 feet. A previously unknown undersea mountain range passed beneath the silent invader.

By 1000, 3 August, *Nautilus* crossed latitude 87 north, the farthest point ever reached by any ship. "With continued good fortune," Anderson announced to the crew,

> *Nautilus* will soon accomplish two goals long sought by those who sail the seas: first, the opening of a route for rapid voyages between the great Pacific and Atlantic Oceans, and second, the attainment of the North Pole by any ship. Thus, our remarkable ship has been blessed with her great opportunity—the discovery of the only truly practicable Northwest Passage. On this historic Sunday, 3 August 1958, let us offer our thanks to Him who has blessed us with this opportunity and who has guided us so truly.

Anderson entered in the log:

> *3 August 1958 eleven men completed all requirements for qualification in nuclear submarines and were designated as "Qualified in SSN" by Commanding Officer on 3 August at the Crossing the Pole ceremony.*
>
> *Sordelet, J. R. EM1 (SS) was reenlisted for six years as* Nautilus *passed over the North Pole, thus becoming the first United States Navy man to ever reenlist while crossing over the North Pole in a submarine at 600 feet keel depth, speed 20 knots.*

Cruising at a fast clip in 13,410 feet of water the *Nautilus* crossed the North Geographic Pole at 2315 (11:15 P.M., Eastern Daylight Savings Time). Without slowing her speed for ceremonies, the jubilant crew pushed the boat ahead. All directions pointed south at the Pole and only the navigational instruments showed the boat's sudden change of course from north to south without the slightest movement of the rudder.

At this moment *Skate* was approaching the ice pack east of Greenland.

At the White House, Captain Aurand and Jim Hagarty were both becoming anxious. A look at the calendar indicated that unless tragedy had struck the gallant boat and her crew, word of success would not be long in coming. Plans had to be made for public release—fast!

The problem they now faced: How would the White House handle the announcement? How would they assure that the news release planned by Jim Hagarty for so many months would receive worldwide attention and that the president would be the first to announce it?

Hagarty wanted to announce the completion of the first successful transpolar cruise at the White House with both the president and *Nautilus* commanding officer present. *Nautilus* was, according to published reports, on another long submerged cruise to Panama. Now she would undoubtedly soon be sighted in the North Atlantic. The top-secret schedule directed the boat to proceed to Portland, England. This had been planned to enhance the overseas part of the exploit and impress European nations with this great U.S. achievement.

Hagarty knew the local news media would cover the news because the crew was made up of local men. If, however, the boat arrived in Europe and the news broke there first, "the President of the United States would be out in the cold." With this in mind, Operation Sunshine's operation order included a tentative plan for just such a possibility: a rendezvous off Iceland.

Captain Aurand outlined his plan.

If they go past Iceland we could pick Bill Anderson off, fly him back to Washington, and to the White House for the ceremony. Then we could fly him back to the *Nautilus* off England, helicopter him out to the boat and he could take her into port. The executive officer could just take her down to the English Channel. Certainly, after all the schooling he had had, Frank Adams would be very capable of doing that.

During one of Anderson's visits to Washington, Aurand had discussed the possibility that should the *Nautilus* skipper ever suffer a heart attack or some disabling illness, his executive officer would have to take the responsibility for the boat. Anderson had readily agreed. "Heck, yes! I have no qualms about turning the *Nautilus* over to Frank Adams!"

Peter Aurand could now see himself winning his one-dollar bet with the press secretary. For months, even with the *Nautilus* crew allowed to return home on leave while waiting for the ice pack to recede, the news had not leaked. Aurand was determined to be certain now at the very end they did not lose that secrecy. But it was still a possibility.

Somehow they had to get Anderson to the Capital and smuggle him into the White House. Some newsmen were already suspicious. Prominent among them was Clay Blair. Aurand and Hagarty both knew that once *Nautilus* was out from under the ice pack they had about 24 hours to act. Aurand decided to fly to Iceland himself, pick Bill Anderson off the boat, and bring him back to Washington.

He telephoned the Pentagon and asked the office of the Chief of Naval Operations to have a plane ready for him to pick up a presidential party. This was to be done in great secrecy; "A party of White House people is over in Europe," he informed Op-53, the flight section, "and they need to be picked up at Prestwich, Scotland. This is a secret mission! We don't know just when they are coming back, but I will give you 24 hours notice. I am going over to pick them up. You have the plane over at Anacostia Naval Air Station 24 hours after I call you."

Nautilus was not yet in clear waters and safety. Their course would take them into the deep-water opening between Greenland and Spitzbergen, close to the same area where Wilkins's *Nautilus* had operated in 1931 and where Anderson himself had passed through the year before.

During the early hours of 5 August the inertial navigation system and Shep Jenks's plotted position, using gyro compass and pit-log figures, were compared. Their position placed the boat at two points just 15 miles apart. By 0230 the bottom dropped suddenly to 2,500 fathoms. There was nothing like that on the chart! Their own sounds recorded in the same area in 1957 showed nothing deeper than 1,500 fathoms.

Suddenly at 0515 open water appeared on the television screen, confirming the ice-profiling instruments. In a few minutes *Nautilus* was on the surface. A top-secret coded message to Arleigh Burke was flashed to the first Navy Radio Station answering the operator's call in Japan, and then England:

> *NAUTILUS*-90-NORTH. NINETY-SIX HOURS, POINT BARROW TO THE GREENLAND SEA.

Captain Aurand made his telephone call to the Pentagon:

> I did not bargain for the effects of my order to the flight section a few days earlier. I gave them the call as I promised. When I arrived at the Air Station there was a great big DC-6.
>
> I was quite sure the pilot had planned to refuel at Keflavik Air Force Base, Iceland, but I did not want to tell him to stop there and create suspicion with a change of schedule. However, he soon confirmed my plans: "If it's okay for you, I will plan for a fuel stop."
>
> It certainly was okay with me! I climbed in the plane with my traveling companion, Chief Warrant Officer Arguello, a writer in my White House office, and as soon as we got into the air I told the pilot: "Okay! Here's your orders. First of all, I am taking off my aiguillettes. I am now Capt. E. P. Adams. Your crew is to be briefed that they should not refer to me in any other way. And second, when you land at Keflavik I want you to simulate a bad engine. But it shouldn't be so bad as to need to call in outside mechs. Yet it should be quite believable." The pilot really wondered whether I had gone nuts!

When the plane landed in Iceland, the pilot pulled it off to one side of the field. He popped and banged one engine according to instructions. Next he put the message out that they had to RON (remain overnight) for repairs.

Looking over the list of people in the local Navy command, Aurand spotted the name of one officer, a Navy captain, who knew him. He quickly informed the officer of his assumed name. Then, of course, Aurand had to tell the man his secret. He was the only person on the island who knew what was taking place. After borrowing a helicopter, Aurand created a story that they were going to fly out and pick up an observer from a submarine. Fortunately an American submarine exercise was taking place in the area.

That submarine exercise had been set up by his old friend Bob McWethy, who happened to be in the Greenland Sea on an unrelated mission, little suspecting his operation was serving to good advantage. He was curious to look into a possibility that the Soviets might use an unusual ruse to make a summer transit along the Greenland coast to reach North America undetected. McWethy, in command of a division of submarines, sent the *Halfbeak* into the area. It was painted white to test its camouflage effect among drift ice moving out of the Arctic Ocean. While the submarine lay in the Denmark Strait off Greenland, McWethy spent two days flying out of Keflavik trying to find his submarine. On the second day, while Aurand headed for his rendezvous with *Nautilus,* McWethy was on board a P2V winging its way westward. "She wasn't easy to find," he said, "even when the weather was clear, the submarine was on the surface, and we knew approximately where to look."

While Bob McWethy was engaged in his operation, Aurand was carrying out his own plans. "It turned out that *Nautilus* was going to arrive 13 miles northwest of Keflavik lighthouse at 0300. At first I was horrified that it would be dark. Local officers assured me, 'Oh no, it is high latitude and plenty of light.' It would have been, except that it was cloudy and darker than the inside of a hat!"

With the DC-6 pilot ordered to be ready for immediate takeoff when they returned, the helicopter headed for sea. Aurand had to find the submarine himself. Sure enough, she was there on schedule. The pilot took the craft down, but couldn't land on deck and the copter did not have a hoist. "The pilot did a terrific job. He hovered the craft over the submarine with his starboard wheels practically on deck. I just reached down and hauled old Bill inside by hand."

After Anderson was safely inside, the first and most meaningful message, among the many honors, letters, and telegrams to follow, was handed down to the men on deck. Inside a plain white envelope addressed to the "Acting Commanding Officer" was a letter that read:

> To the officers and men of the *Nautilus.* Congratulations on a magnificent achievement. Well Done! Dwight D. Eisenhower

Returning to Keflavik, the plane was sitting on the air strip with engines turned up and ladder waiting. The two men ran up the ladder, pulling it in after them. Aurand recalled,

> That huge DC-6 had a nice plush cabin aft. I took Bill Anderson in, locked the door, and told him to stay inside until the plane took off.
>
> I thought I was going to do Bill a favor. I knew that on the trip he had just made he would be up most of the time and pretty tired out. I had brought along a bottle of Scotch. There was a bunk waiting for him and I knew he wouldn't cork out unless I got a lot of Scotch into him. I poured a real heavy one. He drank that down and was still awake. I poured a second.
>
> "Well, don't you think you ought to turn in?" I urged.
>
> About 0300 Anderson was out of bed writing his report. I don't think any amount of Scotch would have toned him down!

Both men rolled out of their bunks about the time the plane neared New York City, en route to Washington. The plane commander appeared at the cabin door:

"Can't you tell me who he is now?"

"No," replied Aurand.

"Well, can't you even give me a hint?"

"Have you been reading Buzz Sawyer?"

Buzz Sawyer, the comic-strip character, had just been flown into the Crimea to help a Russian, a member of the Politburo who was defecting, and help get him out of the country.

A few minutes later the plane commander was back again. "Well, I have asked for customs. Should I ask for immigration?"

"Not only will you not ask for immigration," replied Aurand emphatically, "but you will cancel customs! I don't want anybody around this plane when we arrive!"

Anderson's wife, who had been kept completely ignorant of the plans, had been brought down from New London and was waiting when the plane landed at Anacostia. They all jumped into a White House car and were taken quickly to the White House for the ceremony.

Jim Hagarty had the press conference all set up. It was the first time in the memory of the press corps that President Eisenhower had held a press conference in the Fish Room. The room was so named when President Roosevelt had used the room for his tropical fish collection. It was directly across from the presidential Oval Office. Hagarty had put out a conference sheet: "The President will hold a conference at 12 o'clock in the Fish Room. I recommend you all be there!"

Quite naturally there was great speculation by the press. The White House correspondents had posed some fantastic suggestions as to what was coming off. Aurand had prepared charts showing the route *Nautilus* had taken. After the correspondents entered the room the door was locked, the charts were turned around, and they were told what had happened. As planned, it was a fantastic coverage of the historic cruise.

President Eisenhower pinned the Legion of Merit on the chest of the first ship's commander to take his ship across the top of the world. Absolute secrecy had been maintained and Jim Hagarty paid off his lost wager. Peter Aurand took possession of a one-dollar bill autographed by both. It is one of his proudest possessions marking service in the White House.

News that *Nautilus* had reached the North Pole ahead of them was picked up from a London news broadcast by *Skate*'s crew just a few hours before they went deep under the ice pack from the North Atlantic. The word that they had been beaten to the Pole was understandably disheartening. However, they had a different kind of job to do that required even greater skill and was equally dangerous.

After the White House ceremony Anderson was flown back to England by Pan American Airways. Now, of course, that plane crew knew all about the great voyage. As they neared England the pilot contacted acting skipper Frank Adams by radio and Anderson spoke briefly to his executive officer as the boat was nearing Portland.

Anderson was soon lifted back aboard his boat by helicopter for a triumphant entry into the harbor on 12 August.

Under bright sunshine a band played "Stars and Stripes Forever," bagpipes skirled, and boats whistled, while the crowd of spectators and officers and men of the British and American navies cheered. There was a touch of sadness for Dr. Lyon, however, because missing from the scene was one man. Dr. Harald V. Sverdrup had died the year before while *Nautilus* was under the ice pack.

The world's first atomic-powered submarine docked just 19 days out of Pearl Harbor. Fluttering at the masthead was a newly designed blue flag the crew had made for the occasion which bore the words "Submerged for Transit—*Nautilus* 1958."

In full-dress uniform, Commander Anderson escorted U.S. Ambassador John Hay Whitney aboard. The ambassador addressed the crew:

Men of the *Nautilus*—The President of the United States has in a dramatic ceremony conferred upon your Commander his expression of appreciation for your matchless exploit. I have the honor and good fortune to act on the President's behalf in presenting to you today this same measure of National admiration and respect.

Some hint of the warmth of the welcome you and your men can expect in Portland—and throughout England—may be sensed by the nature of the gathering here and on the dock this afternoon.

With us, and sharing our pride in your performance, are Great Britain's First Sea Lord and Lady Selkirk, together with other distinguished representatives of the British government, the Admiralty, and the local communities whose guests we are on this occasion. Their presence symbolizes the Official Welcome Britain has in store for you. I am sure you will find it hard to believe, as this welcome develops, that Portland was—not so long ago—a center of Anti-Submarine training. Well it may once have been anti-submarine, but Portland today is most definitely pro-submarine. And from what I am given to understand, your unofficial reception both here and in London will hardly be, excuse the expression—icy.

But there is a deeper significance in the warmth of this welcome.

For it is appropriate that, after this voyage, you should first make port in Britain, the island home of such legendary polar explorers as Scott, Shackleton, Sir Hubert Wilkins, and, most recently, Sir Vivian

Fuchs. This tradition is our common heritage. And now—in this one year—our two nations have girded the earth with the two greatest polar achievements of all time—Sir Vivian's overland transit of the southern ice cap, and your creation of a new Northwest Passage beneath the ice of the North Pole. It seems to me there is more than coincidence here. There is a symbol. For these conquests together symbolize the fact that the free world has the imagination, the courage, and the will to lead in the scientific exploration of the unknown.

By their accomplishments at opposite ends of the earth, British explorers and American submariners have expressed better than any words can the similarity of interests, of aims, and determinations that bind the United States and the United Kingdom into the great international partnership of our time.

How gratifying to us and how assuring it must be to the free world to know that while explorers are poles apart, our governments and our peoples are so close.

To you men of the *Nautilus,* I would like only to say what has already been said, and what will be repeated again and again in the accolades to come: Your country is proud of you. You are the latest of a great breed, the American pioneers.

Gentlemen: With the Unit Citation which I will read to you in a moment goes the privilege of wearing the citation ribbon with a special clasp in the form of a golden "N." The right to wear this clasp is reserved to you alone; Naval personnel subsequently assigned to the *Nautilus* may wear the ribbon, but not this special memento of your achievement.

I now read you the President's words, the text of the first Presidential Unit Citation ever awarded in Peacetime:

"For outstanding achievement in completing the first voyage in history across the top of the world, by cruising under the Arctic ice cap from the Bering Strait to the Greenland Sea, passing submerged beneath the North Geographic Pole. This voyage opens the possibility of a new commercial seaway, a Northwest Passage, between the major oceans of the world. Nuclear powered cargo submarines may, in the future, use this route to the advantage of world trade.

The skill, professional competency and courage of the officers and crew of the *Nautilus* were in keeping with the highest traditions of the Armed Forces of the United States and the pioneering spirit which has always characterized our country."

Nautilus's greeting on arrival in New York harbor with fire boats streaming water aloft was a thrilling prelude to an even greater triumphant parade up Fifth Avenue. As a representative of the president of the United States, Admiral Rickover, the "Father of the Atomic Submarine," joined the crew for a hero's welcome reserved by the people of that great city for those few individuals who excel in worldwide achievements. In this case, it was the "technological achievement" sought by men working at 1600 Pennsylvania Avenue, Washington, D.C.

An interesting postscript was provided by Capt. J. S. Kinsey, Medical Corps:

> The two phases of Operation Sunshine provided an opportunity to observe psychological reaction of personnel subjected to a combination of unusual circumstances; an extended period away from home and families, the isolation of prolonged submerged runs, hazardous conditions such as 96 hours under the polar ice cap, and participation in a historic event, the first transit of the Arctic Ocean from Pacific to Atlantic via the North Geographic Pole.
>
> In other words the personnel on board were observed during the anticipation of adventure and trail blazing, the frustration of failure about which they could do nothing but wait, and the satisfaction of success and a job well done.
>
> The entire crew were endowed with a particular zeal and pride to see the successful fulfillment of this historic cruise.

12

A VISIT TO ALPHA

On Saturday, 21 June 1958, a ski-equipped C-54 plane slid to a stop on the rough ice runway of Ice Island T-2 less than 500 miles from the North Pole. Two of the plane's passengers, Elton "Gus" Kelley, a sound expert from New London, and C. W. Senior, an oceanographer from Washington, D.C., climbed down the ladder to join Drift Station Alpha's crew. Several hundred miles across the pack, Richard Hecht, also from New London, arrived in a similar manner at Ice Island T-3.

In the weeks that followed, Kelley and Hecht were scheduled to explode dynamite charges in the cold waters beneath the ice pack to study sound signals between the two ice islands. It was just another front operation for Gus, set up to camouflage the real purpose of his presence.

Unknown to Station Alpha's two dozen occupants, Gus Kelley had been sent to the floating ice research station for a very special mission. Several weeks passed before Gus quietly shared his secret with Maj. Joseph P. Bilotta, the current camp commander. A visitor would probably stop by briefly a few weeks later. Joe Bilotta's reaction was understandably one of great surprise. "Me? A U.S. Air Force major, a U.S. Navy submarine visiting my ice island? You're putting me on! This is too good to be true!" Kelley was forced to repeat the news before Bilotta was finally convinced.

Drift Station Alpha was being used as a floating platform for Air Force Project Ice Skate, another part of the worldwide International Geophysical Year. Early in 1957 several flights of the Alaskan Air Command had taken off from Ladd Air Force Base, Fairbanks, in search of a suitable ice floe. One was finally located some 800 miles from Point Barrow by Lt. Col. Joseph Fletcher and Rev. Thomas Cunningham, a Jesuit priest from Point Barrow who was a student of the ice pack.

The floe had been chosen as ideal because it was near the center of the North Polar Sea. Here, rather than at the North Geographic Pole, were encountered extreme climatic and biological conditions of the Arctic Ocean. With the frozen mass constantly on the move, Fletcher and Cunningham marked the spot with dyes dropped from the air.

Construction began in April and by the end of May a long runway was completed. Drift Station Alpha was finished just in time. The melt season had arrived and the scientists and support personnel received supplies via parachute drops. The official beginning of the International Geophysical Year was 1 June 1957. By that date the small community riding the huge drifting ice floe was in full operation. In the spring of 1958, with some breakup of the floe, Alpha was moved to another floe.

When Kelley arrived in June the station had drifted slowly northeasterly, reaching a position some 800 miles north of Point Barrow and 300 miles from the North Pole. He immediately began preparations for *Skate*'s visit. Both he and Bilotta agreed no radio messages on the subject would be transmitted for fear of a news leak.

Skate entered the ice north of Spitzbergen at 0400Z on Sunday, 10 August. She laid a course directly for the North Pole, stopping only once to surface in a polynya for about two hours over 60 miles into the pack. "With a typical beginner's luck," wrote Commander Calvert, "the first thing we saw under a slight overcast at 33 degrees Fahrenheit was a full grown polar bear clambering up on the edge of the oval shaped polynya."

The day after *Nautilus* ended her long journey amid cheers in England, the second nuclear submarine passed through the North Pole.

With *Skate*'s position established, Calvert and his men searched for an opening large enough to get the 268-foot boat to the surface. Several hours passed without success. Finally a sizable opening appeared as a smooth line on the trace.

Hovering motionless directly below the water level, the submarine slowly had water pumped from its tanks to gain more positive buoyancy. As the boat neared the surface with propellers stopped, the current carried her a few feet out of position. The stern struck the ice. Calvert decided to hold his position there with only the sail out of water. It was not the best position to be in, but he and his crew had reached the surface closer to the North Pole than any ship in history.

Lt. Comdr. John Nicholson, executive officer and navigator, was able to shoot quickly several elevations of the sun for a good position fix. Hoisting the radio antenna, a second message in as many weeks electrified the world. Navy Radio Manila, Philippines, picked up the message and relayed it to the Pentagon:

REACHED NORTH GEOGRAPHIC POLE AUGUST ELEVENTH. NOW IN POLYNYA ABOUT FORTY MILES FROM POLE. ALL WELL.

Four messages were cleared from the polynya without undue difficulty.

At 1758, 12 August Alpha time, the radio operator seated at his desk in the Jamesway communication hut typed out another message, flashed across 300 miles of pack ice from *Skate:*

REQUEST FOLLOWING: A. YOUR LATEST POSITION. B. NUMBER LARGE POLYNYAS YOUR VICINITY. C. INFO AS TO WHETHER YOU CAN PUT NOISEMAKER IN WATER FOR HOMING. IF SO, GIVE APPROXIMATE FREQUENCY.

Overcast skies blanking both the sun and horizon prevented Bilotta and Kelley from immediately checking their own position. To make matters worse, it had been several days since the last fix had been taken. The best position Alpha's navigators had been able to plot even in clear weather was plus or minus five miles. At that distance both submarine and the highest buildings and towers of the station could easily be hidden from each other's view by ice ridges.

Kelly recalled,

> When that first message was received at Alpha, it occurred to me that
> the best continuous noise source we had was the major's 12-foot fiber-
> glass motorboat, equipped with its Johnson outboard motor. That boat
> had irritated me all summer. Bilotta was forever riding around in
> leads and polynyas with that thing, while I was trying to make ambi-
> ent noise measurements and listen by hydrophone for shots set off by
> Ice Island T-3.

The outboard motor as a homing noisemaker for *Skate* sounded
like an excellent idea to Major Bilotta. He was in a joyful mood and
wanted to play a part in the Navy operation. Gus and the major
drafted a message reply:

> STATION ALPHA POSITION LATITUDE 82 DEGREES 58 MINUTES
> NORTH LONGITUDE 136 DEGREES 95 MINUTES WEST. ENTIRE
> AREA COVERED WITH POLYNYAS. BEST POLYNYA 100 FEET
> WEST OF STATION. 18 HP JOHNSON ONLY CONTINUOUS SIGNAL
> AVAILABLE. HOMER FREQUENCY 375 KCS IDENTIFICATION ICE.
> REQUEST STARTING TIME OF JOHNSON.

The *Skate* replied:

> START JOHNSON FREQ AT 1400Z (MIDNIGHT, 14 AUGUST
> GREENWICH TIME)

Right on time Bilotta climbed into his boat and with the Johnson
motor at full power started the marathon circling of the ice lake. Fear-
ing the submarine might surface directly under his boat, throughout
the night the major hugged the ice as close as he dared. He had been
jokingly forewarned by Kelley that any other course of action might
result in the first case in history where an Air Force major might be
skewered by a Navy periscope.

The polynya near the station was huge. It had even been used one
afternoon a day or so before by Bilotta and Dr. Nordert Untersteiner
for aquaplaning. A request to the Alaskan Air Command for a pair
of water skis had not been filled. Water skis at the North Pole?

"The supply people obviously thought it was some kind of joke,"
remembered the German scientist, who had never water-skied before.

"Having been born and raised in the Austrian Alps, I considered skis a natural extension of the human legs."

Undaunted, he fashioned a sled from a piece of plywood. It had been a pleasant but dangerous experiment. "It was, of course, a pretty silly thing to do," said the scientist, "because falling in that cold water is fairly dangerous."

Much to the annoyance of the radio operators, it had been the practice at the small isolated station for men to wander in and out of the radio station. Some talked to their families by amateur radio, which the operators did not mind. Now, however, a slip of the tongue while talking on amateur frequencies constantly monitored by hundreds of listening hams could reveal *Skate*'s impending visit and easily spread the news like a forest fire.

Bilotta realized he could not declare the radio shack off limits prior to and while they were actually homing *Skate* in. This was not practical, due to ham-radio activity and periodic transmission of scientific data. He chose the only alternative: from the moment of the first contact with the submarine the major would clamp the lid tight on all types of transmissions. The radio shack was then declared off limits, not only for the purpose of secrecy but also to prevent personnel from disturbing the operator busy with messages to and from *Skate*. The exchange began:

REQUEST YOU DETONATE A CHARGE EVERY HOUR EXACTLY ON THE HOUR FOR THE NEXT 24 HOURS. PLAN TO REMAIN THIS POLYNYA FOR SEVERAL HOURS. SUGGEST YOU SECURE JOHNSON UNTIL I LEAVE THIS POLYNYA. JUST PRIOR TO LEAVING WILL ASK YOU TO RUN THE JOHNSON AND FIRE A DETONATOR EVERY TEN MINUTES.

Gus Kelley went to work on basic plans he had been working on privately for weeks. He prepared dynamite charges. For many weeks prior to his arrival he had been thoroughly schooled at the Hingham Naval Ammunition Depot in preparation for this assignment. While carrying out sound tests with Ice Island T-3 he had gained more time to practice handling and firing explosives. The tests had been carried out with great care to ensure his safety and that of his ice island shipmates.

On Wednesday morning *Skate* was flooded down. Dropping away from the ice, Calvert set a course south toward the approximate position of the station. In less than 24 hours he was within a few miles of the pinpoint position near the center of millions of square miles of a patchwork pattern of the frozen white mass. Calvert decided to surface in another polynya, hoping for a better position report. He radioed the station commander:

> SURFACED IN POLYNYA AT LATITUDE 85 DEGREES 12 MINUTES NORTH LONGITUDE 135 DEGREES 20 MINUTES WEST. REQUEST YOUR POSITION AND POSITION OF BRAVO. REQUEST YOU GUARD THIS FREQUENCY UNTIL FURTHER NOTICE. CAN YOU DF MY TRANSMISSIONS? REQUEST KELLEY DETONATE 3X AT 5 MINUTE INTERVALS AT 1100Z.

Alpha replied:

> POSITION ALPHA 11 AUGUST 58 LATITUDE 84 DEGREES 58 MINUTES NORTH LONGITUDE 136 DEGREES 05 MINUTES EAST POSITION BRAVO 3 AUGUST LATITUDE 79 DEGREES 06 MINUTES NORTH LONGITUDE 120 DEGREES WEST NEGATIVE OF THIS STATION LAST ITEM COMPLIED WITH

As the day wore on submarine and station exchanged more messages:

Skate:

> REQUEST ESTIMATE OF SIZE AND SHAPE OF YOUR FJORD AND POLYNYA AND ESTIMATE POSITION OF JOHNSON OUTBOARD WILL BE IN IT.

Alpha:

> POLYNYA APPROXIMATELY 3,000 FEET LONG AND 200 TO 300 FEET WIDE POLYNYA APPROXIMATELY 200 FEET NORTHWEST OF CAMP JOHNSON WILL CIRCLE THE OUTER PERIMETER OF POLYNYA UNLESS OBJECTIONS RAISED.

Skate:

> LEAVING POLYNYA. REQUEST JOHNSON NOW AND DETONATE

CAPS EVERY 10 MINUTES COMMENCING 1730Z. MY DISTANCE FROM YOU ABOUT 8 MILES.

At this time both Kelley and Bilotta knew the major obstacles had been overcome. *Skate* was literally zeroing in on a pinpointed location in the vast Arctic. Bilotta eagerly pressed his noisemaker into operation following a zigzag course to clear the jagged ice tongues of the lake's boundary. Kelley commenced setting off explosives. Picked up by *Skate*'s listening sonar, the explosions showed her distance increasing from Alpha. Calvert quickly swung the boat about 180 degrees and closed in.

Later calculations proved Calvert correct, which placed *Skate*'s position 7.8 miles from the station. *Skate*'s sonarmen estimated the outboard motor's noise might be heard a distance of five miles or more.

When Kelley started firing the dynamite charges the uninformed Alpha men soon noticed that they occurred with conspicuous regularity. Dr. Untersteiner said,

> It took us a while to notice that, but when we did, we knew there was something up. Kelley had cut a hole in the ice some distance from everyone. He then lowered the charges into the water. We could hear the shots explode under the ice. To us, it was a strange situation. Our curiosity had first been aroused much earlier when the major had been getting very uncommunicative, avoiding everyone. He had always been a very sociable type. Suddenly he stayed in his hut.

Approximately seven miles from Alpha, *Skate*'s sonar picked up the steady familiar whirr of the Johnson motor's spinning propellers. The sound was unmistakable. With a clear homing signal to follow, Calvert moved toward the huge open lake. At three knots the distance from the position when the first sound was heard would take about two hours. He kept moving slowly toward the gradually increasing signal, when suddenly the sound was directly overhead; then astern. Circling the polynya in a north-south direction, Calvert fired a red flare as a warning to anyone on the surface to stand clear, and then surfaced in the northeast corner of the open water.

At this moment the major was racing down the west side of the lead, heading south with the motor roaring wide open. He had been very doubtful *Skate* would even find the station. He was almost beside himself, he explained later, when the boat completed the turn around the south end and he found himself staring at the submarine, lying quietly on the surface. Bilotta had neither seen the flare nor heard the submarine almost silently break water over the roar of the outboard motor.

Kelley was the only person who actually watched *Skate* surface. It had been a long working day in latitudes where they enjoyed continuous sunlight. Despite weariness everyone had decided to hang around until this thing came up. No one had any idea how it would happen. Even though there was a large area of open water, no one understood the submarine surfacing technique. So far as they knew, *Skate* might poke a hole in the ice. The crew hung around for 36 hours and finally gave up.

"We just got tired," said Dr. Untersteiner, "and sacked out. We had noticed the camp commander climb into the little outboard motorboat. He ran it up and down the polynya for hours on end. That's the last thing I saw. I faded out and turned in, and soon fell asleep."

Skate's visit was a great occasion for both her crew and the station personnel. Tours of the scientific activities were organized and social visits exchanged. With Dr. Lyon on board *Nautilus*, Dr. Eugene LaFond had joined *Skate*'s crew as senior scientist, with Rex Rowray as his assistant.

Calvert had planned a 48-hour stay. However, the temperature was just at freezing. The polynya was constantly undergoing changes.

At about 1700 a wind shift occurred from east to west accompanied by a fresher breeze. The air temperature was 34 degrees, overcast was solid, and the wind was up from 3 to 10 knots. The change in the polynya was fairly dramatic. Several floes began to drift down from the northern end of the polynya. One, estimated by senior ice forecaster Walter Wittmann (from the Hydrographic Office in Washington, D.C.) at 2500 tons, was headed slowly for *Skate*.

"At 1820," wrote Calvert in his report,

we left our mooring position and commenced recalling the crew. At this time it was apparent the entire polynya was becoming smaller.

The south end was closing in and the drifting floes were blocking the north end.

We delivered the last of the ice cream we were leaving for the island, bid our farewells, and at 2001 dropped out of our rapidly disappearing polynya. It is pertinent to note that a new one of corresponding size was opening about a half mile to the west but, at the time, this was not a matter of interest.

Major Bilotta's parting remark reflected the feelings of the 29 men left behind, "It isn't every Air Force major who has a Navy submarine in his backyard!"

The *Skate* submerged and leveled off at 265 feet, on a course of 177 degrees true, speed 16.6 knots, for a planned further exploration of the Lomonosov Ridge, far below on the Arctic Basin floor.

Calvert need not have cut his visit short. The polynya closed in places, then opened up again. His decision to make an early departure, however, had to be based on conditions of the moment. No man could predict what form the constantly shifting ice pack would take with great pressures at work. The mission had been an outstanding success.

By 2300, Sunday, 17 August, *Skate* had passed through the North Pole a second time. After making a 12-mile circle of the Pole in one hour, the submarine turned her nose toward the Atlantic. Another Navy explorer, young Lt. Richard E. Byrd, and his copilot Floyd Bennett had first circled the same spot in the Fokker trimotor *Josephine Ford* on 9 May 1926, on a flight from Kings Bay, Spitzbergen.

With nine successful surfacings through holes in the ice pack to her credit, *Skate* returned to open water in the North Atlantic 18 August. Arriving in Bergen, Norway, the boat's crew was awarded a Navy Unit Citation. Calvert sent a message to Sir Hubert Wilkins:

THE EXPERIENCE OF THIS SUMMER FOLLOWED BY CONVERSA-
TIONS WITH YOUR OLD ASSOCIATES IN BERGEN AND OSLO
HAVE LEFT US DEEPLY AWARE OF THE ACCURACY OF YOUR
INSIGHT AND VISION IN REGARD TO THE USE OF SUBMARINES
IN THE ARCTIC. THE MAJORITY OF YOUR AIMS AND PREDIC-
TIONS OF NEARLY THIRTY YEARS AGO WERE REALIZED THIS

SUMMER. THE MEN OF THE *SKATE* SEND A SINCERE SALUTE TO
A MAN WHO HAS MANY TIMES SHOWN THE WAY.

"The transit to Bergen, Norway," wrote Calvert, "was as routine as
our reception there was heartwarming. The period of 23 August to
12 September was spent in visits to Norway, The Netherlands, France,
and Belgium. An experience none of us on *Skate* shall ever forget."

En route to the United States, Calvert received Wilkins's reply:

SIR HUBERT WILKINS SINCERELY APPRECIATES THE MESSAGE
FROM THE MEN OF THE *SKATE,* AND EXTENDS TO THEM
HEARTY CONGRATULATIONS UPON THEIR SKILLFUL AND
EFFICIENT ACCOMPLISHMENT OF A MEASURE WHICH NO
DOUBT WILL LEAD TO NEW AND FAR REACHING DEVELOP-
MENTS IN SCIENCE, ECONOMICS, AND DEFENSE.

A few weeks later, his work completed, Gus Kelley departed Drift
Station Alpha by C-54. Operations on the ice floe continued without
further distraction throughout the fall and early winter. During September and October, cracking and ridging in the vicinity of the camp
went on almost continuously. Gradually it began to interfere with scientific work. By mid-October serious fracturing occurred inside the
camp area itself and on the runway.

The camp was abandoned 7 November 1958. All personnel were
evacuated to Thule Air Base, Greenland. Of the 31 scientists who
had spent varying periods of time on individual assignments, Dr.
Untersteiner had totaled the greatest number—366 days—on a drifting ice floe.

Calvert said, "The presence on board *Skate* of the Navy's senior
ice forecaster, Walter Wittmann, was a significant value to the ship.
Wittmann has a vast background of ice lore which was of continuous
interest and value throughout the cruise."

13

BURIAL AT THE NORTH POLE

During the winter of 1957–58, Lt. Col. Joe Fletcher and Comdr. Eugene Wilkinson, *Nautilus*'s first commanding officer, had shared an office at the Naval War College, Newport, Rhode Island. They spent time between studies promoting nuclear submarine efforts in the Arctic. They also took time out to visit Sir Hubert Wilkins at his home in Natick, Massachusetts. Wilkinson, promoted to captain, had taken over as commander of the first nuclear submarine division. He invited the famous explorer down for a visit to the modern submarine.

Wilkins was 70 years old. He was a veteran of 9 expeditions to the Antarctic and 24 to the Arctic when he paid his first and last visit to the *Skate* on 18 October. His enthusiasm at viewing the wonders of modern science built into the craft was evident, and he urged continued efforts to learn more of the mysteries locked in the Arctic Basin by the ice canopy.

The seasoned explorer knew the polar regions well. Winter winds in the Arctic Basin are stronger than in summer, and the ice pack is often lashed by howling blizzards. The floes present an unbroken face of white snow and jagged ridges. Polynyas disappear under a fresh layer of ice. The atmosphere grows dark and hostile. The lowest temperatures of the arctic winter occur in January, February, and March. The height of winter, March is the coldest month and when the ice is heaviest.

"Now that you have everything you need to do the job," he told Jim Calvert, "you must go in wintertime. You haven't really opened the Arctic Ocean for scientific investigation, or military or commercial use, for that matter, if you merely demonstrate what you can do in summertime."

"How much open water do you think we'd find in the winter?" Calvert asked.

"Oh, you'd probably find some, but it'd be scarce."

"Not much use of going if we can't get to the surface."

"I think you can," Wilkins said confidently. "Maybe you'll have to bore a hole, maybe blast. I don't know. But you'll find a way."

Six weeks later newspapers reported the end of a long and distinguished career:

2 December 1958: Explorer dies. Sir Hubert Wilkins died 1 December. Explorer of both the North and South Poles was found dead today in his hotel room at Framingham, Massachusetts. He was 70.

Tucked in his pocket was a letter he had written to his old friend and former aide, Raymond E. Meyers. The letter helped confirm the time of his death, and remained as a treasured memento of Meyers's brief period of dramatic exploring and years of close friendship with the famous explorer.

Wilkins had served three countries during a busy lifetime, Australia (his country of birth), England, and the United States (his adopted country).

His widow, knowing of Wilkins's lifelong ambition to reach the North Pole, asked his Navy friends if the next submarine to visit the Pole would carry his ashes there for interment.

In January 1959, the Navy Department began planning the next nuclear-powered trip under the ice. Calvert, his officers, and men, now experienced from their first encounter, were the logical choice. The *Skate* was scheduled to return to the North Pole in March to investigate the possibility of wintertime operations.

But could they really break their way through to reach the surface? If so, the sail would have to act as a battering ram as it rose vertically upward from out of the depths. The sail is filled with nearly a dozen hydraulically hoisted masts, antennas, periscopes, and ventilating pipes that could be damaged without careful ballast control. Although the sail structure had already been strengthened for the 1958 summer trip (in the event the boat might inadvertently strike ice), it was given more attention.

On the 1958 patrol, *Skate* had been equipped with the North American N6A inertial navigator, topside fathometer, and precision depth recorder. In December 1958 and February 1959, she was provided with additional equipment: the Bendix-Friez low/high-level underwater television, improved topside fathometer, improved readout facilities for the N6A auto navigator, a 160-foot floating wire antenna, and a telescoping starboard whip antenna.

Modifications were made to the port antenna to enable it to be stowed pointing downward to prevent damage when surfacing through the ice. An upward beamed light was installed in the sail.

For the special closed-circuit television system, remote controls were provided for the camera. The camera itself was enclosed in a watertight steel container to be focused through a glass window and was adjustable for aiming in various directions. Dr. Lyon had decided to ride *Skate* and was working on his own new, improved topside echo sounder.

In anticipation of future operations, scientists at the Arctic Submarine Facility at the Navy Electronics Laboratory performed beam strength tests in sea ice at their field station at Cape Prince of Wales during 1957 and 1958. The vertical rate of rise chosen was carefully made for the first deliberate ascents against the ice based on the Wales measurements.

Skate's sailing date was set for 3 March. Lt. Comdr. John Nicholson had been ordered to his own command and Bill Layman took over as the new executive officer. Some men had left for other boats, but most of the members of *Skate*'s crew from the summer trip were still on board.

Calvert, Layman, Bob McWethy, and Lieutenant Keller participated in an ice reconnaissance flight that reached the North Pole on 23 February. They searched through darkened skies for free water for a submarine to make a winter surface probe.

Eight civilians were scheduled for the operation, all experts and specialists for equipment and services. Among them were Dr. Lyon as senior scientist, senior ice forecaster Walter Wittmann from the Hydrographic Office in Washington, D.C., and Lt. Bruce Meader, Chief of Information representative.

On 3 and 4 March 1959, three submarines left New London on two separate missions. *Skate* was on her way for a winter cruise to the North Pole. On board were 88 men, the 8 civilian personnel, and 11 officers, for a total of 107. It was crowded. In Calvert's stateroom was a small bronze urn containing the ashes of Sir Hubert Wilkins.

McWethy, as division commander, was off on an operation of his own, heading north with two conventional-attack submarines—the *Harder* under Lt. Comdr. Edward Cooke and *Trout* under the command of Lt. Comdr. Carvel Blair. Their destination was Cabot Strait, which had been traversed by Jack Maurer in *Atule* in the summer of 1946.

McWethy was determined to prove a point. "This was just a sidelight of the main show," he later related. "But that March 1959 operation was designed to show there was a pack ice training area available within easy reach of home port."

While *Skate* pushed on into the North Atlantic toward the arctic approach west of Spitzbergen, *Harder* and *Trout* completed the five-day run to the closer ice field. During the next two weeks, Cooke took *Harder* under the ice up to 14 hours at a time, reaching 75 miles from the southern edge of the St. Lawrence ice pack. It was a new record for conventional undersea boats.

Cooke told newsmen later,

The pack ice seemed to average about eight feet thick. We ran out slowly under it with our periscope elevated to a maximum of 60 degrees above the horizontal. We discovered the underside was not smooth. Great care had to be exercised not to strike the bumps projecting downward. If one propeller was accidentally bent we would have been seriously handicapped. If we bent both, we would have been dead.

Looking through the scope was like watching a huge curved dome revolving overhead. You got a curious feeling that you were about to fall forward on your face. The ice appeared as a great whitish, cumulus cloud, broken by small patches of dull grey water, ribbed with ripples. When we observed a polynya of 1000 yards or so, we would surface vertically. On the surface it was an eerie feeling to look at the endless, empty field of ice. No ships, no birds. Nothing. And dead silence.

During a brief visit to Argentia, McWethy switched boats to lend his knowledge to both crews. The two boats had logged a total of 280 miles under the pack ice of Cabot Strait. McWethy was pleased and later wrote, "We gained enough confidence to carry out surfacing routines at night as well as in daylight."

One Saturday afternoon, four days before McWethy returned home, *Skate*'s radar picked up the coastal mountain range of Prins Karls Forland. A few hours later, while *Skate* cruised at a safe margin of 400 feet, the first drifting floes started passing overhead. It was one indication that the main pack was not far ahead. On the television screen the huge ice blocks drifted slowly under the arctic twilight.

By late evening *Skate* slipped silently under solid ice. Near midnight the engineering officer reported trouble in the engine room when a small seal around one of the propeller shafts started leaking. A small but steady stream of salt water began pouring in around the bottom of the shaft, where it passed through the hull. Calvert was seriously concerned, although the bilge pumps could easily keep the water pumped overboard if it did not get worse. For a moment he thought of turning back before they went any farther under the ice. Fortunately, the seal readjusted itself and the leak stopped.

Early the next morning Walt Wittmann, a veteran of *Skate*'s first cruise, reported not one bit of open water had been recorded by the ice station during the night. It was 15 March. *Skate* was now 190 miles inside the ice pack with nothing in sight but solid ice. The winter freeze had sealed the ice canopy solid.

Calvert decided to make at least one practice surfacing in open water before his boat got so far north,that they might find no opening. So far none had appeared on the television monitor, but the sounder stylus jumped suddenly and was drawing a long flat line. Was it open water? Lyon, monitoring the sonar station, couldn't be sure. Instead of the clean, sharp line that meant a patch of open water during the summer cruise, it now showed a trace of fuzziness. Was the new ice detector faulty?

Calvert circled back and brought the boat to a stop underneath. The black-and-white television screen showed nothing but murky grey. The periscope revealed only a faint aquamarine light that filtered through from the arctic dusk. From the depths it did not look like open water, but at 0900 the sun was only a few degrees above the horizon. Calvert decided to chance it, and he gave the order to surface. Using the trim pump to lighten the heavy load of sea ballast, *Skate* began to rise.

Someone snapped on the floodlights. The powerful lamps lit the underside of the rough ceiling and the Cyclops eye of the television camera was trained around to pinpoint the opening. Suddenly *Skate* started to drop away. Pumping again, the lightened boat began rising behind the narrow cone of light probing the dark waters.

On the first attempt to break ice, the ice was hit at less than five feet per minute. *Skate* rebounded lightly with no effect. Pumping again, the lightened boat hit at about 12 feet per minute. Without any evidence of sensation within the boat, the television screen was filled with a splashing water mixed with bits of shattered ice.

The sail passed through six inches of current winter's freeze with no strain. Calvert wrote,

> With the sail out, the commanding officer should expect to be able to check his general position by periscope. And possibly tell what thickness he had broken.
>
> The air temperatures encountered made the periscope useless. The water film on the objective lens froze the instant the periscope came out of the water. It took the warm-air jet at least 20 minutes to clear the lens. As a result, it was necessary to get to the bridge to see the situation. This was not desirable.

There was sufficient positive buoyancy already established to hold the boat steady and the conning tower hatch was unlatched, but it refused to open. The heavy round steel door was blocked by huge pieces of ice! With a crowbar, a small opening was gained, with just enough clearance for one man to crawl through. Bits of ice tumbled down to the conning tower deck. In minutes they were greeted by the morning sun low on the horizon.

Blowing the main ballast tanks to gain more positive buoyancy, the submarine rose clear. There was no open water visible at the edge of the hull. She was held firmly in a small opening formed by the huge cigar-shaped hull. The temperature stood at 20 degrees below zero—50 degrees colder than the summer average.

During lunch, Dr. Lyon, always eager to catch something for later study, suggested they get some pictures of *Skate* actually breaking through. Particularly he wanted to study the exact manner in which the breaking process occurred. This was a chance to get on film the process he planned later to simulate in his arctic laboratory in San Diego.

It was agreed that it might be possible. *Skate* lay in a frozen lead with plenty of clearance from the main pack on either side.

A party of four men was organized, with Lieutenant Meader in charge. Equipped with emergency rations, a Boy Scout compass, and a waterproof chart of the area in the event that *Skate* was unable to return, the men were put ashore.

With the vents opened slightly, the submarine settled back into the water. The landing party watched billows of white clouds as the relatively warm air vented into the cold atmosphere. From the control room the long cigar-shaped hole recently vacated was clearly visible. Keeping it in sight as a reference point, Calvert brought the boat back through the ice. At 1340 *Skate* was up again without incident only to find that Meader's camera had frozen and he had no pictures. "We were beginning to learn about the winter Arctic."

About 1700 *Skate* submerged and again set a course for the North Pole. Throughout the night scientists kept their eyes glued to the ice detector while others watched the television's changing scene for patches of thin ice. Prospects for surfacing directly at the North Pole did not look very encouraging.

On Monday a strange picture suddenly appeared. The cone-shaped beam of the floodlight passed a school of small fish, none more than eight inches long. Mile after mile as the boat slipped through dark waters at a keel depth of 400 feet the scene continued.

Late that afternoon the familiar fuzzy trace on the sonar screen indicated another fresh layer. Thickness could not be determined, but it looked well worth a try. Plotting smaller than the lead of the day before, it still appeared large enough to use if the sail could break it.

Maneuvered into position the bridge structure hit with a bump and broke through, and *Skate* started to settle. While the crew quickly pumped water, the boat was brought back up slowly for another try. With enough positive buoyancy *Skate* hit with a crunch, passed through, and was held firmly in position. Gently blowing the ballast tanks, the bridge rose clear of the water level.

They were now within four degrees of latitude from the North Pole—less than 250 miles. Beyond nearby pressure ridges, the ice stretched unbroken over the horizon. Inspection revealed the only major damage to the boat thus far was suffered by the radio antenna. Built to telescope within itself for protection, the internal section, being the smallest, had been bent when a piece of ice jammed into it.

This antenna was needed to send a position report. With a radioman strapped to the mast with a manila line, the antenna was raised into the freezing air. Work with gloves for protection was impossible. The radioman straightened the mast but suffered frostbitten hands.

After supper *Skate* again submerged and continued northward. Calvert had not said much to the crew about the service planned for Sir Hubert Wilkins, mainly because he had become increasingly unsure there would be any. If *Skate* was unable to surface directly at the Pole, he had planned to bring the ashes back to the States for interment. Nevertheless, a plan was formulated. When the North Pole was reached, they would start by making several passes through the area in search of thinner ice. The pack was constantly on the move. Assuming the ice traveled at an average speed of 2.5 miles per day, each 24-hour period 5,000 yards of ice would drift past a given point.

Aside from the sentimental part, surfacing precisely at the Pole would be of little military significance. Still, after *Skate*'s return in the fall, many senior officers had wanted to know what the chances would be of surfacing at a given point and time in the Arctic.

At the breakfast table conversation was, as usual, of ice. They began discussing the clumsiness of names used for these areas of thin ice which were so vital to submariners. Actually, they were newly frozen leads and polynyas but difficult to describe in brief terms. Many suggestions were offered. Dr. Lyon heard the captain describe their appearance in natural color through the periscope, although the television was, of course, in black and white. Lyon suggested, "Why don't you just call them skylights?" They were actually very similar to a huge piece of thin blue-green translucent glass commonly found in nursery greenhouses, and they broke an otherwise darker ceiling of thicker floes. These were places where the ice was thin enough for the light to pass through.

When *Skate* reached the North Pole at 1054 on 17 March Calvert started the search for an opening at slow speed. The sun disappeared at the North Pole on 24 September and did not reappear until 19 March. Two days later, every piece of equipment was brought into use. Calvert set up a crisscross search and went back and forth over the immediate Pole area, searching for a possible opening.

Hours passed without success. Finally, at 1443, after finding an indication of thin ice on the sonar operated by Dr. Lyon, they saw it. A lead, not a polynya, but just a long crack was discovered with what appeared to be thin ice.

At first it was just a faint glimmer of emerald green from light of the polar dawn seen through the periscope. It looked much too small for a submarine but was worth investigating.

The first attempt failed. With the motors stopped, *Skate* drifted out of position. Reluctantly, Calvert ordered the boat flooded down for another attempt to align his position.

On the fourth try the diving instruments indicated they were holding their position well. With the order, the diving officer blew the tanks and *Skate* moved slowly upward, breaking through until the upper hatch was far enough above ice to be opened.

Skate made its third surfacing. Calvert climbed to the bridge at 1622 and was struck by the awesome surroundings. The boat was in a small lead which had heavy blocks up to three feet frozen into a matrix of ice about one foot thick. Very high hummocks surrounded them.

It was about three-fourths dark with heavy overcast. A 25-knot wind was blowing snow, the air temperature stood at 26 degrees below zero. "This is a fiction writer's concept of the North Pole," noted Calvert in his report.

Strong freezing winds howled and swirled across the frozen terrain. Snow particles struck faces with stinging blows. The heavy overcast added to the gloomy atmosphere. But with the sail protruding from the ice, the boat was held firmly in place.

The *Skate* had arrived at her goal: the first ship to surface at the North Pole. Where she had been forced to remain submerged the previous summer at the precise 90 degrees north latitude, she had now succeeded under a greater handicap. After the North Pole surfacing, a *Skate* crew member wrote the following:

> *Whereas Peary fought polynya from above the ice in his trek to the Pole and was in continuous exposure to the perils of the frozen wastes, attainment of the North Pole by* Skate *personnel was made by sitting on the main deck on the port side of the sail and sliding down the superstructure about two feet to level ice. At the ice line large blocks laid topsy-turvy in transition line of boat to ice. Because of the thickness of ice there was virtually no open water along most of the ice line. Walking out onto the flat ice surrounding* Skate, *the view of the boat was really breathtaking. The hummocks at the edge of the polynya marked the boundary of thin ice and showed the beginning of treacherous pressure ridges. . . .* Skate *has never looked more beautiful, nor will she ever.*

After a walk on the ice, Walt Wittmann warned Commander Calvert that he did not like the looks of the surrounding ice. He recognized that there had been heavy ice movement recently. With a stiff 30-knot gale blowing there was every reason to expect more.

Immediate preparations were made for the funeral service. Since Sir Hubert had been born in Australia, had performed many of his finest deeds for the United Kingdom, and had made his final home in the United States, in recognition to the three countries he had served crewmen hoisted the flags of all three nations on masts and periscopes.

A small table, fashioned from boxes covered with a green woolen cloth, was placed on the lee side of the boat. On this they placed the bronze urn. Fifteen men formed ranks on either side. Other crewmen lined the submarine's deck, with a rifle squad standing near the bow.

Under the light of a single red flare, the commander read the service from a Navy prayer book:

> I am the resurrection and the life, saith the Lord; he that believeth in me, though he were dead, yet shall he live; and whosoever liveth and believeth in me, shall never die. I know that my redeemer liveth . . .

In a few words Calvert tried to catch the essence of the man:

> On this day we pay humble tribute to one of the great men of our century. His indomitable will, his adventurous spirit, his simplicity, and his courage have all set high marks for those of us who follow him. He spent his life in the noblest of callings, the attempt to broaden the horizons of the mind of man. Some of his personality is expressed in this prayer which he himself wrote: "Our heavenly Father, wouldst thou give us liberty without license, and the power to do good for mankind with the self-restraint to avoid using that power for self-aggrandizement."

Lieutenant Boyd then picked up the bronze urn and, followed by Calvert and the torchbearer, walked about 30 yards through the dusk. Under the glow of the flickering torch, Calvert read the final committal:

> Unto Almighty God we commend the soul of our brother Departed, and we commit his ashes to the deep; in sure and certain hope of the resurrection unto eternal life, through our Lord Jesus Christ; at whose coming in glorious majesty to judge the world; the sea shall give up her dead.

Boyd opened the urn and sprinkled the ashes to the wind. The rifles cracked three times in a last salute. Sir Hubert Wilkins had reached his final resting place with great tribute. (Appropriately, 16 years later, on 4 May 1975 in brilliant sunshine, Comdr. Frank Kelso, commanding officer of the USS *Bluefish* [SSN-675], and Dr. Lyon would commit the ashes of Lady Wilkins to the sea at the North Pole.)

Dinner that evening was a sober gathering. The ceremony had been a great tribute not only to Wilkins, but to all men who have spent their lives in conquest of the North, and all hands were deeply touched. That night the crew built a small cairn of ice blocks. A steel shaft to which an American flag was attached marked the spot. Inside, the waterproof container carried this note:

17 March 1959

Deposited on this date in a cairn at the North Geographic Pole by the United States submarine *Skate*. The *Skate* surfaced at the North Pole on 17 March 1959, and conducted memorial services for the late Sir Hubert Wilkins. The return of this container to the commanding officer of the *Skate,* along with the notation and date and location of recovery, will be a contribution to the cause of international science.

James F. Calvert
Commanding

At 2031, with all radio messages sent and receipted for, the *Skate* submerged without incident and set a course down the Lomonosov Ridge for the New Siberian Islands.

Radio silence reigned from there on.

As often happens when the news reached the Pentagon, *Skate*'s success leaked out. To dispel any speculation, a press conference was held. Commander McWethy, speaking as operations officer, Commander, Submarine Forces, Atlantic Fleet, told newsmen, "The trip was never particularly sensitive insofar as the need for secrecy was concerned. It was kept secret, however, because we did not want to advertise that we were going to do something, and then fall on our faces."

Lady Suzanne Wilkins, upon learning that the *Skate* had fulfilled her husband's last wish, was very happy. Sir Hubert's ashes had been committed to the elements. Lady Wilkins had been undecided what to do with Sir Hubert's ashes since his death. She had requests from England and Australia. Calvert and his men had, in a sense, fulfilled all requests.

On her journey to chart more waters deep in the central basin, *Skate* was brought to the surface through the ice time after time until it became an almost commonplace procedure. The seal around the starboard propeller shaft began to leak again. Behind lay more than 1200 miles to open water. Again, late one evening the leak stopped.

By the second Sunday under the ice pack, *Skate* reached a position 100 miles from the New Siberian Islands, still a considerable distance to seaward in international waters. That evening another leak developed in the engine room. This time a seal in the circulating water

Table 2.
Skate's Transit to the North Pole

New London to ice pack	4,214 miles
Under the ice pack	3,090 miles
Ice pack to New London	4,173 miles
Miles submerged	11,204 miles

pump broke suddenly, spraying water over machinery. A canvas cover was quickly rigged to avoid danger of salt water reaching the electrical switchboard.

Near the spot where the *Jeannette* was crushed and abandoned to sink in 1881, the echo sounder spotted a skylight. This time a small hole of open water about one square yard in size could be seen on the television monitor. *Skate* was brought to the surface. While the boat lay in weather 31 degrees below zero, with the roar of shifting ice sounding through the hull, the engine-room gang worked throughout the night to repair the half-ton leaking water pump.

During the next week *Skate* made four more surfacings and then returned to open water.

"Well done!" radioed Adm. Arleigh Burke.

They had successfully completed their assigned task and pioneered another historic naval achievement. During the two great voyages Commander Calvert and his crew had faced many dangers while learning more of the Arctic Ocean's secrets, and the scientists had gathered a tremendous amount of data in waters never before traversed.

The return to open passage to New London was routine except for transfer of Lieutenant Meader by helicopter south of Iceland on 30 March. The transfer was conducted in a sea state 4 with 20 knots of wind about 30 minutes after sunset. The helicopter from Keflavik did a fine job of picking Meader from the top of *Skate*'s sail.

At the instant Meader got into the yoke, the ship fell away with a large sea and the helicopter surged upward with a gust of wind. Meader shot off the sail with spectacular speed. "He apparently survived the launching," reported Calvert.

14

CONQUERING
THE WESTERN GATE

Following *Nautilus*'s historic transit and *Skate*'s successful surfacings in the summer of 1958, awareness and interest in arctic submarining became high in many commands. A very different atmosphere prevailed compared to the lack of interest of past years; after the recent successes, excitement and anticipation took over many Navy offices.

A few cooler heads pointed out that confused interest could be just as damaging as no interest. To avoid potential problems, some called for a committee to be established to guide and direct submarine and research programs from Washington. Although such a committee could serve a useful purpose for review and deliberation, it could more often prove deadly when it came to getting action to obtain equipment and accomplish field work. The original architects of plans felt it necessary to steer through the confusion and keep guidance on track for a program of all-season warfare capability. Fortunately with the support of nuclear submarine commanding officers, a few succeeded in retaining the initiative and direction within the fleet.

To prove the nuclear submarine's complete superiority over the forbidding ice canopy, it was imperative to learn not only if the submersible could operate effectively year-round but also be able to enter the basin from both the Pacific and Atlantic at will. Calvert's great job removed any doubt that the deep-water approach from the

North Atlantic could be used at any time. Getting through from the west was another matter.

From September on through the winter, pack ice gradually pushes hundreds of miles south, in some years covering more than half the distance between the Bering Strait and the Aleutian chain. Great pressures from the north squeeze the ice pack through the narrow bottleneck, creating a mass with bummocks, which often gouge the sandy bottom to create a scene resembling a huge torture chamber.

One of the most daring exploits in the history of the world on land or sea was planned for the following winter: to enter the basin at a time when the ice pack reached its greatest density and to open a new route north from the Bering Sea.

It was a tremendous challenge to a submarine commander. Looking down on the top of the world, as the astronauts did, the Chukchi Sea–Bering Strait area resembles a huge funnel with the spout lying to the south. The combination of shallow water and rafted ice makes a submarine transit there far more hazardous than in the deep Greenland Sea. Winter storms produce heavy pressure ridges in the pack ice along both the Siberian and Alaskan coastlines. Moreover, with warm summer weather and strong winds, the gigantic pieces of rafted ice break away from the coast and drift into open water to be caught up with the next freeze. Like icebergs with their deep-hanging keels, pinnacles from ice rafting had already been a menace to every submarine.

Ill-equipped for the task, *Nautilus* had been turned back on her June trip. The great boat primarily had been ordered to complete the polar transit as quickly, as neatly, and as secretly as possible to get maximum impact on the world scene. From the scientists' viewpoint the measuring of ice profiles from beneath the canopy was so important it was well worth the entire trip. Indeed, one of the greatest surprises to Dr. Lyon was *Nautilus*'s discovery of those massive ice ridges that literally blocked the strait.

In the fall of 1958 two challenging questions had been posed. Could a submarine operate in winter when no open water was available? And, second, could equipment be provided and a method found to pilot a nuclear submarine in shallow, ice-covered waters, as had been done ten years earlier with the much slower diesel-electric boats?

Commander Calvert answered the first question during *Skate's* winter cruise. Finding the answer to the second question was assigned to Calvert's former executive officer, John Nicholson. His submarine background well qualified him for the task. He had served aboard the *Nautilus* with her first skipper, Eugene Wilkinson, who was among the first to press for arctic submarining. In January 1957 he left to fill the post as executive officer of the *Skate.* That summer cruise had provided Nicholson with firsthand experience in searching for open water holes and maneuvering the boat to the surface. Previously he had been in command of the *Pickerel* for six months and had watched developments with continued interest.

Nicholson was thrilled when he was offered command of *Sargo.* His first nuclear command was not only to attempt a midwinter passage through the strait, but also to make the most extensive under-ice survey yet attempted, under the most challenging and difficult circumstances.

Sargo's cruise was to be of considerably longer duration and of greater distance than previous cruises. However, it faced the threat of cumulative damage by breaking through heavy ice.

After taking command, Nicholson briefed the crew about the cruise. He pointed out the problems in detail with no punches pulled.

Just before they were to depart, the officers tried to send some of the men to service schools in order to reduce the crowded conditions aboard due to the addition of scientists and expert technicians. However, each one of the crew requested to be allowed to make the cruise and permission was given to do so.

Preparations had begun in October 1958 when Dr. Lyon and Art Roshon visited *Skate* in New London to discuss operating sonar needs. Loaded with data, a system was produced in San Diego in time for *Sargo.*

On 18 January 1960, shortly after 0900, *Sargo* backed away from her berth at the Pearl Harbor submarine base and headed for sea. On board to support the operation was the most experienced scientist group in the United States. Headed by Dr. Waldo Lyon, the group included the sonar design engineer Art Roshon, sonar technician

Fred Parker, and ice expert Walt Wittmann. Art Molloy and experts from North American Aviation were there to keep the inertial guidance system operating in top condition.

By Saturday, 23 January, *Sargo* passed through Amchitka Pass, entered the Bering Sea, and reached the first shallow water the next day. Excitement was building as most of the crew looked forward to their first trip to the Arctic.

By Monday morning, 25 January, *Sargo* was in the vicinity of St. Matthew Island. Nicholson decided to bring the boat to the surface briefly for an accurate navigation fix before entering heavy ice.

Ice already began to appear. They were still less than halfway between the Aleutian Islands and the Bering Strait.

Nicholson went to periscope depth with the periscope lowered. Several light knocks were heard just as the sail broke the surface. The officer of the deck raised and then quickly lowered number 2 periscope and ordered, "Flood negative, there's ice ahead." *Sargo* was leveled off at 100 feet and Nicholson stationed the polynya plotting party for the initial surfacing in the ice.

Upon surfacing, they found the only ice in sight was a small chunk on the bridge deck. Visibility was poor and Nicholson continued to lie to. A chill wind whipped snow flurries across the bridge and the temperature was already down to the mid-thirties. The extreme cold-weather bill was placed in effect.

A lonely seal cavorted in open water nearby. Eighteen hundred miles of ice, mostly solid, lay between them and the North Pole.

About 31 miles northwest of St. Matthew the icebreaker *Staten Island* waited at the edge of the solid pack, prepared to provide assistance if the need should arise. This year, however, even her usefulness was limited. On board was Commodore O.C.S. Robertson of the Canadian navy, who for months had hoped that he might join *Sargo* for a short ride before the two ships parted. Now was his chance.

After a navigation fix *Sargo* submerged and headed for the ice-breaker's position.

A vertical ascent was made at 1616 in block ice and Commodore Robertson and the commanding officer of *Staten Island* came over by LCVP. Nicholson later reported,

Since it was late, and we did not have enough time to properly demonstrate *Sargo* to the commodore as requested by the Chief of Naval Operations, we suggested Robertson spend the night on board and he would effect the return transfer the next day.

Robertson eagerly accepted. He just happened to have a small suitcase with him. Captain Larson and I agreed to work our way north during the night. Larson departed and *Sargo* made a stationary dive at 1745.

During the evening while the icebreaker worked its way north, pushing through increasingly heavy ice, *Sargo* cruised beneath the pack while maintaining contact with the icebreaker by underwater telephone.

On Tuesday morning, 26 January, after seven hours of steaming north in company, Nicholson received a report at 0155 that heavy ice had slowed *Staten Island* to three knots. At 0250 Larson reported "Cannot make satisfactory progress with six engines." The icebreaker was stopped by solid pack, three feet thick, with six- to eight-foot ridges. It was snowing heavily in 40-knot gales. The heavy snow reduced visibility to almost zero.

Sargo circled *Staten Island* while waiting for daylight. It was difficult for the submarine crew to imagine the conditions on the surface as they comfortably orbited her at 120 feet.

The polynya plotting party was stationed at 1045. But a succession of pressure ridges caused *Sargo* to abandon the area. Perhaps they could surface in *Staten Island*'s wake.

Given the location of a flat piece of ice by the polynya plotting party, the diving officer brought *Sargo* up. After a short blow on the forward group, the sail punched through the ice at 1435. He blew the after-group and then all main ballast, and heaved the deck through the ice.

When *Staten Island* saw the submarine surface, Captain Larson sent two men across the ice on snowshoes to return Robertson, one of the world's authorities on the Arctic and a "wonderful shipmate." The crew presented the departing Royal Canadian naval officer with a plaque.

Nicholson said he felt sure that Robertson was hoping *Sargo* would be unable to surface so he could continue to ride the submarine on this great under-ice cruise.

Sargo continued her journey north, leaving *Staten Island* to experiment with explosions under the ice, using World War II mines. Dynamite explosions had been advocated by Wilkins, but that method proved literally impossible. The ice was blown upward and fell back in the hole, making it very difficult for a submarine to locate.

While the submarine cruised slowly northward, off-duty men lounged comfortably in the crew's mess watching the movie *Boy on a Dolphin.*

On Wednesday morning *Sargo* broke surface in a frozen polynya for one final navigation fix before entering Bering Strait. Forty-one miles southwest of St. Lawrence Island the storm had cleared, leaving the day bright and clear. In the distance, the hills of the island could easily be seen rising above the horizon. Not far away a few seals searched for food, seemingly unconcerned by this strange visitor. Although no bears were sighted, no one ventured far from the boat.

Wittmann and Molloy headed out on the ice and were soon at work obtaining ice samples. Under the pack's great weight a small geyser squirted into the air when a small core was removed. It was invigorating work as dawn finally broke at 1030. A beautiful sun rose slowly, stretching its oblique rays across the white desert.

Their position fixed, *Sargo* submerged and moved on, following a course to the west of St. Lawrence. They were nearing the most difficult area, but the new scanning sonar gave a good presentation of ice ridges, some reaching 40 feet in draft. The passage around the island went without incident, a very different feeling from that on *Nautilus* in June 1958.

On Thursday, 28 January, the plotting party found a polynya toward which they had been heading. It was just a short distance. Easing up, the bow had come through. However, the sail came through a small pressure ridge and the bridge was full of ice.

The bridge rails were twisted and bent out of shape. The main deck aft was under more than 37 inches of ice, which prevented it from coming through. It was a striking sight to see the bow fast in the ice with only the bow and sail showing. The sun had just set so they had enough light to enjoy the view.

Land was visible to the northwest. The navigator managed to get a radar fix on Cape Prince of Wales.

The boat submerged and, rounding St. Lawrence, *Sargo* pushed northeast toward Bering Strait. The water shoaled soon after midnight on Thursday. The depth stood at 126 feet as the boat eased under ridges reaching down 30 feet as it missed still deeper ridges. Evasive maneuvers enabled the boat to avoid them all, but the course became a twisting, turning, and torturous track to find a safe route.

At one point the sounder ran out of recording paper; simultaneously the stylus wore out on the depth sounder. Nicholson ordered the boat to backtrack briefly and circle while both machines were put back in working order so they could analyze the situation ahead. Was there enough clearance above and below? No one knew.

Moving with caution, they continued on toward the strait. To take advantage of a land fix, Nicholson brought his boat to the surface briefly, breaking through ice three feet thick. For 13 hours the helmsmen worked the rudder as the boat slipped through a winding course, twisting and turning. Finally just at sundown at 1700 *Sargo* again broke surface. The temperature had dropped to six degrees above zero, offset by a beautiful sunset. Ridges rose high above the ice floes and were covered with a foot of snow. Even with heavy winter clothing, it was becoming too cold for comfort and few men ventured from the boat. A comfortable 72 degrees inside was more welcome.

An inspection found no serious damage from the breakthrough, even though the ice so far had been much heavier than anything *Skate* had encountered during her 13 days under the ice on the previous year's winter cruise.

Sargo had covered only about 400 miles since entering the ice. Nearly 500 miles still lay ahead to deep water. With a radar fix on Cape Prince of Wales on Friday the crew rested on the surface for the night. Saturday morning the boat was slowly flooded down and dropped clear. Power was applied to the propellers and the diving officer attempted to gain depth control at 120 feet.

However, the bow planes would not rig out. It was suspected the holes for interlocking pins were blocked by a coating of ice since the bow had been well out of water several hours.

Without bow planes, *Sargo* was difficult to control while using the rudder at slow speed. It was a serious problem when dodging pressure ridges in shallow water and a nerve-racking situation.

Nicholson and his maneuvering watch went to work on a new technique. With a slight increase in speed the rudder would be kept within three degrees of zero, right or left. If a fast turn was required to prevent colliding with an ice pinnacle they might for short periods of time increase the rudder angle to five degrees or more. This required pumping the ballast tanks to keep the keel off the bottom, or flooding for extra weight to prevent smashing into ice above.

Once *Sargo* was well on her way, the diving control team worked the boat about carefully for half an hour before a clear corridor was found leading in the direction they wanted to go.

The water depth remained at 140 feet for the next three hours, when abruptly it began to shoal. The diving officer brought the ship up 10 feet with 15 feet under the keel. The crew braced themselves to bounce off the bottom. Overhead the ice was 3.5 feet thick with pressure ridges down to 55 feet.

Sargo rose just in time, clearing the rise by just five feet! It was a close call and it did not take long for the word to get around about the scare they had.

What lay ahead? The control room grew tense. Men on watch, more aware of what was happening, braced themselves. Now soundings showed a gradual increase in depth. Fast thinking had gotten them clear of the small sea mount.

After word of their narrow escape spread through the boat, virtually everyone came around to take a look at the iceberg detector and watch the officers and scientists conn the ship through narrow passages. The new gear Roshon and his men had designed and built was working as planned.

"It was like taking a slice of the ocean and transferring it to the screen," the engineer explained later. "As the ship moved ahead slowly the signal reached out for new subjects that moved into the top of the scope, measured by markers, and the ship could take evasive action if need be. Even corridors appeared that the ship could move through like a ghost, through the white, clean pinnacles reaching down in clear, blue water."

The instruments reassured the men as they saw how threatening ridges were first spotted and then a course plotted safely around them. As their confidence grew, the tension eased.

Now that *Sargo* was north of the Arctic Circle, a track continuing into the Chukchi Sea was laid out on the chart while popcorn and free candy bars were passed around to celebrate everyone becoming "blue noses." Fresh milk had disappeared but homemade bread was a welcome sight on the mess tables.

When they approached the Chukchi, the sea floor began to gradually drop a few feet lower. Turning northwest, *Sargo* headed for Herald Island. They would take advantage of a long, sloping sea valley running north from the island. Dr. Sverdrup had suggested this to Dr. Lyon in 1948. He had observed part of the shallow valley extending south near the island while on the *Maud* expedition in the 1920s and suspected its extent and usefulness. He had told Lyon to be sure to swing northwest into the Chukchi and look for it. *Sargo* did, and the maneuver was successful.

The water was still only 180 feet deep but a welcome change. The planesman kept working the bow planes to free them. They hoped the water might melt the ice and free the controls. In 29-degree sea water, only slightly below the freezing point of fresh water, there was little help.

By Sunday afternoon *Sargo* was near Herald Island. It was time for another navigational fix. They had safely negotiated Bering Strait and it was time for a report to Pearl Harbor. Without bow planes, frequent blowing of ballast had created a new problem. Air bubbles released through the deck vents cluttered the water, causing pulsating sound signals to scatter. When *Sargo* tried to surface in a suitable polynya, what appeared to be thin ice turned out to be thicker than the instruments indicated. *Sargo* bumped the underside of the ice. Nothing happened. The sail couldn't break through.

Dropping out of that spot, it was difficult to maneuver into a sur-facing position without bow planes. Finally, another try, and sur-prisingly, they rigged out, but not in a full functioning position.

Rising from clear water *Sargo* surfaced off Herald Island through a skylight with ice only 13 inches thick. It was cold and dark. Nicholson remained on the surface overnight to send out some radio messages while his boat was held snugly in the ice. Though the temperature had dropped to 20 degrees below zero, two of the four-man scuba diving team plunged into the freezing water to clear the garbage ejector, jammed by a flattened tin can. Despite precautions the bridge hatch became frozen open, but a Presto-lite torch melted the ice in minutes.

Monday morning found *Sargo* underway heading northwest. In the afternoon, deeper water was finally reached, first 50 fathoms at 1350, then 100 fathoms at 1645. Nicholson ordered speed increased to 16 knots. It was a shock when the iceberg detector stopped train-ing at 1830. Tests proved the training motor was grounded. Without this scanning sonar, *Sargo* had lost her shallow-water eyes. What a fortunate time for it to quit. Five hours earlier and they might have been in serious trouble. The difficult region was now behind, but that equipment would be sorely needed to get back through the strait.

Now they could stay deep enough to avoid the ice without the detector, but making repairs before commencing the return transit was a problem that still lay ahead.

Nicholson decided to surface at the first opportunity on Tuesday to undertake repairs.

On 2 February *Sargo* pushed through seven inches of ice covering a huge polynya. The white surface was clearly visible for some dis-tance even though the first light of dawn didn't start at this latitude until almost noon. The sun, lying just below the horizon, threw its rays across the sky with a brilliant glow.

The roar of grinding ice carried across the pack and could be heard the length of the still boat. The closest ridge was barely 600 feet away. Although the pack appeared solid, groans, loud cracks, and whis-tles rang through the quiet air as the ice constantly shifted under great pressure.

Immediately after surfacing, they started work on the iceberg detector motor. The problem was staggering. The training mechanism weighed 650 pounds and had been installed with the help of cranes in the shipyard. The task of cutting through beams (by two men in cramped quarters, wearing heavy winter clothing in 20 degrees below zero weather) seemed impossible, but an attempt had to be made.

Hour after hour the men struggled in the freezing cold, using torches to cut an access through heavy steel. Because of the position of the mechanism, the bridge hatch had to be left open. Soon a bucket of water sitting on the control-room deck below was frozen solid. It was impossible to work more than 30 minutes at a time. By changing shifts frequently, the work went on through the night.

While crewmen struggled with their job, scientists lost no opportunity to learn more of the mysteries of the frozen north. Although there was no visible sign of wildlife, Art Molloy went over the side with Lt. Frank Wadsworth, who had a .45 caliber pistol strapped to his waist.

It was a scene of fascinating beauty. The ice was covered with salt flowers. Molloy later explained,

> When salt water freezes in this temperature, the salt is leached out quickly and salt flowers about four inches square form on the soft and powdery surface. What looks like grease ice, or water, a short way from the boat, proved to be frozen water without any snow or frost and was quite safe, although the ice in the polynya moved continually. At the opposite side the ice was much thicker and covered with three to ten inches of snow in places. The difference was quickly apparent although there were snow-filled cracks about six inches wide underfoot and hard to see.

Pressure ridges appeared as glazed blocks of ice, lightly frozen together with crevices filled with snow. Heavy rectangular and smaller globular pieces dotted the surface. Footholds were not secure, as small pieces broke off easily, although they gave the appearance of being solid under the snow cover. Some piles of ice formed irregular shapes, more like random pieces of rock thrown together and glued with thin ice. A few snowflakes fell lazily to the deck after the evening meal, but soon the moon was out and bright green rays of the northern lights played across the sky.

Around *Sargo* the polynya changed with the passage of time, cracking and squeezing against the hull as it moved in under pressure. The roar of huge pieces grinding against one another carried through the hull as advancing fragments pushed up on the submarine's deck. "Even with the noise of this comparatively minor movement," Dr. Lyon said, "it was easy for us to visualize the terrifying experience that must have occurred on the *Jeannette* while under constant ice pressure for many weeks and months without any chance of escape."

Sargo's crew grew tense again with gnawing fear for their own boat's safety as work went on feverishly. After 40 hours of backbreaking effort the training motor was inside the boat and, with great relief, on 4 February the ballast tanks were flooded and *Sargo* dropped back into a safer environment.

At 1600 on Friday, 5 February, *Sargo* again pushed her way to the surface through heavy ice. The door to the main deck lay beneath solid pack and could not be opened. Only the sail stuck above the surface.

Once the upper hatch was opened and the ice cleared, the captain could see water four feet below. It was a safe place for the boat. The bridge was covered with 28-inch chunks of ice, which the crew broke apart and pitched overboard.

The only access down to the ice was a Jacob's ladder dropped from the bridge. The main deck was submerged five feet below the top of the ice. It was an incredible sight.

Just the sail from the bottom of "583" could be seen. No trace of the rudder showed.

Many of the crew climbed out on the ice to take pictures.

A stationary dive was started at 0028. The boat was reluctant to go down. With vents open and an extra 4,000 pounds of water in auxiliaries, the keel depth increased three feet, then held. Finally the diving officer ordered 5,000 pounds into negative. That did it. After some crunching and scraping, the sail slid through the ice. Negative was blown and *Sargo* eased down to 350 feet.

Two days later Nicholson brought his boat through the ice for an overnight stay before the final approach to the North Pole.

As the boat made the last few miles, Art Molloy's heretofore barren chart on a new region of the basin now showed numerous submerged mountain peaks and ranges for the first time. The shape of the Arctic Basin, never before known, was beginning to appear as recorders drew hundreds of miles of bottom profile.

Sargo's crisscross track found a sea mount 2,400 feet below. *Sargo* crossed *Nautilus*'s 1958 track twice and the soundings checked closely. The old hands aboard recalled that the *Sargo* put to sea for her first sea trials just as *Nautilus* was making her polar passage.

By evening Molloy was convinced they had discovered a mountain range which was either Fletcher's Rise and the Chukchi Rise or a range that runs parallel to them. Such a range would divide the Canadian basin.

At 0934 Hawaiian time, 9 February, *Sargo* passed 350 feet under the North Pole. Although some men had been there before on other boats, this time they had come the hard way, the shallow, dark, and cold route.

Now to find a place to surface. After a cloverleaf search pattern, they found the ice appeared to be two to three feet overhead. Incredibly the DRT showed *Sargo* only 25 yards from the spot the navigator had decided must be the Pole.

It was shortly after 2200 when the sail pushed through three feet of ice.

As forecaster Wittmann had predicted, the weather was perfect. It was clear, calm, and peaceful with a light breeze. A heaven full of stars and a bright half moon. It was 33 degrees below zero.

The lookout sighted the vapor trail of a high-flying aircraft at 1256. The pilot turned, either because he observed *Sargo* or because he was going to orbit the Pole. A searchlight was turned on and trained on the plane. The pilot flashed his landing lights in reply, then continued on his way. He was too high to identify and radio was unable to contact him.

Nicholson believed it was a commercial aircraft whose route leads across the Pole and whose pilot was astonished to see a light as he pointed out the North Pole to his passengers.

"We celebrated reaching the North Pole with a cake-cutting ceremony and party in the crew's mess."

Dressed as Santa Claus, the head cook ruled over his domain. He
had baked a huge cake in the shape of the hemisphere showing ice
and land limits and *Sargo*'s track laced in the frosting. It was cut and
shared by a happy crew.

The Hawaiian flag was raised alongside the submarine. The *Sargo*
post office for philatelic mail was then opened.

"We honored our home state by raising the Hawaiian state flag
right at the Pole, 25 yards to starboard," Nicholson later explained.
"Harold Meyer, IC1(SS) USN, a Honolulu-born Hawaiian volunteered
to raise the flag."

It was a rather Wagnerian scene, as Nicholson described it, with
floodlights and red flares illuminating the ceremony. The backdrop
was the sail, jutting through the ice to the hull numbers and capped
by a three-foot slab of ice and snow.

Nicholson tried to get through to Admiral Hopwood. Unable to make
the radio connection, they relayed a message through *Staten Island.*

In the evening hours, distinguished only by the clock, kingstons
and vents were opened and tons of sea water poured into the main
ballast tanks. *Sargo* refused to move! Her steel hull had frozen solid,
locked in a vice-like grip of pack ice at the North Pole. Thirty thousand pounds of sea water had to be flooded into her tanks before the
seal was finally broken and the submarine plunged downward.

Quickly the boat was trimmed to the proper weight, regaining control. After a short seven-minute cruise around the North Pole, a
course was set down the 150th meridian leading to Nansen Sound
and the Canadian archipelago.

By this time, electricians had found that the training motor was
beyond repair. Art Roshon, with the help of Parker, Chief Thomas
Walker, and leading sonarman Page, worked out a solution to the
problem, tying the iceberg detector's transmitter, which still worked,
into the receiver of one of the other sonars.

"It was a most brilliant piece of work," recalled Dr. Lyon in tribute,
"and demonstrated the engineer's skill, experience and know-how in

the sonar field. Roshon's genius of finding a solution and guiding the sonarmen on board through a long process of wiring his idea into a workable system was a clear-cut example of the payoff from the scientist-uniformed operator combination, a science-fleet team solving a problem on the scene under the ice." It was this method devised by the Arctic Submarine Facility in San Diego that had accounted for the success on the *Sennet* in 1946.

Nicholson added his own tribute: "Roshon, Parker, and leading sonarman Page had done a remarkable job of coupling two sonars together to replace the disabled iceberg detector."

They were back in shape for the shallow-water navigation with a modified, though somewhat less than ideal, iceberg detector to guide them in safe passage.

Before reaching the Beaufort Sea, *Sargo* was pushed through ice several times for star fixes. She was beginning to show signs of her battle with the ice pack. A stern room escape-hatch wheel had been broken off. The hatch cover was caved in. An eight-foot depression in the after superstructure deck showed grim evidence of surfacing under a pressure ridge shortly after leaving the North Pole.

On 11 February *Sargo* surfaced in what was described as a most interesting skylight off Nansen Sound, covered with very thin ice recently formed, probably within 12 hours. Oval in shape, the frozen polynya was walled in by heavy ridges.

With the entire boat on the surface for the first time in days, it was an ideal time for some work outside. Scuba divers slid over the side to inspect the hull and brought back samples from deep protruding ice ridges. As always, the polynya was in motion, shrinking along one place, gradually closing. The ridges were moving in, narrowing the skylight. The radio operator tried to get off a message but, because of the distance and weak signals amid heavy radio traffic at lower latitudes, he could get no one to reply.

The ice kept closing. When one ridge got too close to port and another pushed in from starboard, the operator tapped out the message blind several times in hopes it might be heard by someone. *Sargo* dropped down and went under a ridge with a draft of 105 feet.

On 14 February, St. Valentine's Day, *Sargo* broke surface in the Beaufort Sea, west of McClure Strait. For the first time in nearly two weeks the sun showed itself, rising over the horizon. "The sun never looked so good to the tired crew," recalled Nicholson. It was Sunday and Art Molloy played his guitar during Protestant services in the crew's mess.

Some of the roughest, heaviest ice of the entire trip was found along the North Canadian archipelago. Ice ridges reached more than 100 feet below the surface and were joined by frozen leads 14 feet thick. High winds sweeping across the ice made the 25 degrees below zero feel even colder.

Sargo's track from the North Pole had led to the west of the smaller islands off Prince Patrick Island, passing near Lands End. Dr. Lyon knew of a plan already being developed for the next arctic probe. *Seadragon,* being built on the East Coast, was scheduled for transfer to the Pacific Fleet. *Seadragon* would go under the ice in an effort to find a usable submarine path through the Northwest Passage from Baffin Bay to the Beaufort Sea, through McClure Strait.

Although *Northwind* had made the McClure Strait passage with ease by remaining along the shore of Banks Island, Nicholson had an ideal opportunity to sound the waters near the center in deep water. Dr. Lyon suggested to the captain that they make a short excursion into the strait for a few soundings. The area was completely uncharted and a few soundings for depth readings would certainly make the next trip easier. Nicholson readily agreed and *Sargo* made a short run to the east before turning back toward Point Barrow.

On Tuesday, 16 February, *Sargo* headed for Ice Island T-3, a massive 500-year-old glacial ice fragment four miles wide, 10 miles long, and about 200 feet thick, according to the latest estimates. It originated on the Ellesmere coastal shelf and was first sighted by the Alaskan Air Command in 1945.

On its westward drift course the ice island had become grounded early in 1960, its keel caught on the continental shelf about 88 miles northeast of Point Barrow.

Sargo reached the floating research station Wednesday morning and contacted the camp by underwater telephone. The submarine made several passes beneath and around the ice island and found it to be a maximum of 160 feet deep. More important, a series of tests was conducted to determine if the modified iceberg detector worked satisfactorily. It seemed to check out all right.

On 18 February one month out of Pearl Harbor, *Sargo* reached the edge of the deep Arctic Basin when the bottom sounder registered just 300 feet. "We were in the most difficult part of the Chukchi Sea," Dr. Lyon later recalled. "We were northwest of Point Barrow then, and the next day were in 155 feet of water where heavy ridges were often present."

Shortly before noon Nicholson ordered the boat to the surface for another fix and a radio report to Pearl Harbor. The conning tower lifted through the ice in a refrozen polynya dotted with small spaces of open water. Scattered bear tracks were seen in the fresh snow but the ice had shifted since the bear had gone by.

In the evening *Sargo* dived with some difficulty to break free and still not take on too much ballast. The water was shallow. Ahead lay heavy going with the makeshift arrangement of iceberg projector and receiving array. Just before 2000 Nicholson spotted two deep ridges ahead, one to port and one to starboard. He ordered a slight change of course to starboard for greater clearance.

At 2003, the sail struck ice. Nicholson later recalled,

Wham! We hit! The boat heeled to port as it was shoved down 25 feet with a steep six-degree bubble, and we slowed drastically. The officer on the conn rang up "all stop" and sounded the collision alarm. In a matter of seconds I had taken the conn myself and rang for "back two-thirds" to kill our way, then stopped. Our depth gauge read 148 feet, almost on the bottom. I ordered ballast tanks blown out with vents open and we came right up. Quickly I rang for "ahead two-thirds" on one shaft and we regained depth control. *Sargo* was clear of the ridge and all compartments reported no damage.

More than a half dozen 60-foot ridges were passed overhead by midnight.

Tight maneuvering continued until Sunday afternoon when open water appeared for the first time since *Sargo* entered the pack.

At 2000, 20 February, *Sargo* was suddenly faced with a solid wall of ice, appearing on the iceberg detector at a range of 800 feet. There was no opening. Nicholson changed course, ran parallel to the ridge, and finally skirted around its end and resumed base course.

Sargo surfaced in a clear polynya off the coast of Alaska where, for the first time in two days, the crew was able to reach the deck to assess the latest damage. From their collision the day before it was extensive. The hand rail on the sail was gone. Heavy plating on the starboard side, which had received the full force of impact, was caved in, bending the forward bridge superstructure to port. One periscope was locked in place.

Sargo remained on the surface for several hours. In the evening she submerged and headed for the Bering Strait.

On February 25, *Sargo* was clear of the ice pack after cruising 6,003 miles during more than 31 days under the ice. She had surfaced 29 times, breaking through ice 20 times. The boat was badly battered, but with great skill her crew had opened the western passage to the Arctic Ocean the year around.

Sargo returned to Pearl Harbor on 3 March 1960.

The *Sargo*'s patrol virtually closed the exploratory period that began with *Boarfish*'s first venture under ice in 1947. Specifications for the sonar and inertial navigator, the two keys to safe navigation under the arctic ice pack, were known. Their technical performance was now confirmed.

15

THROUGH THE NORTHWEST PASSAGE

"Now I would like to see them do it the other way around!" The *Nautilus* had just completed her 1958 historic transit from west to east and enthusiastic President Eisenhower described to Peter Aurand, his naval aide, what he felt should be the next goal: the potential of a short polar route between the Atlantic and Pacific Oceans.

Aurand recalled,

> The president emphasized to me the great advantage of a sea route through the old Northwest Passage for commercial purposes. When you look at a map of the Arctic, commercial nuclear submarines come into the picture to great advantage by cutting the distance between Tokyo and London by thousands of miles. Moreover, if they bring in large oil reserves in the Point Barrow region, in case of war, this route would be the closest supply to Europe by far. These were the thoughts that President Eisenhower had at that time; military benefits as well as the peaceful exploration.

Thoughts of a similar nature brought serious discussion in New London a few months later. Within 10 days after *Skate*'s return to port from her own winter cruise early in 1959, Calvert and his officers were looking forward to a third cruise north. The Northwest Passage was the subject of a new plan: depart in early November, work up Davis Strait and Baffin Bay while trying out the new iceberg detector on deep draft ice, then head west through the passage and

McClure Strait. After spending some time in the Beaufort Sea, conducting sound tests with T-3 and Alpha 2, *Skate* would then move north around the top of the Canadian archipelago and return through Robeson Channel, arriving home around the middle of December.

Quite naturally, Dr. Lyon was in favor of the idea and proposed that Commodore Robertson go along as observer and consultant, both to satisfy Canada's national interest and for his personal knowledge of the area. Lyon and Robertson had been together on the surveys by icebreakers during the 1953–54 era and now the scientist was in possession of original sounding books, field notes, and track charts, plus data the Canadians had worked over.

Military planners felt the next goal should be further charting of the main Arctic Basin itself and perfecting operations under the ice pack in deep water. With the *Sargo* operation, the plan was not considered until the following year when a routine fleet reassignment provided justification for the next move.

"*Seadragon* was scheduled for transfer to the Pacific Fleet at an opportune moment," said her skipper, Comdr. George P. Steele II, "and so it was decided to fit her with ice equipment and send her to Pearl Harbor by way of a northwest passage, if one could be found."

On 28 March 1960, Commander Steele, with his executive officer and navigator, attended a closed conference in the office of the Chief of Naval Operations. This operation was identified SUBICEX 3-60. The plan was discussed and the conferees, interested parties from bureaus and commands, departed to carry it out.

The proposed route from Lancaster Sound into the Beaufort Sea leading through the McClure Strait had been made by icebreakers *Labrador* and *Northwind,* and a part of the way had been covered by earlier ships. However, a usable track for nuclear submarines traveling under the ice in deep water remained to be found. But were there any deep passages that a submarine could get through? There were not enough soundings to show this.

Those earlier surface ships venturing in the Northwest Passage had followed a course near the shore, avoiding heavy ice. Most of *Seadragon*'s proposed track had never before been traveled by any ship. It was assumed in advance that the Parry Channel was at least

100 fathoms deep. Barrow Strait with its sparse soundings was the question mark.

Lancaster Sound and Barrow Strait appeared well charted as far west as Griffith Island. Though little data, except for *Sargo's* brief excursion, were available on McClure Strait, the icebreaker's two north-south soundings across the western part of Melville Sound were helpful and it was believed to be deep enough for submarine passage. The chart between Griffith Island and Parker Island showed few soundings.

Even before reaching that point, a submarine cruising submerged must first traverse hundreds of miles cluttered by icebergs. The *Atule* had gathered some data on bergy bits. Ill-equipped with the depth limitations, Commander Maurer had not attempted to go deep enough to measure the exact distance an iceberg might reach below the surface. Much had been learned about the ice monsters over the years.

The Southern Hemisphere bergs produced from shelf ice of Antarctica extend seaward from the ice cap that projects on the continental shelf of the Antarctic continent. These icebergs are tabular, in contrast to the usually rugged shapes of glacier bergs that calve from the tongues of western Greenland. Antarctic bergs are also less contaminated with material than the north and only about three-quarters are submerged, compared to eight- or nine-tenths of northern bergs.

The submarine's environment under the sea creates problems not always important to the few ships that entered the waters *Seadragon* was to follow.

On 7 July, while the crew made final repairs and necessary installation of last-minute equipment, the captain and his navigator flew to Thule, Greenland, and beyond for a look at the ice they would face.

By Friday, 29 July, *Seadragon* was judged mechanically sound, loaded, stowed, and ready to proceed. By Monday the last of the special riders were embarked. The voyage was ready to begin.

Seadragon got under way from Portsmouth, New Hampshire, for the Pacific Ocean and Pearl Harbor, Hawaii, at 1430, 1 August, amid far happier family farewells than usual. Like any routine transfer from one home port to another, wives and children would join their men at the new home port.

What they did not know was that the boat was bound on a great, pioneering voyage, following a previously untraveled route. *Seadragon*'s schedule included an arctic cruise but the exact route she was to follow was not released.

On board was a familiar team of polar veterans: Dr. Lyon, Art Molloy, Art Roshon, and Walt Wittmann. Unseen by most of those left behind on the dock was Commodore Robertson, then a member of the Canadian Joint Staff in Washington and the Canadian naval attaché. He had eagerly accepted the U.S. Navy's invitation to take passage on board as an observer and expert advisor on the Canadian archipelago.

On 9 August, *Seadragon* entered Baffin Bay, traveling deep at a speed of 14 knots, 200 miles off the Labrador coast, with Greenland some 150 miles to the east. When they approached an area where several bergs had been reported, Steele ordered slower speed. Early in the morning of the tenth, just south of the Arctic Circle, the first ice appeared. More appeared on the iceberg detector. Steele ordered the boat to the surface for a closer look.

Seadragon was on the edge of a large area cluttered with loose ice stretching as far as the eye could see. This was what remained of the solid pack covering Baffin Bay the previous winter.

The operation order directed Steele to learn more about icebergs. The operation planners thought this would be a valuable experiment. If Wittmann could measure the size and shape of the berg's underbody, the International Ice Patrol would have a better understanding of their drift rate and could forecast positions for shipping more accurately.

This would also provide an opportunity to evaluate the equipment. It had been given the name "iceberg detector," and this was the first chance to actually use it for such a purpose. Twelve miles inside the loose ice, Steele headed in the direction of a full-size berg. Slowly he made the approach. The above-water portion measured 74 feet high with a 313-foot waterline. *Seadragon* slowly circled the monster. It appeared blocky on one side, while the reverse was hollowed out. It was clearly weathered, with many visible water lines.

The iceberg detector traced out a huge underwater body. The berg was between 100 and 200 feet in draft. There was no way to check the instrument's accuracy other than to pass under and measure it precisely.

Steele selected his depth to clear by more than 200 feet. The crew was anxious to be the first submarine to do this. They had brought their boat 2,500 miles to find this one. A few runs were made to check results from every angle. The long-awaited trip seemed anti-climactic. The ink trace dipped down and down, to a draft of 108 feet before it began to rise again. Six runs were made in different directions. The maximum length under water proved to be 822 feet, compared to 313 feet above water.

During the week, 12 more bergs were selected and measured. It became routine with speeds up to 20 knots. Icebergs became more numerous. In an area south of Kap York, Greenland, they became so dense that 45 filled the radar screen at the same time.

Entering the Baffin Bay pack at 300 feet, the sonar team watched for an opening. The instruments spotted a great hole, measuring 800 yards long. After crisscrossing the polynya for a good plot, Steele ordered the boat to the surface. The stern rose under a large floe that bounced off the side and slid into the water with a splash.

The engine room had been plagued with hydraulic leaks since leaving port. On board was a reserve supply of oil, but this loss would seriously reduce the supply and three weeks under the ice were still ahead. Plastic bags were tied over valves to try to locate the source of leaks but without success. A close watch on the bilges helped to keep track of the amount of oil lost. The engine-room crew searched without success. Adding to the problem, while diving from the ice lake, a hydraulic pressure fitting had cracked, spewing more oil over the maneuvering room.

On Thursday, 11 August, after running several miles, the iceberg detector picked up another ice-locked berg. It measured 65 feet in width and covered 50 feet draft. A short time later, another one was picked up. The detector showed they must go deeper to clear this one. *Seadragon* moved in slowly to within 1000 yards of the huge berg. It was locked in the ice without a sign of a polynya. Wittmann took his place behind engineer Jonathan Schere, who would operate the upward beamed instrument. The great revolving television camera lens of the underwater Cyclops mounted on the forward deck brought a visual picture to the monitor.

Seadragon moved in, approaching the jagged ice at seven knots. This one appeared far bigger than the first one measured outside the pack.

In 30 seconds the trace began to dip, showing an almost vertical precipice of the berg's keel. The trace passed the mark predicted and it kept going down. *Seadragon* was going to hit! For a brief moment Steele thought of sounding the collision alarm, but in a flash the danger passed. Tensions eased as the trace leveled off and slowly began to rise. The sail had cleared the iceberg's keel that measured nearly 900 feet along *Seadragon*'s track.

Seadragon circled back for more measurements. The berg's overall length was nearly 1,500 feet and Walt Wittmann calculated its size at 3 million tons. It was a great achievement for both crew and scientists.

The crew named the iceberg "*Seadragon*'s Fair Maiden." "Her bottom looked fine," wrote Steele. "Wish we could see her face."

Still in Baffin Bay, *Seadragon* resumed her course to the northwest, dived under the pack, and dodged numerous captive bergs. In central Baffin Bay, they reached open water and surfaced in dense fog, lying five miles offshore. By evening the low sun cast its rays behind a huge glacier, calving more icebergs into the bay.

During the night of 12 August the conning officer dodged icebergs five times. In the morning the ship passed into clear water where *Seadragon* was surfaced and laid to in order to repair the clutch hydraulic line.

Her first task completed, *Seadragon* left the area south of Kap York and on Sunday night was on the way to Devon Island with plans to surface for a position check. In approximately the same position, early explorers had reached this body of water called Lancaster Sound. The exit to the west was a strait that proved to be the Northwest Passage sought by many early explorers. In the winter this channel is completely covered by ice. In the summer the eastern end, Lancaster Sound, is usually ice-free. But the west end as far as McClure Strait usually remains covered by rugged pack ice which, as Robertson found during *Labrador*'s passage, is relentlessly forced from the

Arctic Ocean under pressure generated by the usual currents and circulating arctic winds.

Ships that had traversed sections of the channel stayed inshore in relatively shallow waters where the winds and presence of land frequently left channels through the ice.

Many soundings along the coast clearly revealed that a submerged submarine could not get through. The half dozen or more soundings, sparsely spread along the center of the Barrow Strait narrows, indicated the depth here was shallow as compared to the end of the Parry Channel.

Five islands existed in the narrows, while another island and several shoals were marked as "extremely doubtful" or "position doubtful."

The best passage between the islands (if a passage even existed) was by no means clear from the charts *Seadragon* carried. It was uncertain if the passage could be deep enough for a submerged submarine to pass under the heavily ridged ice that normally was there.

Comdr. George Steele and his *Seadragon* crew were ready to find the answer. During the past two days they had clearly demonstrated the ability of a nuclear submarine to enter an area of high iceberg concentration with safety.

On Monday afternoon, *Seadragon* submerged and entered Lancaster Sound, the entrance to the Northwest Passage. The next day, 16 August, 16 days after leaving port and *Seadragon*'s second birthday, Steele brought his ship to the surface for a position check and a talk with Resolute Bay.

A birthday party was held with a fine cake, special meals, and presentation of awards to the crew. It was a fitting place to celebrate.

At 1240 *Seadragon* submerged until 1801 when she surfaced off the harbor and was buzzed by three helicopters. "We lie off," said Steele, "maneuvering to avoid ice. It will be a minor miracle if ham radio doesn't pick up our presence and let the secret out. Four ships are in the harbor on the annual resupply mission."

Steele wrote in his log,

Squad. Ldr. S. E. Millikan and Flt. Lt. W. Owstan of the RCAF station Resolute, and Mr. Paul Adams, executive officer of the United States

Weather Station, Resolute, came aboard for dinner and presented the ship with a walrus tusk carving of Seadragon. The ship gave the Royal Canadian Air Force station a plaque and sent the Eskimo carver a ship's cigarette lighter.

Personal mail, to be held for a week, and public information is sent ashore. And we depart.

One hundred twenty-five degrees west longitude is a line passing just east of Prince Patrick Island, the northwestern island of the Parry Channel. *Seadragon*'s operation order directed Steele to send a message from this vicinity reporting for duty with Commander, Submarine Forces, Pacific Fleet.

It was planned to make the trip public upon receipt of the report at Pearl Harbor, which indicated they had successfully negotiated the Parry Channel. Then, for the first time, the men's families would learn they had taken a shortcut to the new duty station.

On 17 August, *Seadragon* submerged at the western end of Lancaster Sound and headed into the rapidly shoaling waters of Barrow Strait at slow speed. The strait is about 50 miles wide at its narrow eastern entrance where Cornwallis Island is to the north and Somerset Island is to the south. During the next three days Steele kept his boat never far from the bottom or the surface. Shoals appeared on the sonar trace without warning. Islands were found out of their charted position.

Although there was some ice, fortunately wind conditions had cleared most from the strait. *Seadragon* surfaced six times for navigation fixes and to correct charts. Some of the islands had been charted as much as five miles out of position.

At 1712, Friday, 19 August, the task was complete. From there the charted position of the North Magnetic Pole was abeam at 25 miles. Since that Pole wandered in an elliptical path encompassing *Seadragon*'s position, the submarine added a first: the first submarine to the North Magnetic Pole. In 1831, when first located by James Clark Ross, that Pole was 300 miles to the south.

From *Seadragon*'s three-day survey, there was a charted channel deep enough for any future nuclear submarine to follow, winter or summer, favorable ice or not. Also the survey proved that the equipment on *Seadragon* was capable of leading her through unrestricted channels between land masses.

Seadragon entered the eastern side of Viscount Melville Sound, where some sparse soundings were available, and took a lazy, long zigzag course to collect bathymetric data. The depth increased to 100 fathoms and greater. *Seadragon* went down to 300 feet and increased speed to 16 knots on a straight course west into the deep sector of the sound.

On Saturday, 20 August, *Seadragon* continued west at 16 knots and 300 feet across the deep open water, passing longitude 110 degrees west and through the region which Parry on *Hecla* and *Griper* had found impassable in summers of 1819 and 1820. *Seadragon* quickly entered McClure Strait, passing under the expected eastern edge of the ice pack. In a few hours, *Seadragon* reached the track sounded and charted by John Nicholson on *Sargo* and then sailed out of the strait into the Beaufort Sea.

For the first time a ship had completely and accurately charted a Northwest Passage route available for any future commercial nuclear submarine's use. Setting a course for the North Pole, Steele started looking for a place to surface and radio his message reporting for duty in the Pacific. He had entered the region of responsibility to Commander, Submarine Forces, Pacific Fleet.

Very early Sunday morning *Seadragon* surfaced through thin ice in a long lead. Bringing the boat up with just the sail awash so they could raise the radio antenna clear of the water, Chief Radioman John Evans tapped out the message:

SEADRAGON REPORTING FOR DUTY.

It was a single message, not much different from thousands sent between ships and their commanders each year around the world, but its special significance made headline news. It was yet another great achievement by Navy submarines.

Even in the early hour, the sun was just over the horizon and beginning to warm the air with the temperature in the low 30s. A pleasant breeze came across the ice pack. A lone seal stuck his head up nearby to stare at this intruder into his private domain.

In the mess hall that afternoon, off-duty crewmen watched the movie *The Vikings*. They could easily relate to the movie characters for they were surely modern Vikings.

Most of the Arctic was now open to navigation by any nation having nuclear-powered submarines. It was a great step in future commercial use of the Northwest Passage by submarines as envisioned by President Eisenhower and many others and had been successfully accomplished.

After five hours on the surface gathering scientific data and replenishing the boat with fresh air, *Seadragon* unlocked the hydraulic manifold and opened the vents, and the boat slipped almost silently beneath the surface.

While *Seadragon* headed north, cruising at 300 feet, Sunday Protestant and Catholic services provided an opportunity for the crew to give thanks to Almighty God for a job well done.

Nicholson had discovered in this same area the worst ice conditions of his entire circle of the Arctic Basin. The television showed a good view of pressure ridges that reached 100 feet or more below the surface. Steele ordered the diving officer to take the boat down to 400 feet for a greater margin of safety.

According to the operation order, *Seadragon* was ahead of schedule and had ample time to zigzag on a course for more exploration of the sea floor. At 1200 on Monday Prince Patrick Island lay far to the southwest. Ice suddenly disappeared as they reached a point 600 miles from the Pole. In a few minutes the boat surfaced in a large polynya nearly two miles across. Through a low haze, the sun cast its oblique rays across the desolate but magnificent scene. A light breeze was chilly. But weather and ice conditions certainly were not characteristic of the Arctic in summer so far. The usual northwest wind was coming from the wrong direction and larger openings had not been expected.

Five hundred miles from the north Canadian coast, Steele ordered preparations for tying up to the ice. A rubber raft was inflated and a mooring team carried six-foot steel spikes to the nearest pack. *Seadragon* was soon tied up to her arctic pier.

While members of the crew off watch explored, others made necessary repairs to the boat and removed plankton from sampler nets. Wittmann and Lyon cut a hole in the ice for samples while scuba divers explored the surrounding cold waters.

In the afternoon a special antenna was hoisted. A Washington telephone number was hooked to the single sideband radio providing for official communications, and a few men were given the thrill of talking with families through connections made by Pentagon switchboard operators.

After seven hours the mooring lines were pulled in and, following a circle partly around the huge lake, the boat made its first normal quick dive since entering Baffin Bay.

Sharp edges of open cracks in the ice overhead were clear in detail on the television monitor. Each of the 102 men on board was given a look through the periscope to view the underside of the ice in full color.

"Haven't you ever seen that sort of thing before?" Steele asked Dr. Lyon, veteran of many trips.

"We had no iceberg detector on *Nautilus* or *Skate*," replied the scientist, "and the *Sargo* trip was made in dark winter."

On Wednesday, 25 August, *Seadragon* became the fourth submarine to reach the North Pole. A sounding was 2,270 fathoms with the ice thickness measuring 11 feet.

Immediately the search for a suitable polynya began. Commander Steele described his efforts to surface at the North Pole:

It does not look favorable. During the last eight hours only one opportunity to surface has been seen. An expanding search is begun on a 100 yard execute.

At 1120 on Thursday, a 300-yard opening is seen and we try to cross it again with our Williamson turn and polynya plotting party. Six times the ship crosses the same spot but only much smaller openings are seen—50 yards or less.

The hole must have been very narrow. With periscope up, I slowly pick my way across the area at 150 feet, occasionally recoiling as a deep ridge seems about to hit us. We are all anxious to surface at the Pole.

Finally, Seadragon *is positioned with great difficulty under a narrow opening, with three feet of ice indicated. The exasperating drift of the ice, or the ship, and the difficulty of getting the ship moving, then stopping absolutely still, then turning, then stopping again, only to drift more, wears the conning tower team down.*

As we start up at last, the stylus fails on the topside fathometer. Before it can be replaced, the ship drifts out of the hole above despite all my efforts with periscope and engines. The attempt to find it again fails. The water here, past the Lomonosov Ridge, is from the Atlantic. It is pale green and murky. I cannot see. The TV is almost useless. Seeing is, after all, a prop for novices like us.

Disgusted and hungry, we secure for a quick late lunch while criss-crossing the area some more.

After three hours of frustrating investigation at periscope depth—150 feet—of small openings trying to find our hole again, I secure the polynya plotting party with instructions to the watch to resume the search plan.

At 1552, the party again takes station. I had decided weeks ago not to break ice this thick in order to avoid damage. But my initiation over the so far losing battle, and the single opening in the last eight hours before reaching the Pole, made me change my mind.

Our position report time limit was about up, and I worried about word we were overdue being leaked to our dependents. A flat surface is indicated on all sonars, fathometer, and periscope. The ice proved to be 11 feet thick.

Look some more. Soon a similar but more likely looking spot, perhaps two to three feet at 2220. A welcome opening 225 yards long with very thin ice is discovered.

At 40 feet from the edge of heavy ice, the ship has opened a lead big enough for a life raft. Robinson takes the life raft and proceeds to the ice to find and lay out a softball diamond.

Meanwhile radio has been pleading with me to come below to speak to Admiral Gable. Upon arrival to radio I find it is Admiral Hopwood, my fleet commander-in-chief, that I have kept waiting. We have been talking to McMurdo, Antarctica, Washington, and Honolulu. Admiral Hopwood has been talking to the navigator and I take over with embarrassment.

The encouraging words of Admiral Hopwood and more relayed from Admiral Burke make us all grin with pleasure.

Checking their position with the sun, navigator Al Burkhalter found the *Seadragon*'s inertial navigator amazingly accurate. It had led them unerringly to the top of the world.

The ice was constantly moving, with pressure ridges grinding and cracking close to the boat. At 0100 the sun was obscured by clouds. Plans were made for a softball game. A cold wind blew at freezing temperature across the white landscape, but it did not dim their enthusiasm.

The softball game, with officers and chief petty officers challenging the enlisted men, was a happy occasion, with men struggling for a foothold on a white arctic ball diamond laid out on a nearby floe.

The two-star flag of Rear Adm. Roy Benson, Commander, Submarines Pacific and *Seadragon*'s new boss, joined the Stars and Stripes at the periscope mast.

Dr. Lyon felt it would be important for research purposes to have photographs of a submarine submerging and surfacing through the ice. Three men set up their cameras on the ice while Steele took *Seadragon* down.

Swinging around dark, ragged walls bordering the polynya while preparing to surface, the submarine drifted with the current. Frantically, it was maneuvered about while the men on the ice above waited. They could hear the sound of the sonars pinging against the ice beneath them.

Suddenly the sound grew weaker and there was nothing but silence. They knew the captain would bring *Seadragon* back, but how soon? It was getting cold!

Everyone on board *Seadragon* maneuvering a half mile away watched instruments as never before. Soon the periscope began to show light ahead and Steele ordered the speed increase faster than usual. The polynya plotting party barely had time to plot the edge of the ice. As soon as it showed clear of the stern, Steele gave the order to surface. The sail rose, penetrating slowly through slush. In moments three well-chilled photographers were picked up and *Seadragon* submerged.

During the next five days *Seadragon* cruised south—the only direction possible from the North Pole—over virgin territory. Saturday night around midnight, the depth recorder's extra-sensitive paper had a burned trace that showed a small canyon and a seamount rising 4,000 feet above the ocean floor.

The next phase of the operation was a rendezvous with Ice Island T-3.

"T-3 at this time was aground," said Steele, "and we couldn't get too close." The ice island lay north of Alaska and had broken into six fragments since men first landed in 1952. At 1200, 2 September, *Seadragon* passed under the first fragment which reached 160 feet below the surface. The water grew shallow and the submarine was soon forced to turn around ridges with her keel just 30 feet from the bottom.

By early afternoon Steele had talked with T-3 by radio and commenced his final approach. With the sail awash in open water under bright sunshine, the radar located the main camp five miles away. But Steele couldn't get any closer.

Following a huge, circular course around the ice island, *Seadragon* headed for the Bering Strait, when suddenly the iceberg detector began showing an unusual scope display. Temperature layers of the water were bending sound beams in such a way that ice keels were difficult to detect and targets on the iceberg detector were fading. "It was," Steele recalled vividly, "probably the most frightening moment of the trip."

Ahead lay certain danger. They could not surface since no polynya was known to be close. They could stop and rest the boat on the shallow bottom until the cause for the sonar's strange action was learned, or rise and rest against the ice. To continue through the narrow clearance of the Chukchi Sea, where deep pressure ridges had blocked *Nautilus* and given *Sargo* a lot of trouble, would be impossible.

It turned out there was nothing wrong with the set. The sonar beams were being deflected by thermal layers. Similar bending had occurred in Baffin Bay in the vicinity of icebergs. But it had caused a few tense moments.

By 2100 on 3 September *Seadragon* was out of the Barrow Sea Valley and cleared the ice pack on schedule, entering the fringes north of Bering Strait. The ice posed little danger. By 2230 they knew they were in the clear. *Seadragon* surfaced and while en route to Nome received their first message of welcome.

FROM: GOV. WILLIAM A. EGAN

ACTION: COMMANDER GEORGE P. STEELE USS *SEADRAGON*
CARE STEFFEN ANDERSON MAYOR NOME

THE PEOPLE OF ALASKA CONGRATULATE AND EXTEND ALL
GOOD WISHES TO THE OFFICERS AND MEN OF THE *SEA-
DRAGON.* YOUR EPOCH MAKING JOURNEY THROUGH THE
NORTHWEST PASSAGE AND OVER THE NORTH POLE SIGNIFIES
ANOTHER GREAT ACCOMPLISHMENT OF THE UNITED STATES
NAVY. IT IS FITTING THAT THE NORTHERN FRONTIER PORT OF
NOME ALASKA HAS BEEN CHOSEN AS YOUR PORT OF CALL
AND I KNOW THE CITIZENS OF THAT CITY WILL EXTEND THEIR
PERSONAL HEARTY "WELL DONE" TO ALL ABOARD THE
SEADRAGON. KINDEST REGARDS. WILLIAM A. EGAN,
GOVERNOR OF ALASKA.

On Monday at 1400, *Seadragon* lay to off Nome. The ship sailed
in and moored alongside the icebreaker *Northwind.* All hands had
an opportunity to spend at least seven hours ashore. Hospitality to
everyone was shown by the people of Nome.

"We are treated like royalty," read the ship's log.

At Nome the civilian observers left the boat and *Seadragon* set a
course for the Hawaiian Islands. At 1000 on 14 September the boat
and her crew were welcomed by Adm. John H. Sides, commander-
in-chief, Pacific Fleet.

"The progress of *Seadragon,*" said the admiral, "is in keeping with
the lofty traditions of perseverance and initiative established by
Amundsen's *Gjoa* and the intrepid Canadian ships *St. Roch* and
Labrador in their successful quests of the Northwest Passage. I am
proud to have you with us."

At 1600, 14 September, 1000 local time, *Seadragon* was moored at
the submarine base, Pearl Harbor. Behind lay 11,231 miles from Portsmouth, New Hampshire. 10,415 of those miles were spent submerged.

"We have come UNDER THE ICE TO PARADISE," wrote Steele.

Dr. Lyon's conclusion:

In 1946, the *Atule* penetrated 1000 yards under the ice in Kane Basin.
In 1947 *Boarfish* made a dive of about 30 miles beneath the ice of the

THROUGH THE NORTHWEST PASSAGE

Chukchi Sea. In 1948, *Carp* experimented with diving and surfacing in the ice for nine hours.

The *Seadragon* patrol closed the circle of exploratory arctic cruises by nuclear submarines: a circle of various, typical ice canopies, namely in shallow water, deep water, winter, summer, complete darkness, icebergs, and island channels. The experimental model of the "ice suit" was proven. Sonar has proven capable of handling all types of ice canopy.

16

RENDEZVOUS AT THE NORTH POLE

The last unexplored corner of the world ocean was no longer a great mystery. Much was still to be learned, but nuclear power, coupled with a great deal of human energy and personal ingenuity, now provided the United States with a working knowledge of the sea. New charts showed 26 great ridges, valleys, plateaus, and plains lacing the bottom in a strange design. Most carried new names: Alpha, Cordillera, Fletcher, Plain Arless, Gap, and many others that were unknown until submarines found them. The U.S. submarine force had good reason to be proud of its accomplishments.

However, a single submarine operating alone in the huge basin would be of limited military value. To use the north polar sea effectively in defense of the United States might demand a fleet of boats, often traveling in company without benefit of radar, periscope, or radio, the conventional way to operate in open-sea warfare.

Could submarines rely entirely on sonar not only to navigate, but also to seek one another out under the ice? It certainly would require a high degree of navigational skill.

The next operation was planned for the summer of 1962, specifically to learn if it could be done. Two submarines would be sent under the pack, each to start from opposite sides of the basin. After covering hundreds of miles, with much of the route passing over still-new waters, the two submarine commanders would attempt a rendezvous at a predetermined point and time.

Two polar submarine veterans were selected: *Skate,* now under the command of Comdr. Joseph L. Skoog Jr., and *Seadragon,* by Comdr. Daniel Summit. Both boats were already equipped with many modern tools but, because of the Navy's normal rotational practice, most of the crew now consisted of men inexperienced in under-ice cruising. The old-timers had gone to fill billets on the growing number of nuclear boats joining the fleet.

Three gates to the Arctic Ocean had been swung open: from the north Atlantic, the Bering Strait, and the Northwest Passage. A fourth passage still remained unconquered. Nares Strait was even more formidable than McClure. In recent years, icebreakers had made the passage by hugging the rocky coast with no attempt to sound the bottom in midstream. This became *Skate's* assignment. If she could safely make the transit from Baffin Bay into the Lincoln Sea, still another submarine milestone would be accomplished.

As had been done before, extensive preparations began several months before the two boats went into action.

A Washington, D.C., conference on 5 December 1961 was attended by representatives of interested activities, at which time various tasks, equipments, and responsibilities were identified and assigned.

SUBICEX 1-62 in March 1962, in which *Skate* operated with *Entemedor* and *Tush* in the Gulf of St. Lawrence, was by far the most significant part of this program. Tactical use of the most up-to-date sonar was thoroughly tested.

Commander Skoog, being the senior in service, was assigned the additional responsibility as task unit commander. The task unit included one icebreaker. *Burton Island* was scheduled to join the two submarines for a few days of special operations in the Beaufort Sea.

Wearing two hats as unit commander and commanding officer, Joe Skoog had a great many details to work out. The operation involved tight scheduling with the submarines to start several thousand miles apart. In San Francisco, Skoog met with Summit's division commander, Capt. Mike Moore. With the broad aspects of the operation in mind, Dan Summit joined Skoog on the East Coast.

The commanding officers and *Skate's* leading quartermaster, who was also the ship's ice forecaster trainee, were flown up Baffin Bay, along the Kane Basin–Kennedy Channel, Robeson Channel passage to the Lincoln Sea, and across Barrow Strait, Melville Sound, and McClure Strait during June.

These flights were of great interest to both captains and provided an extended occasion during which the commanding officers of *Seadragon* and *Skate* became well acquainted.

On one of these flights, taking a big Navy reconnaissance plane, the two men headed for a look at a part of their routes. Flying out of the Naval Air Station Argentia, Newfoundland, Comdr. Don Heberling, the pilot and an Annapolis classmate of Skoog, followed the first and most difficult leg of his entire trip.

From Baffin Bay north over the Lincoln Sea the scene below was not encouraging. Still early in the season, the entire area between Ellesmere and Greenland was solid ice. Four hundred miles, from the southern edge of the pack to the Arctic Basin to the north of Greenland, appeared as one solid sheet.

The first leg of the flight ended at Fairbanks, Alaska. While Skoog returned home to New London, Dan Summit had Heberling fly him out over the western route *Seadragon* would follow.

During the following weeks, Joe Skoog made several trips to the factory in New York City, carefully checking the manufacture of *Skate*'s new "ice suit" being built to Art Roshon's specifications. In Washington, Walt Wittmann and Art Molloy were once again at Hydrographic for the latest charts. Much of the planned route was still unexplored and the charts available were of little use.

Skoog held lengthy conferences with Lyon and Wittmann, making a special point to discuss the plans with James Calvert, now stationed in Washington. He also talked briefly with George Steele, who had already covered the route through Baffin Bay. As the date approached, Dan Summit journeyed to New London one last time where the two commanding officers ironed out final details of Operation Order SUBICEX 2-62.

On 7 July 1962, 31 years after Sir Hubert Wilkins's historic departure amid worldwide publicity, *Skate* quietly and without fanfare backed from her berth alongside the submarine tender *Fulton* moored at State Pier and headed down the Thames River into the Atlantic.

On board was the scientific staff headed by veteran leader Dr. Waldo Lyon. Others included Dick Boyle, who as a commissioned officer had made the winter trip to the North Pole under Calvert. He was now a research engineer in San Diego. Also on the staff were Art Molloy, and Jonathan Schere, project engineer for the new ice suit. Walt Wittmann was with a similar group on board *Seadragon*.

There was one great difference in personnel assignments from previous trips. Arctic operations had arrived at a point where the scientists made the decision to be available only if needed. For the first time in the operation of the ice equipment every minute of its use would be handled by the military.

By 10 July the course turned over the Grand Banks of Newfoundland. *Skate* had passed *Labrador* and was working her way north ahead of schedule when *Seadragon* began her trip.

At 2030, Sunday, 12 July, Dan Summit backed his boat from berth S-1-B at the submarine base, Pearl Harbor, left the harbor, then submerged in the Waianae operating area and was soon heading into the North Pacific.

One week out of port, at 0033, Saturday, 14 July, Joe Skoog wrote,

We have our first important event of the voyage. Going past 570 feet keel depth, enroute to 600 feet at 50 percent power to resume transit after the Fox schedule, a three-inch silver brazed sleeve joint in the piping to the port air conditioning units parted.

Fortunately, an adjacent pipe hanger prevented complete disengagement of the pipe sections. Water in large quantity shoots up along the curved hull of the engine room, then cascades down in a way that leads the watch standers to first believe the leak is overhead.

With no ice overhead, the ship is emergency surfaced. By the time we get up, the failure is isolated. Suspect electrical equipment is secured and we start a mass fresh water flushing, wiping, drying, and megging campaign.

Skate was cruising silently through Davis Strait and was in Baffin Bay when she met her first large iceberg. After looking this monster over, Skoog continued to surface periodically to search out and find the middle pack, running on the surface much of the time until they reached the ice boundary.

It was not far away. There were no nights and the low sun showed bright on the white ice stretching as far as the eye could see. The existence of ice in the area was due in part to the current flowing north along the coast of Greenland, circling across Smith Sound, and turning south again into Baffin Bay.

Skate crossed the Arctic Circle at 0733, Sunday, 15 July. It surfaced from 1600 to 1649, maneuvering slowly near a tabular berg of about two million tons with about 20 more bergs shown by occasional single radar sweeps.

After an initial genuinely excited cry of "land ahead," the giant loomed out of the fog. The predominant reaction of topside visitors was quiet awe.

Plans were made for the traditional blue-nose ceremony. A few veterans enjoyed the fun as 100 officers and men were fed whipped cream spiced with Spanish olives and chives and received blue painted noses.

At 2217 the crew heard an iceberg calve to the northwest.

Joe Skoog was anxious to keep on schedule and to make better time. He submerged and was soon under the pack. On 17 July, *Skate* eased to the surface in a large lead. There was no sign of open water to the north or west, but they felt sure they would be out of the middle pack soon.

By Wednesday, 18 July, *Skate* was approaching Thule. In the afternoon, the boat was brought to the surface to replace a leaking circulating water-pump seal. Then it was on through Smith Sound. Glaciers and the mountains of Greenland and Ellesmere Island rose on both sides. The channel narrowed to 20 to 30 miles wide. The surface offered a spectacular view of rugged arctic terrain, topped by rock-hard ice. Radar signals on both sides were conflicting. Small islands and headlands had been poorly charted. The charts brought from Hydrographic were almost useless. Luckily the channel was still deep.

The first real trouble since leaving port appeared in the engineering plant. Commander Skoog for the first time became seriously worried. His log read:

A piece of equipment, critical equipment, had become deranged. It was necessary to repair it so we could have redundancy while we were under the arctic ice pack. It just wouldn't have been wise to go on with everything hanging on faulty equipment.

We spent several blue days there in Baffin Bay on the edge of the ice. Unable, in my opinion, to foresee; in doubt that we were going to be able to make repairs. There was crepe paper hanging all over.

Lt. Bill Johnson, our electrical officer, deserves tremendous credit for his part in diagnosing and supervising repair of the troublesome equipment. When we finally did get it repaired, we went off with a rush and a roar, and with tremendous exuberance.

Friday morning, 20 July, found *Skate* moving slowly at the north end of Smith Sound. In the evening Skoog decided to do some exploring up an Ellesmere Island fjord. His log read:

We go back to 300 feet, 8 knots, headed into Baird inlet. We are on courses that slowly converge with the estimated 100 fathom contour and the OOD is instructed to turn to follow on the deep side of that contour when it is reached.

At 2117 the bottom has been flat at 130 fathoms. Suddenly it begins to rise with a slope of 20 fathoms per minute. The OOD begins to turn away from the near shore, presumedly toward deep water.

One minute later the bottom still is rising rapidly. The OOD backs. I take the conn, blow main ballast tanks—only scattered ice is overhead—then quickly vent the tanks and establish slow headway to continue to turn. We rise 50 feet.

We clear the bottom by 51 feet and I am suddenly thoroughly purged of any desire to investigate uncharted waters not described in our mission. We headed back out of the inlet at slow speed, carefully following our inbound track until well clear.

From the deck, the shore view was impressive, with rugged cliffs reflecting a desolate country. *Skate* was on her way north again with considerable time lost. With the rendezvous date set, the men were getting edgy. The time had to be made up. Ice was overhead and scattered bergs were in the shallow waters. The channel was narrow but was found to be wide enough to maneuver.

Ahead was the passage from Kane Basin through Kennedy Channel, Hall Basin, and then into Robeson Channel. It was an area of scant and doubtful soundings. The captain and his men had searched charts for more details on the passage without success. He wrote in his log, "There had been trips made through these straits by early sailing and steam ships before, but they had been made close to the shore line of Ellesmere Island."

Now it was easy to understand the problem their predecessors had faced. Looking at the coastline, these modern-day explorers found the cliffs to be high and sheer. It was easy to visualize the tense and dangerous hours during that first passage.

Commander Skoog, however, had another type of foe to deal with. He wrote:

> This entire region was solid ice when we flew over it. A distance of about 400 miles was solid with no sign of holes. Now, in July, some polynyas had become available but it was still a jam-packed area. Some openings were large. There was still some intermittent ice all the way through the passage, as well as possible bergs still to contend with.
>
> We did not know, with any degree of certainty, whether this passage was open. That was, of course, one of our missions. To find out! We were not too comfortable about making a transit in a fairly narrow strait where there was no detailed data on depth of water, or currents to be experienced.
>
> We were concerned about our lateral displacement in the channels where we went. Furthermore, there were several entries in the remarks of those early explorers who went through about land masses being present within the channels. There was some doubt as to whether there was land, islands, or just discolored glacial ice. Information reported by those explorers from "eye-balling" during their transits did indicate there might be islands and shallow spots, or perhaps even a shallow barrier might block our own transit.

By 1700, 20 July, Summit had *Seadragon* north of a line between Fairway Rock and Cape Prince of Wales. He changed course to clear more shallow water ahead. At midnight on the twenty-second,

Seadragon leveled off at 95 feet and set a course for Ice Island T-3. By 0600 after running under heavy but scattered ice coverage for nine hours, the ship now seemed to be under the main ice pack.

Men of the *Skate* lost no more time than necessary to be cautious. By Monday morning, the submarine had worked its way clear of the passage and entered Lincoln Sea. Skoog turned across the continental shelf of the north coast of Greenland. The waters were still found to be shallow. At 2030 that evening, the sail cleared an ice ridge that reached downward 105 feet. This was still glacier country.

Just past midnight on the twenty-fourth, Dan Summit established underwater communications on the model UQC (underwater telephone) with T-3 and learned of a large polynya adjacent to the ice station and to the north.

An hour and a half later *Seadragon* surfaced within 600 yards of the ice station.

The rendezvous went extremely smooth. Our position of T-3 and its actual position varied only about two miles at the most.

A slight course change brought us directly under the island from south to north. A word description of the large polynya adjacent to the camp allowed us to surface in record time.

Once out from under the island and in open water, a quick surfacing was executed and we closed to the "shore" nearby the station. A strong, off island wind precluded the possibility of coming alongside. Instead, the bow was held in close and six of the nine ice station personnel were ferried aboard in our rubber raft.

Each member was superbly dressed in the best arctic clothing. The Eskimo cook was by far the most impressive. Each one had a huge pistol on his hip, a grim reminder that this was truly frontier living. They reported that eight polar bears had been killed so far, not for the sport, but in defense.

After a short visit we were on our way.

Eventually *Skate's* track led out of shallow waters into a gradually deepening and far safer polar basin. A new submarine entrance to the Arctic Ocean had been found. The first major objective of the

SUBICEX 2-62 mission had been successfully accomplished.

Time lost while making repairs had dropped *Skate* behind schedule. Somewhere far to the west *Seadragon* was already under the ice pack, feeling her way off the coast of Siberia. Since there had been no requirement, no provision had been made for communication between boats prior to joining up and it was the responsibility of Skoog and Summit to reach the point of rendezvous on schedule.

Having arrived safely under the main pack, it was a part of Skoog's tactical mission to report his position at an exact time specified in the orders, and first to find a lead or polynya in which to surface. Pushed for time, Skoog searched for an opening. On Friday, 27 July, the polynya plotting party found open water. At 1248 he wrote:

> *We plot a lead 50 yards wide, stretching for 200 yards.*

> *We start a vertical ascent with periscope up.*

> *As the periscope comes out I see that it's going to be tight at the stern. We begin to trim. To adjust trim to get the stern down, I twist the stern away from ice to port. The swing continues and I begin a twist in the opposite direction to stop the swing. The latter move is not in sufficient time and I order the screws stopped as the stern approaches ice to starboard. A moment later a man in the stern room hears a "clunk" and reports. I cannot believe the ice was deep enough at the edge to hit the propeller. It must have been the rudder.*

> *Our motion stops and I kick the ship gently with the port screw.*

> *At 1306 we are clear on the surface. It is overcast and snowing but visibility is excellent. The temperature is 34 degrees. After reporting in, we descend and start building up turns to check the starboard screw.*

> *I was wrong! The starboard propeller has been damaged. Vibration sets in hard as we come up to speed. 180 RPM is all that can be made without excess vibration. We resume course. 180 RPM starboard, 260 RPM port.*

> *Tonight the commissary department lays one on in honor of my birthday—bacon wrapped giblets, cake, cherries jubilee, et al. I try to be good company, but it's not been an altogether dandy day.*

*I am persuaded we should not try to work on the propeller blade now,
but should give our competent engineers a chance to see what they
can plan.*

Skate pushed on as fast as was safe, cruising deep to avoid pressure ridges.

*When we began this leg of the route, we entered a new region where we
encountered the heaviest ice of the trip. We never passed close to, or
under what could be identified as a berg. On occasion we knew an iceberg might get up into the main ice pack. Icebergs are of course land ice.*

Skoog surfaced a number of times. The weather was unpredictable
and they never knew what to expect. On one occasion it would be a
beautiful, bright, sunny afternoon. On another it would be windy and
sleeting. On this summer trip, however, conditions were never as bad
as had been encountered by James Calvert and his crew on their winter trip.

Skoog and his men were concerned now about avoiding a collision at the rendezvous. Would noises reflecting from the ice make
hearing difficult? It had been agreed that one boat arriving at the rendezvous point in the Beaufort Sea west of Ellesmere Island would be
within a certain range of depths. Also a generous period of time
would be allowed for the rendezvous.

After the visit to Ice Island T-3 and failing contact with Ice Island
Arlis II, *Seadragon* arrived at that tiny point at longitude 105 degrees
and latitude 82 degrees, designated "India" in the operation order,
on 30 July, close to the earliest allowed time.

Skate was still cruising at a good speed many miles away, but on
schedule.

After Summit failed to make initial contact, he began to worry that
if one boat made a navigational error the crew might not be able to
hear propeller noises and not be close enough to talk to the other on
the UQC.

After several hours during which Summit's sonar men strained to
hear and pick up the sound of *Skate*'s propellers, at 0010, just past
midnight of the thirty-first, they detected a distant noise. One minute

later they were positive. They clearly detected *Skate*'s screws and turbine whine. Summit went deep to his assigned layer for the rendezvous, and speeded up to close the range, in spurts, slowing every few minutes to check contact and attempt communications. He then commenced maneuvering to maintain *Skate*'s bearing, which was fairly constant while closing.

After failing to make contact by UQC, Summit moved out of his assigned depth range, hoping a different water layer might help.

It worked! *Seadragon* was up in just a short time in *Skate*'s depth area when the call came. The voice-modulated sound waves rang through the water so loud Summit thought the approaching boat was almost on top of him. He quickly dove back to his assigned depth while responding on his own telephone.

Summit need not have been concerned. There had been no danger. A range check on their positions at a later time showed the two submarines were 4,800 yards apart. The sound waves traveling through frigid arctic waters had played a trick on Dan Summit.

To Skoog, this meeting was such a success he thought it almost routine. The time problem that concerned Summit was caused by the difference between zone time and Greenwich time. An early agreement was made in New London that the two submarines would use zone time. Later Skoog had decided on Greenwich time, which was in the final draft of the operation order, but Summit failed to notice. Summit took the unknown change in good humor. They had made it.

Having joined up, the two submarines headed for the North Pole. With 500 miles to go they established intermittent contact with their boss, the Chief of Naval Operations.

Before reaching the North Pole, both Skoog and Summit wanted some practice surfacing in the same polynya or lead together. When they found a good-sized polynya, Skoog brought *Skate* up first. Summit broached in a small polynya about 450 yards from *Skate* to establish better communications. Using *Skate*'s information, Summit descended, then passed directly under the other submarine. Seeing her plainly in the periscope, Summit fired two smoke signals and came up. *Skate*'s crew clambered to the deck to watch the 273-foot *Seadragon* rise through the ice pack a few feet away.

The required messages were gotten off in a hurry and both sub-marines dropped back into the depths and headed north, traveling side by side. The two boats covered the last miles while the navigator's team worked to plot the precise position of the North Geographic Pole and compared results with the boat's navigational instruments. The celestial observations placed the Pole at one point. The inertial navigation equipment gave another. A third piece of navigational gear showed the Pole at a third place. The differences were small, but accuracy was important to both captains.

Considering all three positions Skoog put his pencil on the chart and told the navigator, "That is the North Pole, by definition. Take me there!"

On 2 August 1962, at 0630, *Skate* passed through the polar axis. The formation course was changed to take *Seadragon* through the North Pole at the last moment. Skoog wrote,

We all get a laugh when one of the ship's SINS technicians reports that we've gone a little too far and the Pole is south of us.

0642 Seadragon *passes through the polar axis.*

0830 Lt. Comdr. Frank Wadsworth, our very capable exec, has the conn and finds a strong prospect for a suitable polynya. We began to develop this one and it looks better all the time.

We've got a good one.

0855 surfaced, three miles down the Greenwich meridian from the Pole. Weather is glorious. Unlimited visibility, bright sun, strong white and blue colors, three knot wind, air temperature is 45 degrees. Melt pools, and ridges are profuse.

There are several choices of mooring and ceremony locations, with conflicting advantages of terrain and lighting. I will wait for Sea-dragon *to share in the decision.*

We begin to coach Seadragon *in and put over a camera party in the rubber boat to cover* Seadragon's *surfacing. Lieutenant (J.G.) Baublitz, our very sharp young gunnery officer, is first to step out on the ice.*

Dan Summit had broached *Seadragon* in a small polynya that unfortunately was too small for both submarines. He descended to join *Skate,* anxious to participate with Skoog and his crew in North Pole ceremonies. He wrote,

> *While moving under* Skate, *I kept a watch on her through the periscope. The water was crystal clear. I became amazed at the most fantastic sight of looking up at her from 150 feet, seeing not only her underwater hull very plainly but also I could see her superstructure, sail, numbers on the sail, and men standing on deck. I believe this is probably the first time anything like this has ever been seen.*

Skoog continued his description of events.

> *0948* Seadragon *surfaces after releasing smokes to confirm her position. They share our delight with the surroundings and we agree on mooring and ceremony positions that seem best. All suitable edges of the polynya have thick rams three feet below the water, projecting up to 15 feet from the surface ice, so our moorings and landing parties ashore will be a prolonged process.*

> *1035* Skate *is moored starboard side to, with bow and stern lines to ice stakes. We soon have a rubber boat ferry going.*

> *1215* Seadragon *moored ahead of us, bow to bow, and soon begins to land her shore party.*

> *The CO, XO, and senior scientist from each ship meet and greet before color guards from each ship. Letters, plaques, and battalion infantry flags are exchanged on behalf of the two force commanders and the two ships exchange plaques.*

> *I hypocritically prescribe arctic dress for PIO reasons.*

> *A World's Fair Flag is passed from CO* Skate *to CO* Seadragon *for presentations in Seattle. [After returning to the West Coast, Comdr. Dan Summit presented the World's Fair Flag to officials in Seattle.]*

> *Both commanding officers present dolphins in appropriate individual ceremonies. Nine* Skate *men had bored down to qualify in time for this occasion.*

> Seadragon *provided an excellent Santa Claus and fire works.*

> *Norris, EM1c(SS), a former* Skate *crew member who declined to reenlist on board because he wanted West Coast duty and didn't care to*

repeat a previous arctic voyage, is on Seadragon *and is greeted very loudly by his former shipmates.*

With clear, calm water and timing, we attempt to straighten the bent propeller blade. Several non-critical I-beams have been taken from the lower level engine room deck and welded to form two stout clamp members. Using a rubber boat to take up most of the weight, our four scuba divers work in two-man teams, in half-hour relays, and set up on the clamps in form succession in a carefully selected position. The blade top is moved from one and a half to one-half inch out of its normal plane and the general tip area shape is preserved.

1751 Skate *underway, after careful muster. Visibility is reduced to 300 yards. Throughout our voyage we have had this kind of good fortune with weather.*

1846 Seadragon *descends.*

1904 Formation course is set down the 135 west meridian, based on my guestimate as to the final designation of our point Kilo rendezvous with Burton Island. *We build up to 50 percent power, 15 knots without vibration of our starboard shaft.*

About 2130 we cross the Lomonosov Ridge, recording depth of 710 fathoms.

After remaining at the North Pole for 12 hours, the two submarines headed for the Beaufort Sea and a rendezvous with the icebreaker some 300 miles off Herschel Island.

Two days later *Skate* surfaced briefly. From a scheduled broadcast, the radioman typed out a message. Its importance prompted Commander Skoog to deliver it personally to the man concerned. Busy drawing a water sample in the engine room amid the noise of machinery, and with typical modesty, Dr. Lyon read the words, accepted the captain's handshake, and resumed his work with no sign of excitement.

At 0200, 7 August, *Skate, Seadragon,* and *Burton Island* lay in loose pack ice in the Beaufort Sea. On that same Tuesday morning, a group of people assembled at the White House for a very special occasion. Several men had been selected to receive the 1962 President's Award for Distinguished Federal Civilian Service.

They were Ambassador Llewellyn Thompson Jr., State Department; Dr. Francis O. Kelsey, Department of Health, Education, and Welfare; Dr. Robert R. Gilbruth, National Aeronautics and Space Administration; Mr. J. Stanley Boughman, Housing and Home Finance Agency; and Dr. Waldo K. Lyon.

"Dr. Lyon," it was announced to those present, "was absent from the country on a special mission." Mrs. Lyon attended the ceremony in his place.

His citation read:

With Profound Appreciation, Highest Esteem, and Great Personal Satisfaction.

He has been singularly responsible for the pioneering development of the knowledge, techniques, and instruments that made it possible for a submarine to navigate under the ice cap in the Arctic.

In the face of formidable obstacles, he persevered in believing that transarctic submarine navigation could become a reality and directed his efforts toward this objective. His achievement represents a highly important contribution in the Nation's security.

7 August 1962 John F. Kennedy

Among the guests at the White House ceremony were Dr. Lyon's family, James Calvert, Bob McWethy, and George Steele.

At the conclusion of the ceremony, President Kennedy made the following statement:

When one of our employees in the National Government does not meet the high standards which we set for ourselves, it becomes, of course, the greatest news. I hope that it will be equal news, the story of the accomplishments of these ladies and gentlemen. We have so many devoted civil servants, so many public servants working for this government helping and benefiting the lives not only of the people of this country but all around the world that we have really just in a sense symbolically honored them by honoring these ladies and gentlemen. There are hundreds and thousands behind them. So I hope that this ceremony today will call the attention of the people of our country to a very extraordinary group of men and women who are working in their behalf.

So we congratulate you all, we thank you, and we hope that your work will serve as a horizon-making effort by those who work for the People of the United States.

During the next week the three ships carried out tactical exercises. The submarines fired torpedoes to check their operation in polar waters. Whatever the status of naval strategy and tactical requirements the fleet would have in the future, it now had a greater understanding of the environmental conditions prevailing in the greater than two million square miles of ocean and marginal seas known as the Arctic Mediterranean.

The operation completed, *Seadragon* headed for the Bering Strait while Commander Skoog turned east for the Northwest Passage, following George Steele's route in reverse, heading for his home port at New London.

"This was strictly a military operation," said Skoog.

Dr. Lyon made quite a point of this. He very meticulously refrained from offering advice or giving a hand with our material problems simply to demonstrate the fact that, based on the experience of many cruises, the Navy was now smart enough to do the job by themselves.

I watched him very carefully at times for evidence to see whether or not he thought I was making a correct decision. Dr. Lyon was a real Chinese Buddha . . . a real poker face. He left me in considerable doubt at times as to whether he thought I had made the right decision. But he refrained himself, to be careful. No comment. I think that was very important, and demonstrated a real military capability.

Seadragon was working her way westward from the Beaufort Sea. On 16 August, Dan Summit wrote,

At 2113 we came upon a large floe rising 30 feet above the water and measuring 900 feet long by 600 feet wide directly in our track. Presumably this was a remnant broke from Ice Island T-3. We sent a warning message locating this hazard to navigation.

We decided to lie to nearby, photograph the Ice Isle and await weather developments. The Ice Island was breath-taking to view. No icebergs are experienced in this part of the Arctic and this was larger than most icebergs.

Undoubtedly it was a piece of T-3, the whereabouts no one on board knew. It is lucky that we are not charging along submerged, unaware that any ice to speak of, much less this 175-foot deep monster, was dead on our track.

At 2355 we proceeded cautiously on the surface on our way along the Barrow Sea Valley at whatever speed the visibility in the fog would allow at the time.

At 0230 on the 17th, we sighted another large floe and closed to investigate. This was a similar piece rising 25 feet out of the water and measuring 600 feet by 750 feet and so reported it also. A second one in a thousand chance of seeing such a monster. 0233 on our way again.

0650 submerged to make better time. We seemed to be out of the ice, but the visibility remained poor.

0745 crossed the 30 fathom curve, leaving the comfortable water of the Barrow Sea Valley behind and moving into the Chukchi Sea.

At 1443 on the 18th, with a Loran fix, adjusted course to head for the Bering Strait. At 1909 we entered shallower water than expected. Came up to 80 feet and stayed glued to soundings as they came to less than 25 feet under the keel.

At 1958 made a large course change to the right to best clear the shallow water. Immediately, soundings became deeper. Proceeded on this course until well clear of the bank.

The next morning we are south of Bering Strait and so changed course to pass north of St. Lawrence Island.

On the 21st at 2151 sighted the mountains of the Aleutian chain ahead after 40 days without sighting land.

On the 22nd, we are moored port side to the fuel pier in Sweeper Cove, Adak Island, Alaska. Although we are scheduled for only several hours in port, most everyone is anxious to go ashore and feel solid land under his feet once more.

Wednesday, 22 August 1962, President John F. Kennedy called a news conference at the White House. He announced to the world the astounding news that two atomic submarines had, a few days before, made a historic rendezvous at the North Pole. "An exceptional tactical feat!" said the president.

"The Arctic Ocean has become the private sea of the submariner who is free to move in any direction and at any speed under the ice covering the sea." Those are the words of Dr. Lyon, the scientist who helped to make a dream come true.

Military control of the Arctic Ocean is the responsibility of the Atlantic and Pacific fleet commanders. The responsibility is now executed in principal part by the Submarine Force Commanders because the submarine has the capability to operate in any part of the Arctic Ocean during all seasons of the year.

The combined patrol by *Skate* and *Seadragon,* a joint command effort by Atlantic and Pacific submarine forces, had demonstrated the fleet capability. In contrast to all submarine arctic patrols prior to this combined patrol, the equipment and all decisions pertaining to the under-ice operations were operated by and made by ship's regular personnel without reference to civilian specialists.

GLOSSARY

Arched berg A glacier berg eroded in such a manner that a large opening at the waterline extends horizontally through the berg to form an arch.

Berg Arched berg, iceberg, glacier berg, valley berg, and shelf berg.

Bergy bit A massive piece of sea ice or disrupted hummocked ice; also a medium-sized piece of floating glacier ice. Generally less than 16 feet above sea level, and not more than 32 feet across.

Beset Situation of a vessel surrounded by ice and unable to move.

Block A fragment of floating sea ice ranging in size from 6 to 30 feet across.

Blocky berg An iceberg with steep, precipitous sides, and with either a horizontal or nearly horizontal upper surface.

Brash ice Small fragments of floating ice, not more than 6 feet across; the wreckage of other forms of ice.

Bummock From the point of view of the submariner, a downward projection from the underside of the ice canopy; the counterpart of a hummock.

Calving The breaking away of a mass of ice from a glacier, ice front, or iceberg.

Crack Any fracture or rift in sea ice not sufficiently wide to be described as a lead. It is usually possible to jump across a crack.

Fast ice Sea ice of greatly varying width which remains fast along the coast where it is attached to the shore, to an ice wall, an ice front, or over shoals, generally in the position where originally formed. Fast ice may extend over 200 miles from the coast.

Floe A piece of sea ice other than fast ice, large or small. Light floes are pieces up to 10 feet thick. Thicker floes, both level and hummocked, are called "heavy" floes.

Glacier A mass of snow and ice continuously moving from higher to lower ground or, if afloat, continuously spreading.

Glacier berg A large mass of floating or stranded ice broken away from a glacier, often of considerable height. In any case, more than 15 feet above the level of the sea.

Glacier ice Any ice originating from a glacier, whether on land or floating in the sea as a glacier berg.

Growler An iceberg large enough to be a navigational hazard.

Hummocked ice Sea ice, which is piled haphazardly one piece over another and which may be weathered.

Ice The solid form of water, in nature formed either by (a) the freezing of water, as in the case of river or sea ice; (b) the condensation of atmospheric water vapor directly into ice crystals; (c) the compaction of snow, with or without the motion of a glacier; or (d) the impregnation of porous snow masses with water which subsequently freezes. *See also* specific ices.

Iceberg A large mass of floating or stranded ice. If broken away from a glacier it is referred to as a glacier berg; if broken away from an ice shelf it is referred to as a shelf berg.

Ice canopy Ice cover from the point of view of the submariner. In polar regions, the ice canopy is a complex ocean surface containing many different ice types and open water features.

Ice cover The amount of sea ice encountered; measured in tenths of percent of the sea covered with ice.

Ice crystal A single ice particle with regular structure.

Ice island *See* Shelf berg.

Ice keel From the point of view of the submariner, a downward projecting ridge on the underside of the ice canopy; the counterpart of a pressure ridge.

Ice pack A large concentration of sea ice which may include fast ice and which is found in the same region every summer. These concentrations are usually named for the region, for example, the Arctic ice pack.

Ice shelf A floating ice sheet of considerable thickness. Ice shelves are usually of great horizontal extent and have a level or gently undulating surface. They are nourished by local snow accumulation and often also by the seaward extension of land glaciers. An example is the Ross Ice Shelf in the Antarctic.

Ice skylight A polynya or lead from the viewpoint of the submariner in winter. Used to refer to an area of relatively thin ice (usually less than three feet thick) completely surrounded by pack ice. The under surface of an ice skylight is normally flat.

Lead A long, narrow passage through pack ice, navigable by a surface referred to as an ice skylight.

Pack ice Any area of sea ice other than fast ice composed of a heterogeneous mixture of size and age types. Pack ice is usually in motion and is often referred to as drift ice.

Polar ice Extremely heavy sea ice up to 10 feet or more thick and of more than one winter's growth. Heavily hummocked, it may ultimately be reduced by weathering to a more or less even surface.

Polynya Any enclosed sea water in pack ice, other than a lead, not large enough to be called open water. In summer it may be referred to as a lake; in winter with a covering of relatively thin ice it may be called an ice skylight. If a polynya is found in the same region every year, e.g., off the mouths of big rivers, it is called a recurring polynya.

Pressure ice A general term for sea ice that has been squeezed. If the sea ice has been forced upwards, it can be described as hummocked ice or pressure ridge.

Pressure ridge A ridge or wall of hummocked ice where one floe has been pressed against another. Maximum height above sea level in pack ice is about 30 feet. A corresponding ridge may also occur on the underside of the ice canopy and may extend as much as 160 feet below sea level.

Rafted ice A mild form of pressure ice formed by one piece of ice overriding another.

Rotten ice Sea ice which has become honeycombed in the course of melting and which is in an advanced state of disintegration.

Sea ice Any form of ice at sea which has originated from freezing sea water.

Shelf berg A large mass of floating or stranded ice broken away from an ice shelf. The size varies from a few thousand square yards to 250 square miles or more in area; in the Arctic, the thickness varies from about 50 feet to more than 200 feet.

Sludge A stage of freezing when the spicules and plates of ice coagulate to form a thick soupy layer on the surface.

Slush Snow that is saturated or mixed with water. A viscous floating mass in water.

Snow Precipitation of ice crystals. Sometimes star-shaped. At temperatures higher than about 23 degrees Fahrenheit, crystals are generally agglomerated into snow flakes.

Surfaceable feature To the submariner, any feature in the ice canopy through which a submariner can reach the surface without damage.

Tabular berg A shelf berg. Most bergs of this type show horizontal firm snow layers.

Unfriendly ice From the point of view of the submariner, ice with few surfaceable features per 30 nautical miles along the submariner's track.

Weathered ice Hummocked polar ice subjected to weathering which has given the hummocks and pressure ridges a rounded form.

(BIBLIOGRAPHY)

Primary Sources

Anderson, William R. USS *Nautilus* (SSN 571), Final Report of *Nautilus* Trans-Polar Voyage, 9 September 1958.

Bienia, John F. USS *Redfish,* 1952 and 1953 Operation Reports.

Boyle, R. J. Ice Glossary, U.S. Navy Electronics Laboratory, San Diego, California, 10 June 1965.

Calvert, James F. Report on Patrol Number One, USS *Skate,* 22 September 1958.

———. Report of *Skate,* Arctic Patrol, March 1959.

Fletcher, J. O. "Origin and Early Utilization of Aircraft-supported Drifting Stations," pp. 1–13, Symposium Report, Arctic Drifting Stations, Arctic Institute of North America, November 1968.

Icenhower, John B. Patrol Report on Operation Highjump, USS *Sennet,* 1947.

Lyon, Waldo K. The Polar Submarine and Navigation of the Arctic Ocean, Research Report 88, first published 18 November 1948, reissued 21 May 1959, U.S. Navy Electronics Laboratory, San Diego, California.

Maurer, John H. Patrol Report on Operation Nanook, USS *Atule,* 1946.

Naval Examining Board. Evaluation Report on the Submarine *Nautilus* Expedition by OP31B. 1947.

Nicholson, John H. Report of the First Arctic Cruise of the USS *Sargo* (SSN 583), conducted between 18 January and 3 March 1960.

Palmer, James M. USS *Carp,* Operation Report, 1948.

Sater, John E. "Arctic Drifting Stations," Symposium Report, Arctic Institute of North America, November 1968.

Seattle Post-Intelligencer, 1930–31 microfilm reports of Sir Hubert Wilkins's *Nautilus* news dispatches.

Skoog, Joseph L. Jr. Report of USS *Skate* July–August 1962 cruise (SUBICEX 2-62), 28 August 1962.

Steele, George P., II. Report of USS *Seadragon* August–September 1960, Arctic Cruise (SUBICEX 3-60), 14 September 1960.

Summit, Daniel C. Report of USS *Seadragon* (SUBICEX 2-62), 28 August 1962.

Sverdrup, Harald V. Scientific Results of the *Nautilus* Expedition, 1931, Massachusetts Institute of Technology, Cambridge, Mass., 1933.

Turner, John H. USS *Boarfish,* Arctic Operation Report, 1947.

Wilkins, Sir Hubert, *Nautilus* Submarine Expedition Report, to the Naval Examining Board, Washington D.C., 1947.

Secondary Sources

Anderson, William R. *Nautilus-90-NORTH.* New York: World Publishing, 1959.

Beal, M. A., F. Edvalson, K. Hunkins, A. Molloy, and N. Ostenson. "The Floor of the Arctic Ocean, Geographic Names." *Journal of Arctic Institute of North America* 19, no. 3 (September 1966): 215–19.

Calvert, James F. *Surface at the Pole.* New York: McGraw-Hill, 1960.

Dugan, James, and Richard Vahan, eds. *Men under Water.* Philadelphia: Chilton Books, 1965.

Fletcher, J. O. "The Arctic: Challenge to the Air Force." *Air University Quarterly,* no. 3 (1953).

LaFond, E. C. "Arctic Oceanography by Submarines." U.S. Naval Institute *Proceedings* (September 1960).

Lyon, Waldo K. "Ocean and Sea-ice Research in the Arctic Ocean via Submarine." *Transactions* (New York Academy of Sciences) 23, no. 8 (June 1961).

———. "The Submarine and the Arctic Ocean." *The Polar Record* 11, no. 75 (1963).

Nicholson, John H. "Sargo." In *Men under Water.* Philadelphia: Chilton Books, 1965, 53–67.

Steele, George P., II. *Seadragon: Northwest under the Ice.* New York: Dutton, 1962.

Strong, James T. *The Opening of the Arctic Ocean.* Washington, D.C.: Smithsonian Institution Press, 1963.

Wilkins, Sir Hubert. *Under the North Pole.* New York: Brewer, Warren & Putman, 1931.

INDEX

About the Author

Marion D. Williams joined the Navy in 1927 as an apprentice seaman and served thirty years, all of which were in radio communications. He spent ten years in the submarine service as a crew member on four submarines. As a senior radio operator he handled the sonar equipment on a submarine that operated in and out of Pearl Harbor for the four years prior to the 1941 war. He met Raymond Meyers when they were both senior radio operators on "O"-boat submarines, the same model as the Wilkins boat. Much later, Meyers related to Williams his role in the arctic adventures.

As an enlisted man, Williams entered and graduated from an advanced military electronics engineering school. He was commissioned in 1943 as an officer, following completion of a second advanced military electronics engineering school. After the war in 1945 he was assigned duty as officer in charge of shore radio stations. He had a tour on the carrier *Hancock* as communications officer. Comdr. Peter Aurand, one of Williams's shipmates on *Hancock*, later became naval aide to President Eisenhower.

Following his Navy retirement in 1957, Williams was hired as an engineering writer by General Dynamics, San Diego, for his expertise and technical background in electronics. His training and experience with sonar, and operation of both a submarine and its radio and sonar equipment, have given him the knowledge to tell the story of the arctic conquests.